MISS O: MY LIFE IN DANCE

Miss O

MY LIFE IN DANCE

BETTY OLIPHANT

with a foreword by
MIKHAIL BARYSHNIKOV

TURNSTONE PRESS

Turnstone Press
607–100 Arthur Street
Winnipeg, Manitoba
Canada R3B 1H3

Turnstone Press gratefully acknowledges the assistance of
the Canada Council and the Manitoba Arts Council.

Front cover photograph: Official portrait of Betty Oliphant, CC,
LL.D., D.Litt., a gift to the National Ballet School by the
Board of Directors on the occasion of the twenty-fifth anniversary.
Photo by V. Tony Hauser.

Back cover photograph: Prime Minister Pierre Trudeau enjoys
the alumni party of the twentieth anniversary celebrations, 1979.
Photo by Andrew Oxenham.

Front flyleaf photograph by Jeannette Edissi-Collins

Back flyleaf photograph by Peter Varley

Design: Manuela Dias

This book was printed and bound in Canada by
Friesens for Turnstone Press.

Canadian Cataloguing in Publication Data

Oliphant, Betty, 1918–

Miss O: my life in dance

Includes index.
ISBN 0-88801-210-1

1. Oliphant, Betty, 1918–   2. Dance teachers –
Canada – Biography.   3. National Ballet School (Canada) –
History.   I. Title.

GV1785.O45A3 1996   792.8'092   C96-920122-2

For my daughters
Gail and Carol

The true teacher defends his pupils against his own personal influence. He inspires self-trust. He guides their eyes from himself to the spirit that quickens him. He will have no disciple.

—Amos Bronson Alcott

Contents

Foreword
by Mikhail Baryshnikov

It was with considerable pleasure and the happiest of memories that I learned about the making of this book. Even before I first came to Canada in 1974, I had heard about the National Ballet School. If I did not have a perfect image of its founder in front of my younger eyes, nevertheless I knew what she was accomplishing because of the high regard for the school she started. It was talked about even as far away as Leningrad. Actually, *especially* in Leningrad!

So it was fate that brought me to Toronto in 1974. When I decided to thank Canada for being such a welcoming and generous host to me during a very dramatic and difficult moment in my life, I offered a performance of *La Sylphide* to the people of Toronto at the Ontario Place Forum. I asked that my fee—my first independent fee for dancing in Canada—be given to the National Ballet School of Canada.

What higher tribute to the achievement of Betty Oliphant can I make than to acknowledge that the school she created became known as one of the great ballet academies anywhere? Her graduates are all over the world and she made an institution which brought great honour to Canada.

I salute her and the noble experiment she began all those years ago, nurtured, and passed along. The National Ballet School is not so much her monument as a living testament to her courage and wisdom.

—Mikhail Baryshnikov

Acknowledgements

Before acknowledging the people who have contributed in a practical way to the production of this book, I wish to thank those whose affectionate support helped me through a difficult period when my confidence in my ability to succeed in this project was sadly lacking.

First, my children, to whom this book is dedicated. I spent delightful weekends with Gail. As she read the manuscript, she made excellent suggestions, and we laughed a lot at some of the memories that were engendered. Carol was less close to the project, but her understanding, through the years, of why my job has caused me to be less available than we would have wished, has always meant a great deal to me.

Second, my thanks go to my friends: to Stan Greben who encourages me and picks me up when I feel unable to continue; to Margaret and Gethin Hughes who are constantly making generous gestures to help me; to Shirley Porter, my secretary, who remains interested and helpful even though I have left the School; to Donald Urquhart who has always been there for me; to those with whom I worked at the National Ballet School, and the many other friends and neighbours who make my life worthwhile.

Finally, the hands-on people, whose assistance I deeply appreciate, no matter what form it has taken. When this book was just a gleam in my eye, John Fraser—at that time editor of *Saturday Night*—mapped out for me, as we lunched, just how I should set about writing a book.

Some years later, when the idea became a reality, I met Shirley Knight Morris, a former director of publicity at Macmillan of Canada and a freelance editor. Her contribution, from start to finish, has been inestimable. She has read, suggested changes, and, above all, given positive feedback without hesitating to criticize in an objective way. I thank her for her patience and for believing in me.

Keith Walker, my son-in-law, was the technical adviser. As I semi-mastered the word processor we bought together, he dealt patiently with my trepidation. I was convinced that I was going to lose everything and was often on the end of the phone as he calmed me down. As each chapter was finished he cleaned it up; I only learned to "indent" in time for the last chapter!

Thanks to the late William Kilbourn, I was introduced to Donna Ivey who worked with him on his book *Intimate Grandeur: One hundred years at Massey Hall*. Donna has been responsible for many areas of research. Her professionalism and enthusiasm have been truly valuable.

Margaret McBurney has organized the launch at the Arts and Letters Club and she and her husband, Rod Austen, have helped me in numerous other ways. Gail and Jonathan, my grandson, worked for hours as we struggled to make up my list of invitations and flyers.

When I started I had no publisher, therefore no advance payment to cover my basic expenses, so I am very grateful to Pauline Traub (née Patey) for her generous financial contribution.

Finally, I am very happy working with Jamie Hutchison, my editor at Turnstone Press. He is creative, sensitive, and highly intelligent. I thank him and his staff.

Significant Events in Betty Oliphant's Life

1918   Born August 5, 1918, Nancy Elizabeth (Snookie) Oliphant, London, England.
Death of Betty's father in September.

c. 1923   Betty's first dance lessons in London.

1930   December 13, sees last London performance of Anna Pavlova before her death in January, 1931.

1933   Assistant director of a nativity play at the Duchess Theatre, London.

1936   November, first person to pass Advanced Stage examination of the Imperial Society of Teachers of Dancing (I.S.T.D.) in all subjects.
Obtains trust fund advance and opens her first school at 72 Wigmore Street, London.

1939   August, at age twenty-one the youngest person to be appointed a fellow and examiner of the Stage Branch of the I.S.T.D. and a licentiate, later examiner, of the Cecchetti Branch.

1940/41   Arranges dance numbers for a pantomime in Cardiff, Wales.

1942   June 27, Betty marries Frank Russell Grover in London.

1943   April 25, first daughter, Gail, is born in London.

1944   October 10, second daughter, Carol, is born in Edinburgh.

1947	Carol diagnosed with tubercular spine.
	Betty, Frank and Gail immigrate to Canada, leaving Carol in England.
	Invited to create ballet for *Hansel and Gretel*, Eaton Auditorium, December 18 and 19..
1948	Teaches first dance classes at Jesse Ketchum Hall, Toronto.
1949	Mildred Wickson, Betty, and their colleagues found the Canadian Dance Teachers Association.
1949/50	Arranges dances for *Mother Goose* at the Royal Alexandra Theatre, December 26, for two weeks.
	Performs first and last recital at Hart House Theatre.
	Frank and Betty separate.
1950/51	Arranges dances for *Mother Goose* with Wayne and Schuster, Montreal (one week) and London (one week), December and January.
1951	Appointed ballet mistress of new National Ballet of Canada by Celia Franca.
	First performance of National Ballet of Canada.
1957	Betty's mother suffers stroke, dies a few months later.
1958	December, Betty marries Reginald Mawer.
1959	National Ballet School of Canada founded.
	Betty retires as ballet mistress of the National Ballet of Canada.
1967	Invited by Erik Bruhn to reorganize the ballet school of the Royal Swedish Opera.
1969	Appointed associate artistic director, National Ballet of Canada.
	Tenth year as director and principal, National Ballet School of Canada.
	Guest of honour at the First International Ballet Competition, Moscow.
1971	Company performs in Europe.
	Marriage to Reg Mawer ends.
1972	Betty's physical and mental health suffers.

1975	Betty resigns as associate artistic director, National Ballet of Canada.
1977	Member of jury for the Third International Competition, Moscow.
1978	Invited to Denmark to reorganize the ballet school of the Royal Danish Opera.
1979	Twentieth anniversary, National Ballet School of Canada.
1981	Member of the jury for the Fourth International Competition, Moscow.
1984	Twenty-fifth anniversary gala performance, National Ballet School, November 21.
1986	Member of the jury for the International Ballet Competition, Jackson, Mississippi, U.S.A.
1988	October 17, the official opening of the Betty Oliphant Theatre.
1989	Retires as director and principal, National Ballet School, remaining as artistic advisor and continuing to teach for two years.
1991	Member of the jury for the 1991 Prix de Lausanne.

(For a list of awards and honours, see page 259.)

My first tutu.

Childhood

Guilt is very destructive. Obviously I did not feel guilty when I was born prematurely in London on August 5, 1918, but as a child I always felt that if it hadn't been for me, my father would still be alive and I would have a daddy like everybody else.

When I was six weeks old my father was killed in a train accident while travelling from Scotland to see me for the first time. My mother would never speak of my father to me or my sister, so it took me years to find out what had happened or even to see a photo of him. Only twice in my life did my mother mention him. Once when I was singing the war song "Take Me Back to Dear Old Blighty," she told me to stop because it reminded her of my father. On another occasion I was deeply hurt when I told her I missed my daddy and she said sharply, "How can you possibly miss someone you never knew?"

Eventually I managed to piece together some details of my parents' lives. All four grandparents and ten of my father's siblings had died before I was born. Remaining were his younger brother Jack and his older sister Margaret, who was bitterly resentful of my mother. Auntie Nan was my mother's only sibling. My parents were first cousins; my mother's father was the brother of my father's mother, but their lives went in very different directions.

My mother, Yvonne Marie Frances, was born in 1885 on the island of Shameen in what was formerly Canton, China, where her father, Robert William Mansfield, was the British consul general. His wife was a French woman whom he had met while on leave. They fell madly in love even though they could not speak a word of each other's language. Naturally my mother was brought up speaking fluent French. The early years of her life were happy ones. She loved China and spoke of it often, but when she was seven tragedy struck.

My mother's family was burned out during the Boxer Rebellion. As a result of the hardship she suffered, my grandmother died, and from then on my mother's life was intolerable. My mother was sent with her young sister, Nancy, to Scotland to live with my father's parents, Thomas Truman Oliphant and his wife Georgina Elizabeth.

My father, Stuart Oliphant, had been born on June 12, 1872, in the family home known as Rossie House, in Perthshire, Scotland.

"Queen Mary's House," Perthshire, Scotland. The picture of the Three Kings which hangs to the left of Mary Queen of Scots is now in my home.

The Oliphant family name, originally spelled Olifard, and since spelled in many different ways, is found in the ancient chronicles of Scotland as a Norman surname that ranks as one of the oldest. It appears in the Domesday Book which was compiled in 1086 by William the Conqueror and in many other old manuscripts. In the sixteenth century the family split into three main branches: the Oliphants of Gask, of Condie, and of Rossie.

Oliphant of Rossie coat of arms.

One of my ancestors, Sir Walter Olifard, was the son of the famous Sir William Olifard, sometimes spelled Olifaunt, who defended Stirling Castle in 1304 against the armies of King Edward I of England. He married Lady Elizabeth, the sister of David II of Scotland and the daughter of Robert the Bruce. Robert was the king who, while watching the spider's efforts to rebuild its web each time it was destroyed, coined the phrase "If you don't at first succeed, try, try, try again." Another ancestor, Caroline Oliphant, later Baroness Nairne, wrote several ballads including "Charlie Is My Darling" and "Will Ye No Come Back Again?"

The Rossie branch has its own coat of arms. It consists, ironically, of an elephant—I was always called "baby elephant" at school—and a lion supporting a red shield with three silver crescents. At the top stands an eagle with its wings spread. Our motto, which appeals to my idealistic nature, is *Altiora Peto* (I seek higher things).

Just one more piece of history, and then I will get on with my story. Having sold Rossie House in the early 1880s, my father's family had moved to Queen Mary's House in St. Andrews, Scotland. In 1904 my grandfather, T. T. Oliphant, or Uncle Tom, as he was called by my mother, co-founded St. Leonards, a well-known private girls' school in St. Andrews. In the grounds of the school are the Oliphant gates, built in his honour. My father's home, Queen Mary's House, is now the school library. I remember, when I was a girl and we visited the school, how annoyed the headmistress was that as the granddaughter of the founder I had not been sent there, but my mother's memories of that frigid east coast of Scotland were painful. If I had attended the school, I could never have had a career in ballet.

Two little girls, Yvonne and Nancy, my mother and aunt aged seven and four respectively, arrived from the Far East to join this large, boisterous family that thought nothing of walking ten miles on Sunday before consuming a hearty lunch of roast beef and Yorkshire pudding, with all the trimmings. The motherless girls were not strong and had been pampered by their beloved amahs in China. Their father, whom they adored, was thousands of miles away, and the searing winds were bitterly cold. My mother developed inflammation of the cornea in both eyes, which, in those days, was incurable. She was completely blind. She told me stories of living in this creepy old house, and how she would feel under the bed at night convinced that someone was hiding there ready to pounce.

The relatives were not unkind but they were insensitive to my mother's suffering. She eventually regained about five percent of her sight. Despite her handicap, she managed years later to make and embroider beautiful dresses for me and my sister. During her time at Queen Mary's, my mother idolized my father. There were thirteen years between them, so he was twenty when they first met. He was very kind and understanding and probably took the place of the father she missed so much.

Things were even worse when my mother and her sister went to boarding school in England. My great-aunt, Mrs. Meyrick Heath, whom we had to call Granny Kitty, had founded and was headmistress of a private school called Mortimer House in Clifton, a suburb of Bristol in Gloucestershire. She was a tyrant, although a superb educator. In every way she was far ahead of her time. Her enthusiasm for sports led her to insist on shortening the girls' long skirts. She came up with the first "gym tunic."

My mother's life was miserable. She was treated and felt like a charity child. She did all the dirty work in the school. Every morning she had to get up to ring the six o'clock bell, and for the rest of the day she was at my great-aunt's beck and call. She only found out when she had left the school that her father had been paying handsomely for his daughters' education.

When I was a child, Granny Kitty lived in the flat below us, and our cook prepared her meals. She was never satisfied. I resented the way she treated my mother, who waited on her hand and foot, but I loved her kind, gentle husband, my great-uncle Meyrick. This selfish woman died leaving a considerable fortune to charitable organizations. My mother never attached much importance to money, but she must have been hurt when she was ignored in the will. She had done so much for my great-aunt, who knew how hard it was for her to make ends meet.

My mother was seventeen when she matriculated. She won a scholarship to Oxford University, but her father did not want his daughter to be a "blue-stocking" so, happily for her, he whisked her off to China to be his hostess at the consulate. This naïve and unsophisticated young woman was catapulted into entertaining her father's distinguished guests. She told me of the graciousness of the Duchess of Connaught who assured her that it was acceptable to eat asparagus with one's fingers. As children we benefited from my mother's attitude toward accidental breakages. It had been established on a social visit when she saw a Ming vase knocked over by a guest and smashed. The owner simply smiled and said, "Don't worry, it's nothing," as she rang for a maid to sweep up the pieces. Once my mother had prepared the dining-room table for a banquet, decorating it from end to end with some glorious lilies she had picked. Having gone upstairs to dress she returned to find that they looked like a bunch of weeds. The flowers were the kind that closed at night. In spite of these minor contretemps, my mother spent six joyous years with her father until he died when she was twenty-three years old.

Deeply upset by the death of her father, my mother returned to Britain. Feeling rather at a loss, she enrolled in a midwifery course at Edinburgh's Royal Infirmary, where many years later my youngest daughter Carol was born. My mother worked there for several years, delivering babies in the dreadful slums of

Edinburgh. She had never lost a single one, she told me proudly, but she also spoke of the pain she suffered as she had to stand by in silence while young, inept doctors—too proud to accept help—would, through their clumsiness in the delivery room, cause the death of perfectly healthy babies.

My mother always had a wonderful knack with small children and animals, but she was almost as unaware of my psychological needs when I started to grow up as her aunt and uncle had been of hers.

In June 1914, my parents were married by the Bishop of Kensington in London, where my mother was living at the time. My father was now, at forty-one, a writer to His Majesty's Signet, which is a rather classy type of Scottish lawyer. As children, we knew he had the initials W.S. after his name and thought it a great joke to change them to W.C. His law firm was in Edinburgh, but when my parents married they bought a country house called Pondtail Lodge in Fleet, Hampshire, England, where my sister Mary was born in 1915. I have no knowledge of this period, but I assume that my father commuted to Edinburgh. He was there, tied up with a trial, just before the fatal train journey occurred.

The little I came to know of this incident convinced me that it had ruined my mother's life and affected my sister's mental health. Mary had been on the train with her nanny and my father, whom she adored. When I was having psychotherapy, in my fifties, the therapist remarked, "Your mother must have been very angry with your father for leaving her." I was astounded. Being a very practical person I could not see how anyone could be blamed for being killed. I understand now that practicality has very little to do with one's emotions.

My mother had had a difficult time at my birth and was still weak, six weeks later, when she was waiting for my father at Euston Station in London. The train was five and a half hours late, and she heard rumours about an accident on the line. In Hatfield, not far from London, my father had opened the exit door, presumably instead of the lavatory door, and he had fallen out of the train and been killed.

When the train arrived my mother was greeted with this news. With me in her arms, she had to deal with her own shocked reaction plus that of our hysterical eighty-year-old nanny, who had brought up three generations of the family, including my father. Three-year-old Mary was also screaming her head off. She had been badly frightened on the train by the commotion and by overhearing remarks about "what was to become of the poor fatherless wee bairn." Her nanny was too distraught to calm her down. Years later, when Mary was mentally ill, the doctors explained that this trauma, which had not been dealt with at the time, had left her emotionally damaged.

At the inquest my mother had to deal with insinuations that my father had committed suicide. She showed them his letters, which expressed love and joy that he had another daughter. His death was never explained, but he was blind in one eye, and, like many Scots, he drank pretty heavily.

My mother destroyed all my father's letters and photos. Apparently this was the only way she could deal with his death. My father's will was extremely complicated. He had not taken into account the possibility of his premature death, nor had he known that income tax would increase from sixpence on the pound to ten shillings and sixpence at the end of the First World War. Consequently the annuity he had left to my mother of five hundred pounds per annum was hopelessly inadequate. The rest was all tied up in a trust for us, and, because they were entailed, the furnishings of my parents' large house could not be sold until Mary and I were twenty-one. Three family heirlooms—a locket with Bonny Prince Charlie's hair, a brooch which had belonged to Mary Queen of Scots, containing strands of her hair, and a Raeburn picture—were lost in the war.

My early years were happy ones. My mother had decided to make her home in London. She bought a large house in Hampstead which had two self-contained flats attached to it. We lived in the upper flat. It was some years later when the lower one was occupied by Granny Kitty and Uncle Meyrick. Before they moved, we had often stayed in their beautiful country house at Farnham Common. I loved being out of doors and spent all day playing in the thick gorse that covered the common outside their house.

The visits were not as pleasant for my mother. She was sensitive to my great-aunt's criticism that I was unladylike because I loved to be outside either alone or helping the gardener. I blotted

Me in 1919.

my copybook forever when I fell into the lily pond. My poor mother never lived down the fact that Granny Kitty's rare lilies never bloomed again.

Our new house, the rooms attractively decorated by my mother, quickly filled up with residents requiring bed and breakfast. My mother ran it with some domestic help. Our cook-housekeeper was Mrs. Wheatley, whose husband and son also lived with us, and Eva, from Wales, cleaned the rooms. Eva had a lovely singing voice, and she would come over and sing me to sleep when my mother was out. We also had a series of fourteen-year-olds who came to us to be trained as housemaids. They were Welsh and had names that sounded like music: Bronwyn, Credwyn, Alwyn, and so on.

We had our own kitchen, but I used to sneak down to the big one where I was thoroughly spoiled. I would read the *Daily Mirror*, a forbidden tabloid, consume all kinds of junk food, and make a general nuisance of myself. The staff ate such things as winkles, tripe and onions, and jellied eels. I was fascinated, when I was older, to see the eels still wriggling after they had been cut up. Mrs. Wheatley told me it was their "last nerves" so I promptly wrote a play called "The Prostrate Foe." In it the numerous people who died but did not lie still were suffering, as I explained to the audience, from "last nerves"!

They adored me in the kitchen but once in a while I would go too far. When I did they knew how to get rid of me. I had a horror of raw fish and they would chase me with one. On one horrendous occasion, I decided to try to help Mrs. Wheatley get over her morbid fear of mice. I put two of my pet mice in my pocket and sauntered down to the kitchen, intending to show her how sweet and harmless they were. I changed my mind when I got there, but I must have looked guilty because she asked me if I had them. I was a hopeless liar and one of them peeked out. All hell broke loose, Mrs. Wheatley fainted, and her husband and son chased me upstairs.

My sister was a beautiful child with huge dark brown eyes. I had blue eyes and dimples and was always laughing—cute rather than pretty, I am told. I was christened Nancy Elizabeth but, as a baby, I was called Snookie. When I was five, I objected strongly to this and wanted to be called Betty. None of our friends would take me seriously until my mother gave me permission to charge them a penny in aid of Doctor Barnardo's homes every time they forgot my new name. I can remember rattling a tin box under their noses until, in sheer self-defence, they made the change.

Before the advent of the Wheatleys, who were with us for twenty-five years, we had another cook. Her little boy, Ronnie, shared the nursery on the second floor with us. One day, when we were toddlers, we were playing "horses" on the back of the sofa. It was next to a window which our nanny, who was in the adjoining bathroom, had left wide open. Ronnie suddenly disappeared. I trotted through the door and said, "Nanny, Ronnie has fallen out of the window." I can always remember my indignation at being ignored as Ronnie became the hero of the

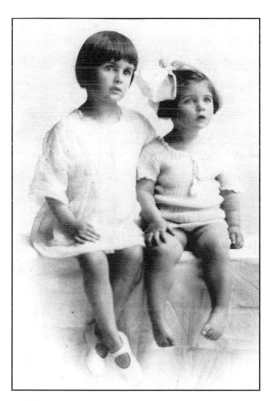

Mary and me, six and two years of age.

hour. Luckily he only broke his hip, but everybody was so concerned that I made a mental note: in future I would not take any action that would draw attention away from myself!

At the age of four, I went to kindergarten at South Hampstead High School. I was so proud of my uniform: a gym tunic, blouse, tie, blazer, and hat—velour in the winter, panama in the summer. The school colours were orange and black. I was somewhat swamped by all this paraphernalia, but I felt very important. My poor sister had to take me to school every day. It was quite a long walk, and once, when we were halfway there, I said, "Mary, my knickers are wet." She was furious as she took me home to change and we set out again.

With nearly four years between us, my sister and I had very little in common. I think she was thoroughly bored with me. As we got older she went to boarding school, while I was at home, absorbed in my ballet. I was very good at sports, and she hated them. I was a good student and she would not apply herself. She used to tease me mercilessly and I would retaliate by hitting her. I was always blamed because I appeared to be the aggressor. In fairness, however, she was afraid to hit me as I would become very dramatic and say, "My career, my career, you have ruined it!"

Our relatives accused my mother of favouring me. I believe there was some truth in this, especially when I started dancing. On the other hand Mary was extremely stubborn; she refused to wear the lovely clothes my mother made for us, because she wanted to look like everyone else. She was not affectionate, while I was cuddly, and she insisted on going away to school. I was much closer to my cousin Lolette, who lived with us. Her father, Jack Oliphant, was in forestry. Her parents were stationed in the former British Honduras and later in Malaya. Lolette was treated as another daughter by my mother. She was a year older than I was, and even though she went to boarding school with my sister, we were inseparable when she was at home.

I was a highly strung, imaginative child who believed in fairies. I used to leave notes for them in a secret mailbox that was hidden in the bushes outside our house. The fairies always replied. Many years later I learned that our postman had known of the box and had taken the trouble to keep the correspondence flowing. I frequently had nightmares, always the same two: a mass of snakes seethed towards me until it reached my neck, and a huge polar bear came through my bedroom window. He was going to crush me with a big hug. I used to wake screaming and my mother would rush in to comfort me. I have often wondered how Carl Jung would have interpreted those bad dreams.

I loved the outdoors and was a real tomboy. One day my mother saw me climbing, three floors up, along a narrow plank between our house and the one next door. Afraid I would lose my balance if she called out, she kept very quiet until I was safe. She was not over-protective and, I am happy to say, gave me a lot of freedom.

As a small child I had frequent bronchial problems, and after three bouts of double pneumonia I finished up with a patch on my lung. The doctor recommended exercise classes and was enthusiastic when my mother mentioned that she had a friend who taught ballet. So it was arranged that I would have private lessons with Miss Sheen, my first and most important ballet teacher.

At that time well-brought-up girls were supposed to sit around waiting for a husband. Having a career was frowned upon. A career on the stage was akin to prostitution. Although she was broad-minded and not at all influenced by our stuffy relatives in Scotland, my mother had no intention of allowing me to get hooked on the idea of becoming a dancer. Consequently, at her request, my lessons consisted of exercises at the barre without music. To relieve the monotony I used to watch my badly behaved little puppy, who had to be tied to the barre with my stocking.

It is hard to understand why this dry and apparently boring introduction to ballet would inspire me to fight to continue when my lung was healed and my mother wanted me to give it up. When my pupils tell me how they discovered ballet, it is always through some moving experience: they have seen a great dancer on stage or on T.V., or they love music and interpreting, through movement, the emotions it evokes. For me those things would come later. On looking back I think I enjoyed the marriage of mental and physical effort: the challenge of mastering a difficult and, dare I say it, abnormal technical skill.

"I'm going to dance," I—who never argued with my mother—said belligerently. "I don't care what you say or what you do, I won't give it up." Luckily Miss Sheen supported my urgent pleas to be allowed to go on with my classes. She confirmed that I had talent. She said I had beautiful arms and was very musical, but she warned my mother that I must have lessons every day. Reluctantly, my mother gave in, although she knew she would face severe criticism from all our relatives.

I was never allowed, as many young dance students were, to neglect my academic education. When I was seven I was sent to Queen's College on Harley Street as it was close to my ballet studio. I was given permission to leave school at the mid-morning break for a daily ballet class. I returned in time for an afternoon of study. At 4:00 p.m. I went back to the studio for another class in pointe work or some related form of dance such as national, Greek, or character dancing.

It was understood that I would make up anything I missed at school. I was threatened with having to give up ballet if I did not remain in the top three of my class. I felt somewhat miffed but relieved when I was told that I need not take singing or art as I showed very little aptitude for them. My days were long and I did not get home until 7:00 p.m. Once there, I still had to have supper and do any homework I had not been able to do on the bus travelling to and from school.

When I was totally exhausted I had a ploy that helped me to relieve the tension. I would put talcum powder on my face and soot from the fireplace to emphasize the circles under my eyes. My mother, with her bad sight, was taken in completely. She would not let me go to school in spite of my phoney protests. The trick was gradually to eliminate my pallor so that I was considered well enough to go to my afternoon dance classes. It always worked!

It was a solitary life. At school they could not understand my passion for ballet. At the ballet studio most of the students went to a governess for three hours a day and had no homework. My friends told me that if I planned to be a dancer, it was ridiculous for my mother to place so much emphasis on my academic subjects. How wrong they were. The days of the so-called "dumb dancer" no longer exist. In fact the dancers were not dumb, simply poorly educated.

It was my own experience that led me to insist on high academic standards when the National Ballet School was founded in 1959, and to introduce an enriched curriculum with music and art as core subjects. These essentials for a dancer had, in my case, been sadly neglected. Also, I remembered the loneliness of having to make a commitment at such an early age, and the gulf it created between me and so-called normal children. These memories caused me to provide, for our students, a professional counselling program. I wanted to ensure that they were not trapped into a dance career or that if they had one they would be equipped, when they retired, to follow a second career.

I was lucky to have Miss Sheen as my first teacher. A big, Junoesque woman, she dressed beautifully and had lovely legs. She taught ballet in the old Russian style, as she was a pupil of two famous Russians, Laurent Novikoff, a former partner of Anna Pavlova, and Madame Pruzina. They had immigrated to England and opened a school in London. Theirs was not the Vaganova system which, years later, was recorded and introduced into the ballet schools of the U.S.S.R. Theirs was the training that had taken place in the old days at the Imperial School in St. Petersburg. This school, with its superb teachers, is movingly described in *Theatre Street*, a book by Tamara Karsavina, one of the great ballerinas of the early twentieth century. In the thirties Karsavina was another teacher who had a profound influence on me.

I adored Miss Sheen. She was very strict about our appearance and made us work very hard. We wore white organdie tutus which my poor mother had to wash every day. In these days of practical leotards, I often look back and recall how the white tutu made me feel like a dancer and how wonderful it looked on Armistice Day with a scarlet poppy at our waists.

As soon as I was strong enough, I had pointe shoes, and we worked in them for at least half an hour every day. My feet were practically ideal for pointe work: square, like a peasant's, with a good instep and four toes almost the same length. This gave me a broad base to stand on. It should not be hard to imagine the pain suffered by dancers when each toe is shorter than the one beside it, or when the second toe is longer than the big toe and it gets all scrunched up. The blocks in pointe shoes are made of hardened gum and often cause blisters, especially when they are new. The

I still had to learn to tie my pointe shoes!

shoes get soft very quickly and are then usually discarded, so one spends many hours sewing on ribbons and breaking in new shoes. They are handmade, expensive, and very hard to fit. I used to try on a dozen pairs in order to find two or three that were comfortable. Each maker, usually an Italian, has his own letter on the sole of the shoe, and the letter *K* was the signature of the man who made my shoes.

Because our feet were often sore from the morning ballet class, we used to look forward to the afternoons when we would study other forms of dance. I especially loved Greek dancing. I have never seen it being taught in North America, but I feel it is a valuable adjunct to ballet. For those classes we wore mauve chiffon tunics which went across one shoulder, and our feet were bare. It was such a relief. In ballet there is not much freedom until a certain amount of technique has been mastered. In Greek dancing, the technique is much less demanding, and one can move freely from the beginning. We learned the eight positions taken from the Greek friezes and lots of little steps with intriguing names such as *roebucks* and *komats*.

In this class we had to compose "nature rhythms." We were told to imagine we were something in nature. I was too shy to let myself go by emulating the waves in the sea, or a tree in the wind, so I curled up in a little ball. When the teacher asked what I was I said I was a stone. She replied, "But that isn't nature." I was incensed and rolled over a few times, saying, "Yes it is; I'm gathering moss." This was not acceptable and I was humiliated.

I was in trouble again, in a much more serious way, when we had a Scottish dance class with one of Miss Sheen's assistants.

This woman had lost the top of her thumb. The end was red and shiny and had what looked like a piece of string at the end. It reminded me of a sausage, and I was terrified of being touched by that thumb. I was squeamish about many things: I could not tolerate seeing people who had been injured in accidents; I had a horror of raw fish and raw meat; I always crossed the road to avoid passing a butcher's shop. In a vain attempt to cure me my mother offered me a puppy providing I was willing to take care of it. She made me cut up raw liver for his dinner. Not a good idea! I did it because I wanted to keep my puppy, but it increased my revulsion. My heart was broken one day when, on the way to school, my dog stepped into the gutter to do his business. He was hit by a car and killed.

The class in Miss Sheen's studio was a joke as the teacher didn't know the first thing about Scottish dance. It so happened that every year, while vacationing in Edinburgh, I had studied with a famous teacher of Scottish dancing. I knew all the traditional dances and was extremely adept at the sword dance. We had to learn it with bare feet and real swords, which made us very careful about where we placed our feet. In the class, being an absolute brat and feeling very superior, I proceeded to act up. I informed the other students that what we were learning was all wrong, and I showed them how it should be. The poor woman was embarrassed and I was merciless. As you can imagine, I did not get away with my shameful behaviour. The next day I was called into Miss Sheen's office. She tore strips off me and sent me sobbing back to my ballet class, where I sat under the barre and cried until the class ended.

I cried very easily and frequently. I feel, on looking back, that I was always put in situations that I was too immature to handle.

My mother expected a great deal from me at a very early age. I appeared independent and confident when, from the age of seven, I travelled all over London, but I was often a frightened little girl. Once when I was supposed to meet my mother at a downtown store she didn't turn up. There was some misunderstanding about the meeting place. By the time she found me I was hysterical, and she could not understand why I was in such a state.

On the other hand, I could be very enterprising. By the time I was ten, I had moved to Saint Mary's College in Lancaster Gate. Miss Sheen taught social dancing to the girls at that school. Because she knew the authorities, they were more sympathetic to my ballet than the ones at Queen's College had been. To get to and from my new school, I had to catch one bus and transfer to another at a department store called Selfridges. Each ride cost a penny, and one day my friend who was travelling home with me had lost her two pennies. I lent her one of mine for the first part of the journey. When we got to Selfridges I marched in and said, "Please can you give me tuppence?" I continued, "You can charge it to my mother's account." I had often seen my mother do that and felt it should have worked. However, the shop assistant laughed heartily and said, "Here are two pennies but I can't charge it!"

I cried the most when I was taken to the professional classes at Novikoff's school. For my age I was very advanced at ballet, and Miss Sheen was proud of me. However, I was overwhelmed and intimidated by all the grown-ups who looked thoroughly scruffy but were superb dancers. I was in my little white dress, beautifully groomed, and feeling totally inadequate. It was not long before I started crying and had to leave. I knew my mother was very disappointed in me, and I suffered my usual sense of failure.

On one of these disastrous visits I was shocked, when the class was over, to see Hilda Butsova (née Hilda Boot), who had been a leading dancer in Anna Pavlova's company, wringing out her pants. As soon as we got outside I whispered, "Mummy, that lady has wet her pants." My mother explained that they were rubber pants, designed to make one sweat, and that what I had seen was perspiration. Dancers, who are a stubborn lot, still wear them although it has been proven that they are not good for the muscles.

I was extremely happy during the years I spent at Saint Mary's College. I was a born organizer and was given many responsible positions. As well as being form prefect and games captain, I was in charge of raising funds for our charity project, a club called Senior Street, which had been founded to help poor children. When my mother was invited to the school to be told that I was too bossy, she suggested that they take away some of my leadership roles. "That is impossible," they said. "She is so good at them." "Then I'm afraid I can't help you," my mother replied.

We always had wonderful holidays. We stayed at home for Christmas and went to lots of parties. Only once do I remember an unhappy Christmas. I feel to this day that my mother overreacted, but the reader can decide. My sister, my cousin, and I had gone to bed with our stockings hung up beside us. In our family we would wake to find not only filled stockings but all our presents. This year we found nothing. In the night we had woken and decided it would be okay to open one present, so we all went to sleep hugging whatever we had found. On discovering this, my mother saw it as a breach of trust and removed everything. After breakfast we were allowed our presents, but because we felt so ashamed, our day had been spoiled.

In the Easter vacation we went to Auntie Margie's flat in Edinburgh. I had a great time playing with the boys in the street. We played cricket with a lamppost as the wicket. At first I was only allowed to be the "cop-watch." Since it was illegal to play ball games in the street, somebody had to look out for a policeman. When one appeared the boys would throw the bat and ball over the wall and disappear, leaving me to play Miss Innocence. Although gruff, the cop usually got taken in by my smile and my big blue eyes. After all, there was no evidence to make him doubt my assurance that we had only been playing tag, a game that did not need a ball.

As I climbed the wall to rescue our equipment I felt the stirring of feminist feelings. "Why am I always left to face the music?" I asked the boys. To appease my ruffled feelings they promoted me from cop-watch to active team player. That a girl could bowl straighter than they could, run faster, and catch a ball nine times out of ten was in their view a freak of nature, so I was accepted as one of them.

As I have said, I loved being out of doors. In Scotland I used to spend all day roaming the hills around Edinburgh. I would find a cave and build a fire and fry sausages. My mother trusted me to behave responsibly. On those holidays she only made me do one thing that I hated and dreaded. I had to dance at Whitehill, a home for mentally retarded children. Once again my squeamishness took over. I could not stand the smell of these children, who often could not control their bowels or their bladders, and their abnormal appearance upset me terribly. I was not proud of these feelings, but needed a bit more understanding from my mother. She accused me of a lack of generosity when I had so much and the children so little. She said it wasn't too much to ask me to give pleasure when I could, and she totally discounted how I felt.

My favourite holidays were in the summer. From the age of twelve until I was fifteen we went to Duinbergen, a small place on the Belgian coast. We took trips to hear the carillon in Bruges or to see Brussels. Sometimes we went across the border to Holland. I was happiest when we stayed at the resort. I used to dig a big hole in the sand and put a seat all around the inside, then invite a number of children on the beach to join my nursery school. I kept them amused for hours and their parents were delighted. A kindergarten teacher was the only career I was tempted to consider aside from ballet.

In Duinbergen they had a casino. It was more like a community centre than a gambling place although it did have slot machines. As we were there for six weeks I had plenty of time to find some kids who had studied ballet, rehearse them, and put on a show at the casino. My mother made the costumes out of crêpe paper and the audience was very appreciative. In my spare time I was a ballboy for the tennis tournaments. I took great pride in keeping my players supplied with balls while being as unobtrusive as possible.

As I have said, I loved organizing, and my insistence on perfection in all my efforts eventually became a curse. My mother encouraged this and would persuade me to repeat my ballet exercises over and over again until I was exhausted. Once I entered an essay competition. My entry had to be perfect so I wrote it out about ten times. When I won a bicycle, she pointed out that it had been worth all the work, but I had doubts.

At home our living room was designed for me, with a parquet floor, a big mirror, and very little furniture. When relatives visited they always wanted me to do a little dance. I refused, saying, "No! We don't do 'little dances.' We just do exercises." My mother always supported me in this; she knew I felt it was unprofessional. However, I was constantly putting on plays. We would rig up a curtain and arrange the chairs for the audience. We were allowed to charge a penny as long as it went to charity. I told my sister that one of the seats was free. She objected, "But, Betty, you can't see from there."

"That's why it's free," I replied.

My happiest times were spent in the studio and on my frequent visits to the theatre. My mother made great financial sacrifices for me. She would buy tickets for all kinds of shows: the D'Oyly Carte Opera, dramas, comedies, musicals, and of course dance performances. I saw Mary Wigman, one of the great exponents of modern dance. I was thrilled with two young East Indian dancers, Uday Shankar and Ram Gopal. I think I was too young to appreciate the flamenco dancers, Argentina and Argentinita, but I loved the company of Kurt Jooss, who choreographed the famous ballet *The Green Table*. I went to inspiring performances of Diaghilev's company and many other visiting ballet companies. Although I saw many wonderful dancers, Anna Pavlova was the great love of my life.

Her death in The Hague on January 23, 1931, affected me deeply. I had seen her very last performance at the Golders Green Hippodrome in London on December 13, 1930. I had waited for her at the stage door. She came out wrapped in a fur coat, and as always I gave her a big bunch of violets. Although I was only twelve I had seen her dance some thirty times. Whenever she was not on stage, I felt empty. When the performance was over I would go home longing for the next time I would see her. When I knew I would never see her again I grieved deeply. At school everybody thought I was crazy to make such a fuss about a dancer.

I saw Pavlova in many different roles, but the two that I loved the most, *Amarilla* and *The Dying Swan*, were tragic ballets full of drama. Comments on Pavlova's dramatic ability by Valerian Svetlov, a distinguished St. Petersburg critic, are quoted by Oleg

Kerensky in his book *Anna Pavlova*. He is speaking of her first performance in a revival of Petipa's *Bayaderka* in 1902/03 at the Maryinsky Theatre:

> To write about *Bayaderka* is to write about Pavlova; all the rest remains in the background and colourless. When this young beautiful and graceful ballerina appears on the stage one feels exalted, seeing her sincerity and her simple charm. Not for a second does one doubt her love for Solor, her hate for the Brahmin, her tragic grief when the man she loves betrays her, and her great suffering before she dies. Her face marvellously reflects all her feelings. The role does not possess her. She is in full possession and control of the role. Pavlova's talent for mime has the elements of a real tragic artist.

This talent is rare in the ballet world. As in *Bayaderka*, it was very evident in her performance of the two ballets I have mentioned. In *Amarilla* and *The Dying Swan*, Anna Pavlova sent shivers up my spine.

Pavlova played the part of a gypsy girl in *Amarilla*. She had to dance at a wedding celebration for a count who had once been her lover. She hoped to win him back with her dancing, but when all she received was a purse of gold she fell senseless to the ground in despair. I found this ballet passionate and unbearably moving. In a short space of time the role covered so many emotions from love through betrayal, jealousy, hope, sadness, to despair. I think I grew up a little each time I saw it.

Since Anna Pavlova's death I have seen many people dance *The Dying Swan*, including some world-famous dancers. These sentimental performances always made me feel very angry. This ballet was created by Fokine who expressed his intention in these words: ". . . that the dance could and should satisfy not only the eye but through the medium of the eye should penetrate into the soul." When Pavlova danced *The Dying Swan* I experienced this depth of feeling, but I was never to feel it again.

To the music of Saint-Saëns, in her white tutu and feathered headdress, she glided on stage, and I became aware that I was seeing the final struggle for life of a dying bird. In the centre of her breast she wore a large green emerald which, I imagined, represented the hole made by an arrow that had pierced her heart. I cannot describe adequately the poignancy of the final moments so will leave it to Cyril W. Beaumont, the British author and critic, who wrote in his book *Anna Pavlova*:

> There is something at once fascinating and agonizing in watching this painful ebbing of life, which ever retreats before the conquering advance of death. The arms extend like wings and flutter feebly; but the effort to rise is too much and she sinks to the ground. Gathering all her strength she rises, her head thrown backwards and her body quivering from the effort. Her body becomes more erect. Again the wing-like arms rise slowly, higher and higher. But her strength fails, her head droops to peer despairingly from under one outstretched arm. Now she moves slowly in a circle. Suddenly one arm leaps upwards towards the sky in a supreme effort to escape from the invisible force that bears her down, but the figure falls helplessly to the ground. The arms quiver pitifully, the body is shaken by a few faint tremors. The arms close stiffly above her head and fall forward on the outstretched leg. Her head drops on her breast. Then all is still. The swan is dead.

Half an hour before she died, Pavlova tried to cross herself, and whispered to her maid, "Get my Swan costume ready." I believe that this dance should remain sacred to the memory of Anna Pavlova. I will never forget the memorial performance organized in her honour by the Camargo Society in London. The curtain was raised on an empty stage, the lights were dim, and we heard the music of *The Dying Swan*. The audience was hushed, sharing a moment of grief and a feeling of unbearable loss. As the music continued a strange sort of collective psychic image was evoked. To this day I could swear that I and many others saw a ghostly figure gliding across the stage.

Soon after Pavlova's death my whole life was turned upside down. My mother had a terrible fight with Miss Sheen and would not let me return to her school. The trouble started when I had a huge blister which covered my little toe and the one next to it. My

21

mother wrote a note saying she thought it would be better if I didn't go on pointe until my foot had healed. Miss Sheen replied that she would not be dictated to by parents and that she would decide what I would do. When I went to the studio I had to do pointe work for approximately three quarters of an hour. This was very cruel and I was conscious of being a victim of Miss Sheen's stubbornness, but I didn't for a moment think of leaving her. Dancers expect and tolerate a lot of pain and in my day heroism was embraced.

My mother, Yvonne, circa 1920.

I returned from the class and the blister had burst. It was bleeding and looked horrible. In spite of my mother's efforts it became infected. She said to me, "You are not going back there." I replied, "I have to go back. I have to go back."

"Look," she said, "I can't get her not to put you on pointe. You have an infected foot."

"Just wait until my foot's better and then I can go back," I pleaded, but my mother was adamant.

As well as feeling happy and secure at the studio, I had a very special reason for not wanting to leave at that time. Miss Sheen was putting on a professional show at Saint Mary's College and I was to be the star soloist. Having always undergone a great deal of teasing from my peers, I was looking forward to the chance to show that my passionate commitment to ballet had not been in vain. I knew I was good and wanted the staff and my schoolmates to recognize that fact. With more confidence I wouldn't have needed that boost to my ego.

Much later I met a former pupil of Miss Sheen in England. She had been one of four little chickens while I had been the mother chicken. That lady, Phrosso Pfister, had become the principal of the London College of Dance. We laughed as we remembered the recital at London's Scala Theatre. The chickens had been dressed in yellow marabou and I had worn a tutu in the same colour. I told her I often felt very lonely being a soloist and used to beg my teacher to let me be part of a group. She pointed out that I should be thankful because I was more advanced and could cope with the challenge of solo roles.

From the moment my mother forbade me to return to Miss Sheen's class, I had a bewildering time. As an adolescent I was rebelling against my mother, who rarely took the trouble to find out what I wanted or how I was feeling. I was full of repressed anger.

Rehearsing for the Tricity Restaurant at age fourteen.

Adolescence

Leaving Miss Sheen's studio left me completely shattered. My mother started searching for another school and would read out advertisements from the various dance magazines. I was too angry with her to show any interest so she decided to send me to the Euphen MacLaren School, which was described as a stage-dancing school. They taught all forms of dance, including ballet, tap, musical comedy, and baton twirling. It turned out to be a third rate commercial institution and I was there for less than a month.

In a way this descent from the sublime (Miss Sheen) to the ridiculous (Euphen MacLaren) taught me something important. Miss Sheen had high standards and excellent taste. I had absorbed these qualities, but was not conscious of them until I had a chance to make a comparison.

The next school my mother chose for me was vastly superior. I was enrolled at the Zelia Raye and Joan Davis School of Stage Dancing. At the time my mother and I were at loggerheads. I was a "ballet snob" and looked down on all other forms of dance. My mother, in her wisdom, wanted me to be more versatile. She was afraid that my future in classical ballet was uncertain. To increase my chances of getting a job, she wanted me to learn more commercial dance techniques.

Her fears were well founded. In the early thirties ballet in the United Kingdom and North America was in its infancy. British dancers were still having to change their names to get jobs with rapidly disappearing Russian companies. The high level of professional dance that exists in the West today was not yet in evidence.

My new school was near Leicester Square tube station in London. It was on the outskirts of Soho, which was then somewhat unsavoury. Soon after I went there, we moved into a beautiful building at 77 Dean Street in the heart of Soho.

Zelia Raye was an older woman, extremely garrulous. I didn't like her, but that was not important because I had all my lessons with Joan Davis. Before becoming a teacher, Joan had performed in her own act as a male impersonator. She was an attractive blonde with a masculine hairstyle.

For my first class with Joan Davis I wore tap shoes with toe and heel taps. I found them clumsy. Our uniform was a checked gingham romper—a far cry from my white tutu! I felt ridiculous, out of place, and somewhat piqued that nobody knew I was a very good ballet dancer.

I soon found out that in tap dancing the toes and knees must face front and that my ballet turnout was unacceptable. As I struggled with single, double, and triple timesteps, I decided that tap was for the birds and that I would never master the intricacies of this new dance form. Gradually, however, I became interested, realizing that in the world of stage dancing I had much to learn. I made up my mind that if I had to do it I was going to be the best.

In Joan Davis I found, once again, a teacher with taste and high standards. As well as tap, she taught us limbering and stretching, musical comedy dancing, modern ballet, and acrobatic dancing. I became an acrobatic dancer, but the cost in terms of stiffness and bruises was great. My mother with her usual enthusiasm encouraged me to practise each new trick until it was mastered. I used to feel very proud when I heard her telling her friends that I was so stiff and sore when I woke in the morning that she had to help me out of bed.

When I was twenty-one I wrote a book entitled *What Is an Acrobatic Dancer?* It was accepted for publication, but the war

Drawings of acrobatic positions
from my unpublished book.
Top: splits; left: back bend;
right: walk-over.

caused a severe shortage of paper and the project was shelved. As I excelled at this type of dance and performed it at many professional venues, I would like to describe it by quoting part of my first chapter:

An acrobat is described in the dictionary as 'a highly skilled gymnast, tight-rope walker, tumbler etc.': I expect you have held your breath as you watched acrobats perform some particularly daring feat; I know I have and envied them their perfect timing, balance and control. Very often these men or women have been trained from babyhood by their parents who have learned from their parents before them, thus handing down the great traditions of the theatre and the circus.

Another person who is sometimes styled acrobat is the contortionist. Again, referring to the dictionary, we find that: 'he or she, usually she, is an acrobat but one who twists her body into unnatural postures.'

At some time or other everybody must have seen a contortionist. Let us make a brief mental picture: a small slender figure, minimally dressed in white or silver, steps on to a raised platform in the centre of the stage. She is followed by a bright beam of light; she twists and turns like a snake until it seems that her body must break in two. Soft music and the roll of drums in the background grow louder as the climax is reached; some particularly breathtaking feat followed by thunderous applause.

What then is the difference between this imaginary performance and that of the Acrobatic Dancer? In the first place, you have a series of clever tricks strung together. In the second, a dance, with pattern and form, arranged to music that has been specially chosen. The dancer covers the stage, very often wearing a flowing dress which makes a circle of colour as she performs an acrobatic movement with grace and ease. You would not think of applauding this trick for its own sake; it is blended into the whole effortless picture.

In reality the title of this book should be reversed, for the acrobatic dancer is first a dancer and then an acrobat.

Some years after my early classes in acrobatics with Joan Davis, I was introduced to Laurie Devine. Perhaps some of the older generation may remember her famous Lorelei in C. B. Cochran's London revue *Bitter Sweet*. This great artist had been born in a circus. Her mother told me that when Laurie was three, asleep in her crib at night, she would sneak into Laurie's room and tie her legs into the splits. Laurie had made the transition from circus acrobat to a superb acrobatic dancer. It was from her that I learned the finishing touches that enhanced my performance of this controversial form of dance.

This controversy arises, and with good reason, from the belief that the body can be damaged from learning acrobatic tricks. This is only true if the pupil is in the hands of a bad teacher. I was lucky. My teachers were very careful and emphasized the importance of protecting the spine. We were given very comprehensive limbering, stretching, and strengthening exercises before attempting any tricks. Great attention was paid to this so that our back and abdominal muscles became strong and gave us plenty of support. A sway-back, which one sees frequently in gymnasts, was unacceptable because it puts too much strain on the lumbar area.

Most dancers are flexible; in my case, too much so. I was hyper-mobile, somewhat like an overcooked chicken, so I needed little in the way of stretching, but a great deal of strengthening. The extreme suppleness of dancers like me creates a myth that I must explode. There is no such thing as being double-jointed.

Once I had decided to give up the role of "ballet nun," my tap dancing progressed rapidly. Joan Davis had been taught by a pupil of Fred Astaire's teacher, Hermes Pan, so the tap we learned was very balletic and covered a lot of space. I became proficient at myriad steps and was helped by my natural sense of rhythm. "Winging," first with two feet and then with one, was the ultimate technical challenge. By the time we moved to 77 Dean Street, I could wing with the best of them.

Within a year at the Zelia Raye school, I was one of its most advanced students. I shared this position with a girl called Dorothy Workman. She sang as well as danced and was more stagey than I. We were about equal in tap and acrobatic dancing, but because of my years of training in classical ballet, I was the better dancer when it came to musical comedy and modern ballet.

My classes in the latter gave me a chance to shine and Joan Davis was excited to have such an advanced pupil. Unlike my training with Miss Sheen, the emphasis was on showy theatrical steps and the class included all kinds of spins and

My first modern ballet costume.

29

pirouettes. I was very good at these, and at one time Joan suggested that I would do well with a vaudeville act that consisted of nothing but turns. I would become "Betty Oliphant, the Queen of the Spinners!" I shuddered at the thought.

Approaching my thirteenth birthday, I was happy at the studio, but my life at home and at school was rather bleak.

My cousin, Lolette, was moved from our home by her parents. No explanation was given, but I believe that my uncle Jack's wife, Amina, was jealous of her daughter's affection for my mother. We were all very hurt by this action, and I, who had suddenly lost someone I thought of as a sister, was inconsolable. We did not know that Lolette had been told we didn't want her back, so we were surprised when we didn't hear from her. She had been hurt too.

The truth came out quite recently when Lolette and I were in our seventies. I obtained her address from the family trustees in Edinburgh, and when I was on the Isle of Capri, judging a ballet competition, I went to Naples to visit her. It was a moving reunion. There was a strong family likeness between us which amazed her husband, but it is not unusual in first cousins.

She told me her parents had left her in a convent in England when their leave was over, and they returned to their station abroad. She was miserable and ran away five or six times. She could not understand why we had abandoned her.

Lolette and I agreed that her mother had been a very difficult woman. Her parents' marriage had broken up when Jack could no longer tolerate his wife's total disregard for anyone but herself. As for the two of us, we felt as close as when we were children. We regretted the sixty-odd years that had been wasted through a silly misunderstanding.

When I changed dance studios, I continued to attend Saint Mary's College but was not as happy. I no longer left school in the morning to take ballet. Instead, I went to the studio after school every day and took at least two classes between four and seven o'clock. This meant giving up all after-school activities. The one I missed most was leading the netball team in matches against other schools.

I suffered a great deal when Miss Sheen put on her show at Saint Mary's and I was not a part of it. Needless to say, I could not bear to watch it. With nothing left but academic classes, I no longer had a feeling of belonging to the school.

This feeling of estrangement may have accounted for some reprehensible behaviour on my part. I was caught climbing the ropes in the gymnasium in the lunch break. The teacher who found me imposed a punishment that I felt would be totally humiliating. I was to change in the junior cloakroom every day for a month. Being very tall for my age, I could imagine how the younger kids would snicker. To the teacher's amazement, I burst into tears. "Why are you crying?" she asked. "Because I haven't got a daddy," I sobbed.

From that moment everything changed. The punishment was cancelled, and I was treated with great sympathy. Since then I have been known to be manipulative with board members and with politicians, but never again to avoid consequences of my behaviour. I will not forget my feelings of shame.

Although easily hurt and prone to tears, I had always been, at least outwardly, a happy child. I was known to laugh a lot and to be full of mischief. A born leader, I am sure my peers did not always appreciate my attempts to organize them. Yet on the whole I was popular with them and my teachers.

As puberty approached, my life seemed to get darker. My gloomy thoughts were not helped by the onset of my period, about which I had been told nothing. I was terrified when it happened and thought I was bleeding to death. As usual my mother dismissed my fears as childish nonsense. She had a way of making natural things seem ugly, and that was how I felt when she told me it was called "the curse." Luckily I got a much healthier response when I went to the studio. My mother had phoned Joan Davis as she believed my physical activity should be limited. On arriving at the studio, I expected to be handled with kid gloves. Not a bit of it! I took two very demanding classes in tap and acrobatics and was not spared in any way. From that day forward, in spite of much pain and nausea each month, I did not allow myself any concessions.

When I was unhappy I transported myself to an imaginary life in which I was the hero. I read constantly. In the early days I had all kinds of schoolgirl magazines, but as I grew older I loved Tennyson, Rudyard Kipling, Sir Henry Newbolt, D. K. Broster,

Henry Williamson, and many others. Most of the authors I read and the poems I memorized were idealistic and, in many cases, patriotic. Some were also chauvinistic and patronizing in their belief that men, and British men in particular, are a superior group. At the time I did not recognize this aspect of their works; I only knew they moved me deeply.

To this day I have two ways of dealing with unhappiness: I either soak in a hot bath or I recite poems to myself. Tennyson's "Mort d'Arthur" is one of my favourites, and I have arranged to have his "Crossing the Bar" recited at my funeral.

By the time I was thirteen I had a mad crush on Joan Davis. It manifested itself in my efforts to be helpful to her. I took attendance, dusted the piano, answered the phone, and kept the appointment book up to date.

Unfortunately Joan and Zelia Raye discovered that I was a good teacher. I had vague feelings of resentment when I was taken out of my own classes to coach or even to give a private lesson. They charged a guinea (one pound, one shilling) for me to teach for half an hour and pocketed all of it. My mother was paying hefty fees for my training, but I would gladly have died for Joan, so I didn't let on at home how much I was being used.

Nor did I tell my mother that I was sometimes left alone in charge of the office at the studio. I was terrified one day when the milkman arrived with his face bleeding from razor slashes. I have always been squeamish and it took all my courage to help him clean himself up.

Still in my early teens, I was virtually an unpaid assistant. I was relieved when my mother decided I should look older. She bought me some very nice, more grown-up outfits. I also had my first "perm." In those days it was a big deal; I was strung up to a machine and the whole thing took about four hours. Lesley, the hairdresser with whom I continued until I came to Canada, was an absolute darling. He did a wonderful job and people were amazed at how much prettier I looked. My mother was afraid I would look common, a horrible snobbish English expression meaning not good class.

I have to say here that by and large my mother was not a snob. She was actually very socialistic. When we moved to Hampstead, she made a bonfire of any of our ancestors' portraits that she considered were not good paintings. I suffered because, unlike my school friends, I was not called Miss Betty by our maids. When I protested, my mother said, "Why should a thirty-five-year-old woman have to call a little twerp like you 'Miss'?" I had no answer.

Although I was enthusiastic about my stage-dancing classes, I missed taking lessons in my first love, classical ballet. The one class a week in modern ballet was hopelessly inadequate.

Once again, my mother arranged for me to leave school in the mornings, this time to study with Marie Rambert, a former dancer with Serge Diaghilev's Ballets Russes, who had her own school. She was also the founder of the Mercury Theatre in Ladbroke Grove.

Despite my classes with Marie Rambert and, later, Karsavina, I still spent most of my time at 77 Dean Street. Joan Davis was very fond of me and I was extremely useful to her and Miss Raye. I had far too much work and responsibility for my age and I suffered severe indigestion because of irregular, hurried meals. Even so, I was very happy. I had my place at the front of the class and was highly thought of as a teacher. Then things started to go horribly wrong.

A woman called Vivien Davies enrolled at the school. She and Joan Davis fell in love with each other. I realized something weird was happening when Vivien started to model herself on Joan. She copied her hairstyle, her clothes; they were like clones. Most mystifying of all was when she changed her name to Peter Vivien.

I found myself being ignored by Joan. I was receiving little or no attention from her and was banished to the back of the class. It was obvious that Peter was so jealous of me that Joan could only please her by ostracizing me. I was deeply hurt and bewildered.

My fellow students were clearly sorry for me, and I overheard one of them saying that Joan and Peter were lesbians. I went to my mother and said, "What is a lesbian?"

"Oh! It's just a woman that sleeps with another woman," she replied. I thought, Well, that's impossible, how could it work?

My mother never gave me clear explanations, and one day she paid a price for this. I asked her in a loud voice, "Mummy, what is an illegitimate baby?"

"Hush," she said. "It's just a baby which is very small." Two days later I rushed up to a baby, saying, "Mummy, look at this darling little illegitimate baby." She was embarrassed, but I think it served her right.

I really had no one to talk to about the pain that Joan was causing me. The other girls at the studio were much older than I, but they were almost as naïve. One of them told me you could catch a baby by going to a swimming pool.

At the tender age of fourteen, I danced nightly at the Tricity Restaurant on the Strand in London. The paradox of attending a Girl Guide meeting as a patrol leader in my short blue uniform with long black stockings and then going home to change into more sophisticated clothes, fur coat and all, made me very uncomfortable. I still wanted to be a child, but my mother was very ambitious for me.

I was performing at the Tricity with Joan Davis and was deeply hurt when she replaced me with Peter Vivien. It was there that their relationship came to an abrupt end. Peter Vivien killed herself.

Coming to terms with suicide, especially when it is so close, is not easy for a youngster. Yet I had suffered so much at the hands of this woman that I had feelings of gladness which made me feel thoroughly ashamed. As always, I could not express myself to my mother, so I felt very much alone as I nursed the confusion in my head.

Meanwhile, my life went on. Once again I was where I most loved to be—in the ballet studio. I will always remember Marie Rambert, known to her friends as Mimi. She taught and took lessons at the same time. She was not a good teacher. She wore a pink tunic with a frill and black tights. She looked like a little frog. The studio was huge and bitterly cold. Since she stood right beside it, she was the only one who benefited from the great big stove at the end of the room. The rest of us started class in coats and gloves and we could see our breath as we exercised.

Many of the dancers who were in the class with me were to become well known. Diana Gould became the much-loved wife of violinist Yehudi Menuhin. Prudence Hyman changed her name to Morosova and joined a Russian company. Pearl Argyle, a stunningly beautiful girl, died at an early age from a brain tumour. These dancers were much older than I, and woe betide me if I accidentally took one of their places at the barre.

Madame Rambert was brilliant at discovering creative talent. When I was there, Frederick Ashton was just emerging as a choreographer, as was Antony Tudor. The latter had given up his job as a porter at Billingsgate fish market when Rambert offered him a scholarship. In return he had to teach and do odd jobs around the school. Agnes de Mille was also there working with Tudor. All these people and many more, including Celia Franca, were able to hone their talents at the Mercury Theatre's Sunday evening performances.

I took afternoon classes with Antony Tudor. He often asked me theoretical questions. Although I had a strong technique, I had no memory of how I had acquired it. One day he asked in exasperation, "Don't you know any theory?" I muttered a negative reply. It was a great revelation; I hadn't been aware that there was any theory to know. If I wanted to teach, I told myself, I would have to do something about this.

Although she was good at finding people with great potential, Marie Rambert was too unpleasant to keep them. They often moved on to be developed by Dame Ninette de Valois, the founder in 1931 of the Sadler's Wells Ballet, now the Royal Ballet. This lady was also difficult, autocratic, with a very sharp tongue, and merciless if subjected to criticism by her underlings.

An incident typical of the way Marie Rambert treated people caused me to leave her school. Just before class I ripped my tights on a nail. I wore my tunic but my legs were bare. I was ordered to the centre of the room and told that I was trying to attract the men in the class. I was terribly shy and blushed profusely. While I admit that I am over-sensitive, I found that was a very cruel remark to make to an adolescent. In spite of my mother's protests, I refused to return to Rambert's studio.

Most of the artistic directors I have known were insensitive when dealing with staff and company members. I always felt that Celia Franca modelled herself on Dame Ninette. In Celia's case, her arrogant behaviour was probably due to insecurity. She was in a new country, faced with an enormous challenge. Grant Strate was honest about Celia when interviewed by Max Wyman for his book *Dance Canada*. "She was hell on wheels," Grant said, "but there was a wonderful side to her as well . . . more so in the early years. Later on, she became embattled." I agree wholeheartedly.

It is only recently that I have seen dancers treated with more respect by a new breed of artistic directors—people like Erik Bruhn, Rudi van Dantzig, and Reid Anderson. Perhaps those who wish for a career in ballet have to submit to the discipline of ballet too early in life, and consequently they do not rebel when as adults they are treated like children. I am proud to say that graduates of the National Ballet School have been encouraged to have a good self-image. They will not accept the cavalier treatment that was inflicted on me and my peers.

After my experience with Rambert I was lucky. I spent the next few years studying with Tamara Karsavina—first in the ballroom of a big hotel on Marylebone Road, later in her own studios in a mews on Baker Street, which is well known for its connection with Sherlock Holmes.

From St. Petersburg, Tamara Karsavina had the same background as Anna Pavlova, although she was four years younger. In 1910 she received the title of prima ballerina at the Imperial Theatre, where she had danced since she graduated from the school. She was on a leave of absence when, partnered by Nijinsky, she appeared in Diaghilev's company which opened in Paris in 1909 at the Théâtre du Châtelet.

Nijinsky was a great artist who had a fabulous jump. It was said that he literally seemed suspended in mid-air. His exit leap through the open window in Fokine's *Spectre de la rose* brought gasps from the audience. According to Karsavina in her book *Theatre Street*, when he was asked if it was difficult to stay in the air while jumping, he replied, "No! No! Not difficult. You have just to go up and then pause a little up there."

I had seen Karsavina dance but not as frequently as I had seen Pavlova. Karsavina, with her training in Russia and her tours with Diaghilev, obviously preferred to be part of an artistic whole—a company served by the best masters in dance, choreography, design, and music, under an artistic director who could combine all these talents to produce fine art.

Pavlova, on the other hand, wanted to take her great talent to the four corners of the world. To achieve this, some of the factors mentioned above had to be sacrificed, and they were.

Anna Pavlova has been seen and adored by many people who knew little or nothing about dance. Tamara Karsavina has

36

entranced a smaller but vital audience. Both of them have left a legacy to ballet for which we can never be sufficiently grateful.

As a teacher, Madame, as we addressed Karsavina, was gentle and kind. When teaching, she wore the most extraordinary clothes: a blouse of purple, a black shawl, an orange skirt, and wrinkled stockings. Her bloomers with elastic to the knees were full of holes. She used to retire behind a curtain at the beginning of class to wash her hair while her assistant supervised our work at the barre. Once she poked her head out, her hair wringing wet, to say to me, "Put down your sholdaas." We all loved her.

Under Karsavina I became much more aware of the difference between a mere technician and an artist. When she demonstrated, every movement came from her heart: the flow of her arms, the subtle use of her head and shoulders, the striving for simplicity, and the avoidance of affectations and mannerisms which are so common in dancers in this day and age.

It was fortunate that I already had a strong technique when I went to Karsavina, because when teaching she paid little attention to our feet and legs. She concentrated almost entirely on the upper body and was pleased that I had naturally good arms. This is important, as it is well nigh impossible to develop in a student with stiff arms and hands anything more than correct positions and a moderate flow when moving from one position to the other. I was also very musical. Although many unmusical dancers exist today, musicality really is an essential gift—one, I am pleased to say, that is very much in evidence in many of our Canadian dancers.

At sixteen, after three happy years with Karsavina, I had no intention of leaving her. I stayed with her until she left England with her husband, Henry Bruce, a diplomat who had been posted to Hungary as Britain's ambassador. However, mindful of Antony Tudor's remarks, I was also looking for a teacher of an accredited method.

Although most of my training was Russian, it was not codified as is the Vaganova system which is now recorded in detail. While searching for a codified method that was close to my own training, I was introduced to Margaret Saul. In order to obtain teaching qualifications, I wanted her to prepare me for the examinations of the Cecchetti Society. Founded in 1922, it preserves and promotes the work of a great teacher—Maestro Enrico Cecchetti. In 1924

37

the Cecchetti Society became a branch of the Imperial Society of Teachers of Dancing (I.S.T.D.).

To quote the Cecchetti Society's brochure:

> Enrico Cecchetti, the celebrated Italian dancer and teacher, was born in Rome in 1850. At the height of his career he migrated to St. Petersburg where he joined the Imperial Russian Ballet. So prodigious were his technique and his gifts as a mime, that he created both the virtuoso role of the Bluebird and the mime role of Carabosse at the premiere of *The Sleeping Beauty* in 1890. Cecchetti eventually taught the Maryinsky dancers and amongst his pupils were Pavlova, Karsavina, Preobrajenska and Nijinsky.

In 1905 when Anna Pavlova had been officially appointed a ballerina, she persuaded Maestro Cecchetti to devote himself exclusively to her for two years. She was weak and he gave her exercises to develop strength. To this day the Cecchetti method, when well taught, is recognized for the technically strong and accurate dancers it produces.

Pavlova's rapid promotion to prima ballerina in 1906 was an indication not only of her great talent but of the help the maestro had given her. When speaking of her talent, he is reported to have said: "I can teach everything connected with dancing but Pavlova has that which can be taught only by God."

When Diaghilev took his Ballets Russes to western Europe in 1909, Cecchetti joined him as mime artist and company teacher. Here his pupils included Léonide Massine, Alicia Markova, Ninette de Valois, and Marie Rambert.

Karsavina has said: "Cecchetti's reputation was that of a wizard who could make dancers. In fact he was the only absolute teacher of the academic dance in our time." Rambert has called him "the greatest teacher of his generation," while de Valois has written that "Maestro Cecchetti left a great imprint on the English School."

Geared to training professionals, the maestro had devised a system whereby the vocabulary of movements was grouped into six sets of exercises, one for each day of the working week. The great advantage of this is that we teachers are human and tend, when teaching, to concentrate on the area of our own strengths and preferences. For example, I excelled in the adages (exercises for balance and control). I was very good at turns so loved *enchaînements* that included pirouettes of any kind. Also having strong elevation, I enjoyed combinations of big jumps. It was a different story when I had to perform quick little fussy steps. I was tall and supple, so it was hard to pull everything together in order to move with speed. As a student, and later a teacher, I might have avoided those steps, but they were all in the Friday program so that was not possible.

When he was tired of touring with Diaghilev's Ballets Russes, Cecchetti opened a school in London to which dancers flocked. It was said that no one could become a finished dancer without passing through his hands. When, in 1923, he returned to Italy, his work was handed down through his disciple, Margaret Craske, to a whole generation of British teachers and artists, one of whom was Margaret Saul.

When, at sixteen, I was first introduced to Margaret Saul, we were amused to discover that I had taught her tap at Zelia Raye's studio. She told me that although I had been a good teacher, I was obviously resentful that I had been taken out of my own classes to give her private lessons. I remember her rosy cheeks, her twinkling blue eyes, her warm smile, and keen sense of humour. Unlike me she could not get rid of her balletic look when tap dancing, mainly because her feet were so turned out she looked like a duck. However, I felt ashamed when she described how I sat there looking bored and saying, "That's not right, do it again."

Poor ballet training can be harmful to a dancer. The knees, feet, and hips, as well as the back, can be permanently affected. As an orthopaedic surgeon, shaking his head, once told me, "You have to do things with your body which I have learned are impossible." He was wrong in the sense that the movements are possible after years of training, but right about the fact that the ballet technique is abnormal.

Only one aspect of my ballet training was bad, and it was a common one when I was a student. I paid a price for having a fantastically strong technique at the age of fifteen. Instead of learning that we could grow strong by expanding our muscles to their fullest extent, we gained strength much more quickly by gripping and contracting them. The result was overdeveloped legs—both thighs and calves—and sometimes, especially in Russia, big buttocks.

Poorly constructed and overly heavy classes contribute to this problem of bulging muscles. Poorly constructed classes are those where the students are given a succession of exercises that each use the same group of muscles. In order to give a well-balanced workout, the exercises should be varied, using different groups of muscles, tendons, and ligaments. Classes that are "too heavy" overwork the joints and the muscles supporting them. This often happens when men teach girls. Used to more athleticism, they do not always take into account the differences between male and female physiques.

The consequences of my own training have led me to devote my whole professional life to studying this subject. I have looked at teaching methods all over the world—in England, Russia, Denmark, France, etc. I have experimented. I have changed what I felt was bad and sometimes I have changed back again. At last, I feel I know what ballet training is all about.

Years later I was to teach flexibility without distortion.

At the National Ballet School I have been able to develop in my students an aesthetically pleasing physique; also, to protect each individual from distortions caused by forcing the body beyond reasonable limits. Unfortunately that still happens, but less so in this day and age. It will shorten a dancer's career and cause much discomfort in his or her later years.

Musical tempo can also affect the musculature. This reminds me of a funny story which results from the slower than average tempos that the Russians favour.

I was teaching a professional class in Sweden. It included Erik Bruhn, the director of the Royal Swedish Opera ballet company; Rudolf Nureyev who was there to produce his version of *Nutcracker*; and Margot Fonteyn, the great British ballerina. I was very nervous, and I was not helped by the fact that Rudi and Erik were making frequent trips to the piano and whispering in the pianist's ear. The poor man looked thoroughly uncomfortable. He was between the devil and the deep blue sea. Erik was his boss, Rudolf a temperamental guest.

I knew what was going on. Erik with his slender legs wanted the music faster. Rudolf, with stronger legs and different training, was asking for everything to be slower. I was ignoring the whole situation except for simplifying the *enchainements* (exercises) so that even if they were slow they would not be too tiring for Erik. Margot sailed through the class, totally professional, as always. She appeared not to notice her colleagues' silent struggle.

Recalling this incident reminds me of my definition of the word temperamental, which has amused and jolted many of my students: "Temperamental means half temper, half mental!" This saying is most effective when temper tantrums are the order of the day.

As I studied the Cecchetti method with Miss Saul, I felt I had made the right choice. The system appeals to me because it is professional, logical, and its technical demands are totally revealing. There is no way of cheating in the set adages, centre practice, and allegro steps that must be executed in the examinations. There is great emphasis on the use of the head, *epaulement* (shoulder movement), and the small nuances that are disappearing rapidly in these days of instant ballet. Finally, the eight *port de bras* (arm movements) are known far and wide for their simplicity, purity of

photo: R. Cadwallader

Margaret Saul, the Cecchetti teacher who was to join my staff at the School.

line, and their sheer beauty. To quote Sir Frederick Ashton, "If I had my way I would always insist that all dancers should daily do the wonderful Cecchetti *port de bras*."

I was frustrated at Miss Saul's studio because, instead of the usual one-and-a-half-hour classes, she only gave one hour. However, she was a superb teacher, very positive and respected by her students. Once, when she was away, I organized a group of them to paint her studio. She was surprised and delighted when she returned.

As I approached adulthood, Miss Saul had a great influence on me. She encouraged my rebellious feelings towards my mother. It was wonderful to find a sympathetic adult who listened to me. On looking back, I believe that her support aggravated the situation. I was really quite unkind to my mother.

Because of my strong background, I managed to pass the first two major Cecchetti examinations in July and December 1935. This was my year for exams. In November, Joan Davis entered me for the I.S.T.D.'s Intermediate Stage Branch examination. This was a new branch of the society with a syllabus created, with me as the guinea pig, by Zelia Raye and Joan Davis. The following November, when I was eighteen, I was the first person to pass the Advanced Stage exam in all subjects. When I reached my majority in 1939 I became the youngest person ever to be appointed a fellow and examiner of the Stage Branch of the Imperial Society of Teachers of Dancing and a licentiate, later examiner, of the Cecchetti Branch.

Examinations do not make a dancer. Their value lies in giving pupils and teachers a specific goal to work towards at a particular stage in training. I also found it helpful when, as a young teacher in London presenting my first candidates, I was able to get an objective opinion from an experienced examiner. In my case it was Kate Forbes, who helped me tremendously. I felt dejected when she saw my first batch of pupils and told me that they were too well trained, too correct, and that I must give them more freedom. On her return one year later, her comments were the opposite: my students were too free, and as a result their technique was sloppy. I threw up my hands, but she comforted me. "That is the way it is, Betty," she said. "It is the swing of the pendulum; it goes too far one way and then the other. One day you will find the happy medium and you will be a very good teacher."

When I opened my school in London, Margaret Saul taught some ballet classes for me. Many years later she came to Canada and was a much-loved member of the staff of the National Ballet School. When she died at eighty-five in Indianapolis, dancers and colleagues across Canada raised enough money to buy two seats in her name at the Betty Oliphant Theatre.

When I was fifteen, in order to cut down on travel, my mother had taken me away from Saint Mary's College and sent me to a school near my home. I hated it so I left and had a wonderful year with a tutor whose name was Dermot Morrah. He was a leader-writer for *The Times* in London, and was famous for an obituary he had written on the death of King George V.

Dermot Morrah was a brilliant graduate of Oxford University. There was a great chasm between his education and mine. When it came to mathematics we were so far apart that his wife had to take over. It was in English that he excited me. I will always be grateful for the way in which he broadened my knowledge, my understanding, and my vocabulary.

Through my tutor, who had written a charming nativity play, I was offered the chance to assist the director when this play was produced at the Duchess Theatre. It was a high-class production with music composed by Sir Walford Davies. The prologue was spoken by Robert Speaight, a British actor with a superb speaking voice. As assistant director I was highly thought of because, even at that tender age, I was well organized, authoritative, and paid great attention to details.

After a year of tutoring, I gave up my formal education and devoted myself to studying dance. That was the period when I took daily morning classes with Margaret Saul. The rest of the time, except for my classes with Karsavina, I spent at the studio with Zelia Raye and Joan Davis. I was not happy there and my duties became more onerous. To compound my unhappiness was the fact that I was putting on weight. I received no help with this problem from my mother or my teachers.

photo: Wallace Heaton

The splits.

After being rejected by Joan, I had transferred my affection to Laurie Devine, who had been hired to teach acrobatic dancing at the school. She was a gentle soul with large brown eyes. I often went to visit her when she was performing at the Alexander

Palace. It was the centre for English television, which was in its infancy. She danced with her brother Tom, who was tall and handsome. They were both under the thumb of a domineering mother—the old circus matriarch who tied her sleeping baby's legs into the splits.

Laurie and Tom, with Mama as a chaperone, were invited to act as host and hostess for the 1934/35 winter season at a very posh hotel in Wengen, Switzerland. Laurie suggested I should go with them to perform twice a week in the cabarets they were expected to present. I would stay in a small hotel close to them, and my expenses would be paid. However, my mother would have to pay the fare and provide me with pocket money. I was desperate for a change so I begged her to let me go. I am afraid that, with the selfishness of an adolescent, I didn't think of the financial burden I was imposing upon her. The rate of exchange was terrible. She had to outfit me and did so with superb good taste. I had beautiful clothes which must have cost a fortune.

I was supposed to travel with the Devines, but Laurie got a last-minute T.V. job. It would cost too much to change my travel plans so I had to go alone. It was a daunting prospect. A friend of my mother was to meet me in Basel. I must have been very eager to make a good impression as I remember washing my hands about twenty times before I met him. I spent the night at his house. He was very kind and put me on the train for the last lap of my journey.

When I reached Wengen, I found my way to the hotel. Much to the amusement of the proprietors I made a huge *faux pas* on the first day. I had broken a glass and went downstairs to find something to use to sweep it up. I intended to ask, in my best German, for a *schaufel und burster* (shovel and brush). Instead I used the word *bruster*, meaning breast. I was painfully shy, and although the laughter was well-meaning, I felt like an idiot.

Wengen was a beautiful little town, surrounded by mountains. I was there from November to April so was able to see the snow melting and the arrival of spring.

Laurie and her family arrived three days after me. I was very homesick and Mrs. Devine was no help. I think she resented my being there. Tom was nice but not interested in the feelings of a young girl. Laurie was her usual gentle self. Unfortunately her preoccupation with the job left her little time for me so I was virtually alone. I tried skiing on the nursery slopes. Seeing a number of people hopping around on crutches with their broken legs in casts made me afraid for my career, so I decided to limit myself to skating and lugeing. The latter, akin to tobogganing, was actually very dangerous. On my luge I would come careering down the luge run. The surface was solid ice with huge walls of ice on either side. On one occasion I went over the wall and finished up with a severe concussion. However, because my precious legs were not damaged, I was not concerned.

On the skating rink I met Ted, a seventeen-year-old English boy. He was a good companion. For the time that he was there I did not feel as miserable as I had before his arrival.

The whole trip was a disaster. Laurie, who had promised to give me lessons, never had time. I performed twice a week. That was fun, but otherwise I felt sad and neglected, and was counting the days to my departure.

When the time finally came, I went back to a new home. While I was away my mother had moved from Hampstead to Tavistock Square in Bloomsbury. I became very depressed. It was partly due to the change in climate, but mainly because of my mother's obvious disappointment with my career-threatening weight problem. Although I was welcomed by Margaret Saul, Zelia Raye and Joan Davis were only interested in using me to learn their syllabi. I didn't see Laurie for several weeks. Already depressed, I was shocked to learn by telephone that she had died of tuberculosis.

As a civilian volunteer, I choreographed a musical revue for the troops with The Blue Pencils, 1941. (I am in the centre of the back row.)

The War Years

Soon after my return from Switzerland, I decided to make a career of teaching. I still had a weight problem, and I was becoming very tall for a dancer—the same height as Karen Kain, five feet seven and a half inches. In those days that was taller than most of the male dancers. When you added the extra inches gained through standing on pointe, it was clear that I was at a disadvantage. Also, ballet was in a slump and I had little hope of joining a company.

Once she knew I had made the crucial decision to teach rather than perform, my mother planned a project for me that was extremely painful. She applied on my behalf for a teaching job in Holland. I was qualified to meet all their requirements except one. As well as ballet, tap, and musical comedy, they wanted me to teach ballroom dancing. I was sent to study with Victor Silvester, the world's champion ballroom dancer. His school was on Bond Street and was very posh. At seventeen I was quite unsophisticated, and the teachers and the students at the school were dressed to kill. I felt like a fish out of water.

I hated ballroom dancing. It wrecked my feet, and like most people trained in ballet, I was no good at it. I studied four dances:

Another dance in my modern dance repertoire.

tango, slow foxtrot, waltz, and quickstep. For the examination of the Imperial Society of Teachers of Dancing, I had to pass each one in practice and theory. I had never failed an examination in my life, but in this one I was given a high mark, ninety-eight, for theory but only forty-five for my practical demonstration.

I went home to announce the result, and my aunt Margaret, who was a converted Roman Catholic, said, "Well, I'm sure you didn't pray." Always too honest for my own good, I replied indignantly, "If God would pass me in an exam I'm not ready for, I don't think much of Him." I was banished to my room without supper for my rudeness.

I had to return to the ballroom school, but something happened that made life more bearable. As a qualified member of the Stage Branch of the Imperial Society I was invited to teach at their annual Congress. Victor Silvester belonged to the Ballroom Branch and happened to be there when I was teaching.

After my class he came and said, "I didn't know you were

important in another field of dance. I'm afraid we have been treating you as a total failure." I explained that was exactly how I felt. I was no good at ballroom dancing. I didn't wear the right clothes or have the appropriate jewellery. My nails weren't painted. I was, in fact, a disaster.

From the moment they knew how intimidated I had been, Victor, his wife, and the staff were really good to me and I was much happier.

Three months later I scraped through the exam with the same mark in theory but fifty-five in practice. Ironically, we were not able to get a visa for Holland as I was not yet eighteen. Imagine my horror when I realized that I had gone through all that hell for nothing.

At that point I decided to take charge of my life. I told my mother that I was going to open my own school. I planned to go to Edinburgh and demand some of the money my father had left in trust for my sister and me. Although we were supposed to wait until we were twenty-one, there were provisions in the will which would allow the trustees to release money in certain circumstances.

At seventeen I arrived at the fusty offices of Lindsay, Jamieson, and Haldane in St. Andrew's Square. I presented my project and demanded five thousand pounds. I also told them what I thought of the way they had treated my mother. When she had needed money for our education, they had insinuated that she wanted it for herself. She had struggled to bring us up on a very small annuity while all that money was in their hands. I pointed out that my father would have been furious had he known what was going on. Anyway, they gave me the money to open my school. I think they were amused at my youthful vehemence—also a little ashamed.

I found premises to rent at 72 Wigmore Street over Twinings Tea Emporium. It was a very good central district near Portman Square, where Wallis Simpson lived. We often saw the Prince of Wales' car outside, but there was no scandal at that time.

I had the upper two floors of the building. On the first, I made a studio with a wonderful sprung floor, an office in which I slept, and a changing room for the students. On the top floor there was a kitchen, a large living room, and a bedroom. Although we kept our house on Tavistock Square, my mother and sister moved in with me.

In 1936, soon after my eighteenth birthday, I was open for business. A young student of mine, Pauline Patey, became my assistant. Her mother had sent her to me because she liked my Scottish name. I gave Pauline a scholarship and she helped with the phone, appointments, finances, etc.

The school was an instant success. I was well known in

photo: Pauline Patey

My first school opened in 1936, over Twinings Tea Emporium in Wigmore Street, London.

52

London and abroad as a result of having taught—from the age of thirteen—when I was training with Zelia Raye and Joan Davis. My pupils came from all over Great Britain, South Africa, Sweden, Holland, and the United States. I offered a full-time course in dance which included ballet, tap, musical comedy, limbering, stretching, and acrobatics if they wished. I sent them to Victor Silvester for ballroom dancing and he in his turn sent me, among others, the international ballroom champion who wanted me to "theatricalize" his work so that he could become a cabaret artist.

I had a lot of fun with my students. On April Fool's Day they put in a wake-up call for me at 5:00 a.m. I spent the next few hours planning my revenge. First I coated the barre with syrup. In the washroom I put soap that would turn black when they washed their hands. I put dough in the toes of their tap shoes so they would feel slimy. Finally, I asked Pauline to phone Mr. C. Lyon to cancel his lesson. She came back looking puzzled; he had hung up and been quite rude. I had given her the number of the zoo!

A famous film star who came to the school was Merle Oberon. I remember her as Cathy Earnshaw, opposite Laurence Olivier's Heathcliffe in *Wuthering Heights*. She was married to Alexander Korda and he wanted to make a film called *The Red Shoes*. It did not materialize until many years later when it was made with Moira Shearer, and I will tell you why.

When they called me from the film company to see if I could teach Merle enough ballet to fake a few scenes, I said I would try. They made strict rules. All my students must make themselves scarce when the star arrived, and she should have her lessons in complete privacy. We agreed on a fee and made an appointment for her first lesson.

Merle Oberon arrived but from then on it was a complete farce. It was obvious that she didn't want to work and she cancelled her lessons frequently. The crisis came when she had to wear pointe shoes. She insisted that the shoes must be broken in so that they would not be too hard. Her feet were tiny so this job was undertaken by Pauline Patey whose feet were the same size. Merle made one attempt to go on pointe and that was the last time I saw her.

For the first time in years I was happy and enjoyed each day. As tangible proof of my success my photo—one of the first action pictures ever to be taken in England—appeared on the cover of the June 1937 issue of *The Dancing Times*. Then tragedy struck. My sister's fiancé, Donald Munro, had broken off their engagement while my mother and I were on holiday in Europe. They had been engaged when Mary was seventeen. At that time, his wealthy father had lost everything in a stock exchange crash. My mother had used her influence with friends to find Donald a job in China. He came home on leave after five years, and he and Mary went to Scotland together.

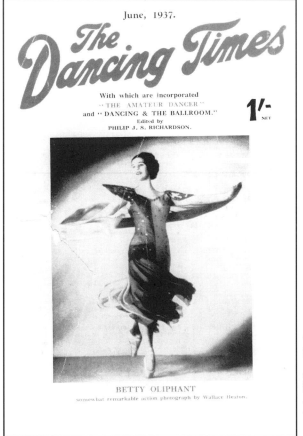

photo: Wallace Heaton

When action photography was in the experimental stages, the camera caught me in motion.

Then my mother got a telegram saying Mary had tried to commit suicide. We rushed back from our vacation and went up to Edinburgh. When Donald told Mary that he no longer wished to marry her, she had gone to Aunt Margaret's flat in a dreadful state. This was the same aunt I had offended in London. She used similar tactics, trying to convince Mary that prayer would solve everything, and only realized it wasn't working when she was faced with the suicide attempt.

We took my sister home, and I resumed teaching. It was a nightmare. She was always disappearing and leaving farewell notes. I used to roam the streets at night searching for her. When she finally came home, she was usually filthy from hiding in the subway and seemed to be somewhat gleeful at the trouble she had caused. Eventually she was hospitalized, but that too was a disaster.

In the hospital Mary was so heavily dosed with paraldehyde that we were shocked when we saw her. I doubt if she would ever have recovered had it not been for a wonderful nurse. She was about to leave the hospital to take up a position as head of a mental hospital in Birmingham. She had three months' leave and told us she would come to our house with Mary, whom she felt was getting the wrong treatment. She was very fond of my sister and wanted to wean her off the drug and help her get over her depression. Mary was much better for many years, but sadly, after my mother's death in 1957, she broke down completely and spent her last fifteen years in a mental hospital in England. Thankfully, it was a wonderful place.

Life was grim, but it had its compensations. Apart from my love of teaching, I also had some boyfriends. The first was George Stent from South Africa. He was unbelievably handsome. I was just eighteen; he was twenty-four. He was on his way to fight against Franco in Spain, which made him a hero in my eyes. He came to Wigmore Street through friends and returned there whenever he was on leave.

I was totally naïve and knew nothing of sex, except that I didn't want it. However, I thought I was in love. George took me everywhere—to theatres, the opera, the ballet, and to dine in fine restaurants. He kissed me and it was heaven. He was a socialist who believed in free love. I didn't know that, so when he said, "I don't believe in petting and pawing, do you?" I agreed. "No," he continued, "I believe in sleeping with people." He could see I was totally flummoxed, so he let the matter drop.

That little romance ended when I overheard a friend, Janet, telling my mother that George was having an affair with the Spanish ambassador's wife. Janet was kind when I asked why he had abandoned me. She explained that I reminded him of his little sister, and he enjoyed taking me around. I felt humiliated but it was not a shattering blow as, although I liked his kisses, I had been afraid of where they would lead.

Derek Maude, a cadet at Sandhurst Military College, was the next admirer. I went to the June Ball, which was a big affair at the college. They served only champagne, probably to avoid the hangovers that the cadets would suffer if they mixed their drinks. I made Derek take me out on the lake because I wanted to avoid dancing, and we had a good time.

I could have married Derek, but he was destined for a career in the Indian army. Apart from having a horror of snakes, I knew I would never give up my career to be an army officer's wife. He was posted to India when war started in 1939 and wrote to me faithfully until I married in 1942.

My most serious relationship was with John Wilkinson, a young businessman. From 1937 we saw or phoned each other every day. I cannot say I was in love. I think now I have never been in love. Not even later when I had two marriages which turned out to be very unhappy. I was such an innocent. I had tried to work out sex from romantic novels, but they always drew a veil over the final moment. At one time I thought the penis could be inserted into the navel, but decided that wouldn't work because the couple would not be properly aligned for kissing.

It must have been hard on John. When he tried to kiss me, he told me I was frigid. I didn't understand although I knew I was disappointing him.

I was so stressed in the three years at Wigmore Street that I became very ill with what I suspect was a migraine tension. I was in bed for ten days, I lost fifteen pounds, and my head was so painful that I could not bear any noise or a flicker of light. The doctor told my mother that I needed help. She pooh-poohed the idea and said it would make even more work for me if I had to pay the doctor. I regret deeply that I missed the chance to deal with my emotional problems at that time. I would be fifty-five before I had another opportunity.

In July 1939, the end of the third year at my school, I was a bridesmaid for a friend. She was marrying a young diplomat who was stationed in Afghanistan. After the wedding in London, I was invited by her aunt to spend time with them at her villa in the south of France. It was situated on a little island across the water from Hyères near Toulon.

I was driven there from Paris by another good friend, Claude Chauvet, whom I had met on one of my frequent visits to France. We were very close and his mother was terrified that she was going to lose her son to a British girl. However, we were not romantically involved, so she need not have worried.

Claude drove me all the way to Hyères. We had a wonderful picnic in the country: tuna fish, a baguette, dark chocolate (which is wonderful with fresh bread), grapes, and white wine. He left me at the ferry which took me to the Îles de Porquerolles where I was met by my friends.

It was truly beautiful. I had a superb holiday and was looking forward to returning home for a big twenty-first birthday celebration in September, although my actual birthday was in August. Unfortunately, this was not to be. One day all visitors on the island were told by the French authorities to leave immediately as war was imminent.

The French inhabitants, of whom many of the men were called up, organized a huge farewell party. It seemed like a gesture of defiance toward the Germans. We left the next day, soldiers and civilians alike. My friends came as far as Marseille and went from there to Afghanistan. I was all alone—a young girl surrounded by good-natured, but very drunk, French servicemen.

The journey to Paris was a nightmare. A blackout, nowhere to sit except on my suitcase, no food, and because of frequent stops it took twenty-four hours. I got very frightened and was comforted by a young French lieutenant. I fell asleep on his shoulder and woke to find we had arrived in Paris.

I phoned Claude, who met me and intended to take me to Dieppe to catch the boat to Newhaven, which was the only route to Britain that had not been closed. As we sat in a café, his officer class was called up on the radio, and he had to leave immediately. I was to see Claude for the last time when he turned up at Tavistock Square after France was defeated by the Germans. He was on his way to fight for the Free French with General de Gaulle. I believe he was killed for I never heard from him again.

Once more I was alone. I made my way to Dieppe, left my luggage there, and sailed on a boat in which we were packed like sardines. We finally arrived in England. From there it was a train to London and a taxi home. The Londoners were filling a few sandbags in a desultory way, and my mother couldn't understand why I had come home early. Her main concern was that my bed was not made up. My luggage turned up at Victoria Station three weeks later.

In September when war was declared, Derek and John came to see me on the same day. I had one of them upstairs and the other in my office downstairs. I confess they did not know of each other's existence, so I had an awkward time but they finally departed without having met.

Derek went to India. John, who was an officer in the Reserve, remained in London before going to Kenya. I suffered his prolonged cooling off, which was very cruel. Just when I was trying to face it, he would phone. Once he sent me his regimental pin, which was generally looked upon as a commitment. A clean break would have been much easier.

Air raids were expected as soon as the war started but did not materialize. I tried to keep the school open for a few months, but was so idealistic that I felt guilty and unpatriotic, and finally I closed it. We continued to live at Wigmore Street, but when we had suffered some terrible air raids, we moved back to Tavistock Square which was much safer.

Before committing myself to the war effort, I accepted a contract from a West End producer named Prince Littler. Prince was his first name. He had a very big company which produced musicals and pantomimes all over the United Kingdom. He wanted me to be principal dancer and to arrange all the dances and ensembles for a pantomime, *Sleeping Beauty*, in Cardiff, Wales. To this day, I will not use the word choreography in this context. Most people do but I find it pretentious.

A pantomime is a British phenomenon that is almost

impossible to describe. Suffice it to say that it is a Christmas show, based on a fairy tale and beloved by children and adults. It has acting, singing, and dancing and is full of humour thanks to the comedian. He is dressed as a female and plays the part of the "dame," the mother of the leading character, who might be Aladdin, Cinderella, or, as in my first pantomime, the Sleeping Beauty.

My job was to choose the music and create a ballet in which I would dance the leading role. I was responsible for all the spectacular chorus numbers and any dancing the principals had to do. There were forty girls in the chorus, chosen by me and the director, who staged the whole production. With my height, I looked older than I was. This was fortunate, as I was younger than most of the girls we hired.

During rehearsals, I was accused by the management of being too soft with the dancers. There were no unions, but I always treated them with respect. I gave them proper rest periods and coffee breaks. On being challenged, my bosses admitted that I achieved excellent results, so no more was said. Although I had no ulterior motive for my treatment of the dancers, they rewarded me by saving my job.

I was designing the big ensembles for the opening and closing of the show. Although there were all girls in the chorus, half of them would be costumed as boys with short jerkins and tights. In rehearsal, however, they wore their own practice clothes.

I was very aware of this when I started planning, with boys and girls alternating. At the end of the second movement, they finished up in twos (i.e., two boys, two girls, etc.). But after that I forgot all about their gender. Imagine my horror when I saw them in costume for the first time, just hours before the brass arrived from London to see the final dress rehearsal. I told the girls what I had done, and they were unbelievably supportive. When the big moment arrived, they went through all the numbers, arriving in logical order at the end of each sequence. I will never know how they managed it, but I was very grateful.

I learned my lesson. From then on, at the first rehearsal I pinned pink papers on the girls and blue on the boys.

The twelve-week run in Cardiff, 1940/41, was incredibly

tiring. We did two shows every day and three on Saturdays. Sunday was a much needed day of rest.

One day I had a nasty accident in the highland scene when, to make up the numbers, I had replaced a chorus girl who was ill. After the scene opened with a shepherd and his dog, we marched down a long and winding ramp in fours, each group wearing the kilt in a different tartan. We all had swords and that was my downfall. As I left the stage to run up to my dressing room, I stumbled upwards and ran the sword down through my foot. Although the swords were blunt, it was a deep wound. The management representatives rushed up to me, waving a piece of paper; I ignored them because I was angry at their lack of concern for me. I learned later that the paper was a waiver absolving them of any blame. Anyway, I wouldn't have sued them for my own clumsiness.

I worked for Prince Littler on two more pantomimes, one at Streatham Hill Theatre on the outskirts of London, and the second at Golders Green Hippodrome, a major London theatre.

At Streatham Hill, in 1941/42, I did not dance. Instead, as well as arranging the dances, I took on the job of assistant stage manager to learn the technical side of theatre production. By this time, the bombing was fierce, and we had a difficult time getting home after the show.

The Londoners showed great fortitude during the war. Along with their cheerfulness and humour, they had a strong sense of fair play, especially when it came to the endless line-ups for ration books, food, and transportation. Once I was waiting for a bus in the blackout and had reached the front of the line. When the bus arrived I climbed on. As it started, a man dashed past the queue and jumped onto it. The conductor rang the bell to stop the bus. "You can't put me off. I'm a rabbi," the man said. "I don't care if you are Popeye," the conductor replied in a strong cockney accent. We all clapped as the man stepped off the bus.

My last pantomime, in 1942/43, was to be after I married, and was pregnant. In one of the breaks the girls decided to name my baby. Somebody suggested Gail, a name I had never heard before. My married name would be Grover and Gail Grover sounded good, so it was decided, and we went back to work.

In early 1941 when I finished in Cardiff I went back to

London to find some war work. They were very rude to me when I applied to the armed services, saying that as a dancer I would only be useful for washing dishes. I was incensed and decided to look elsewhere. I finished up as a temporary clerk, grade three, in the Ministry of Pensions. My salary was two pounds ten shillings a week.

I was working on supplementary allowances for people who were suffering severe hardship as a result of enlisting or being called up. As the servicemen earned practically nothing, we had many applications. The rules as to what was allowed were ridiculous, and all we were authorized to give, whatever the circumstances, was either eleven, sixteen, or twenty-one shillings a week.

We had some extraordinary requests. In one case a man had a wife and another woman who was common-law. The first needed new false teeth and the second was pregnant. His application was disallowed. The job was so futile and so boring that I couldn't stand it. After two months I went to the big boss, whose office was carpeted. He asked why I was leaving, and I explained what my profession was and how I hated the inactivity. He said I was a very good worker and that he had heard only one complaint about me; I laughed too much! The interview ended with his wishing me luck and asking if I could provide some entertainment for the annual concert given by his church. I declined.

After my short career as a civil servant, I joined the ambulance service. I drove a big white fever ambulance and had to double-declutch with every gear change. We did twenty-four-hour shifts, and the station, at night, was a veritable brothel. All the married men and women whose spouses were away or working elsewhere felt free to enjoy their sexual freedom with their colleagues. The younger ones, like me, were protected by being given a separate room, but we knew what was happening next door.

We saw practically no action. The Blitz was still ahead of us. I would have stayed on but saw an interesting advertisement in the *Daily Telegraph*, a respectable national newspaper. They wanted civilian female volunteers, all expenses paid, to perform in an army concert party.

I was somewhat suspicious when I applied, but everything turned out to be above-board. Brigadier O. W. Nicholson of the

40th A.A. Brigade interviewed me with Captain T. Y. Benyon, the director of the show. They engaged me to dance and, as in the pantomime, to arrange and rehearse the dances.

The company, called The Blue Pencils, had already been formed. It comprised ten talented male members of an anti-aircraft corps and six girls. Captain Benyon had put together a slick army revue which was called *Go to It*. They performed not only for the troops, but also for the public to raise money. The proceeds went to the A.A. Corps Welfare Fund.

When I joined the group, as the sixth volunteer, it was already in performance. I discovered that I was displacing the girl who had been chosen as dance captain. I was furious and wanted to leave, but she insisted that I was more experienced and that she would be happy to become one of the dancers.

I was with the concert party for approximately eighteen months. I joined in the summer of 1940 and was given leave at Christmas to do the Streatham Hill pantomime, which only took five weeks. I left at the end of 1941 when I became engaged to Frank Russell Grover, a Canadian soldier who was billeted at our Tavistock Square house.

The Blue Pencils were a very happy group, but we found our entertainment officer, Captain Benyon, both difficult and devious. After a few months, he was replaced by another officer, Lieutenant H. S. Denton, who made life more interesting for me as he loved ballet and gave me the opportunity to create something serious and less corny than my previous work.

Our second revue, *Winning Through*, consisted of sketches, songs, dance numbers, and a ballet, *Flirtation Fantasy*, to the music from *La Boutique fantasque* (Respighi/Rossini). To my surprise, it was greeted enthusiastically by servicemen and public alike.

Brigadier Nicholson was a great supporter of The Blue Pencils; we were, after all, his brainchild. As we became better known, we were promoted to divisional concert party, which meant that we travelled further afield. The girls were billeted in private homes, the men in army quarters. They had plenty of food. It may not have been appetizing, but things were much worse for us. We were dependent on our ration books. Many items were rationed on a monthly basis. We often found after spending two days in one place that the coupon for our pot of jam or pound of sugar had been taken, so we were out of luck until the end of the month. The same happened with the weekly allowances of butter and margarine, two and four ounces respectively, and meat, a shilling's worth, which equalled about one lamb chop. We also met some wonderfully kind people who could not do enough for us.

We suffered a great deal from the bombing. At one big military base, concise instructions were given to all personnel as to where to go in the event of an air raid. I chuckled to myself as I realized that no plans had been made for us. Presumably we would remain on stage. Another night, when we were billeted in a hotel, the air-raid warning sounded and we went downstairs. It was a heavy attack and lasted about four hours. The guests were frightened so we decided to entertain them by dancing the can-can. The next morning we read of our "bravery" in the local newspaper. On another occasion an acrobat, Merial Gaunt, was poised on her elbows on a raised platform with her legs in the air, toes beautifully pointed, when a bomb fell very close to us. Her toes gave a little quiver and then she continued. A year or two later, Merial danced numbers I had created for her at the Coconut Grove in London.

Some of the company members were former professionals, the others talented amateurs. One of the latter, Bill Waddington, who had been a butcher before the war, became famous in Britain as a result of his work with The Blue Pencils. He is a banjo-playing, George Formby-type comedian with a Lancashire accent and a wonderful sense of humour. He never resumed his former trade.

Recently, a reunion was held in England to celebrate the fiftieth anniversary of The Blue Pencils. Only five members attended, but here are three excerpts from the letter they sent me. From Elizabeth Darlow (Colville) with whom I danced:

> How we all wished you had been here. . . . Don't let it make you sad, we all talked of you often with love and admiration.

From Alex Denman, the pianist and music arranger:

> You will surely remember the pianist who played for the Can-Can and that exquisite "Deep Purple." We should have loved to have seen you here.

From John Ingram, our advance manager:

> As the organizer of this small reunion of The Blue Pencils, I thought a few lines might not come amiss, to remind you that even after fifty years you are not forgotten and are certainly missed on this occasion. [Signed] Inky.

It warmed my heart to be reminded of those happy times.

What is to follow is much more difficult to write. With the exception of the pantomime at Christmas 1941, I cannot recall many pleasant moments after I left the group and returned home.

Like our home in Hampstead, Tavistock Square was a bed-and-breakfast place. It was four storeys high with a kitchen in the basement. When I was at home, I took approximately twenty breakfasts up endless flights of stairs. The rooms were tastefully decorated, and we had many interesting tenants, including that famous old man Max Beerbohm and his wife. I was always welcome in their big front room on the ground floor. It was like going back to Victorian times. Their furniture was very old-fashioned. They refused to use electricity and continued to use oil lamps.

I had become engaged to Frank when I was home on leave from the concert party. My mother seemed quite pleased, but I learned later that she was very unhappy. If only she had told me how she felt! The whole thing was a disaster from the start. He was a private in the Canadian Fusiliers, but—as a dispatch rider—he moved from unit to unit. I was to learn, very painfully, that he was a pathological liar with no moral scruples. Even when we were courting, I heard he was sleeping around, but my mother was very keen on trusting people and said I should give him the benefit of the doubt.

Why did I agree to marry him? It must be clear by now that I was naïve and totally inexperienced, but the answer would be amusing if it were not so sad. One evening we were indulging in some heavy petting, which I wasn't enjoying but couldn't stop. I had my first experience of sexual arousal, a tingle down my spine. I immediately thought, So this is love! In those days my emotions were a closed book to me or I would have known that I wasn't happy and that I was making a horrible mistake. It makes me blush now to think of my mother choosing the engagement ring for him. She probably paid for it, as well as a very pretty pearl and diamond bracelet which he gave me as a wedding present.

We were to be married on June 27, 1942, but first I had to go out of town to meet Frank's colonel to get permission. The poor man. He did his very best to dissuade me. He told me horror stories of other girls who had gone to Canada and how disappointed they had been. He suggested that Frank and I came from completely different backgrounds, so I immediately decided he was a snob. He could not convince me. I was trained to see loyalty as one of the most important virtues and did not really hear what he was trying to tell me.

The wedding took place in a church round the corner from our house. In the limousine my mother told me it was not too late to change my mind if I had any doubts. I was so surprised; it was unlike her to express her feelings to me. I wish I could have reciprocated, but I was too confused. All I could think about was not causing trouble for everybody, so I went ahead. Had I not, I remind myself now, I wouldn't have my children whom I love dearly, and I would never have had the opportunity to found the National Ballet School.

We went to a farm for our honeymoon. It was a nightmare. The walls were so thin one could hear every sound. I was intensely shy and filled with trepidation. Frank was insensitive and brutal, and satisfied his appetite five or six times. In the morning I was stiff, sore, and disillusioned.

The final humiliation came the next morning. Frank slept in; I got up and sat in the room feeling miserable. At noon, the landlady banged loudly on the door, saying, "I know you are newly married but this is disgusting!" I opened the door, fully dressed, and said with great dignity, "My husband is in the army and he needs his sleep." Her face was a picture and it gave me great satisfaction to see her embarrassment.

We left the farm soon after this incident and went home. Frank returned to his unit when his leave was over, and I continued my dreary life.

At the end of July, I came down to breakfast and could not face the two things I love most, coffee and marmalade. I knew I was pregnant, but my mother said it was much too early to tell. A month later it was confirmed. I was sick and nauseated for the whole nine months, but my pregnancy was uneventful except for one frightening incident.

Two months before the baby was due, I joined my husband in a small town near Eastbourne, an English seaside resort. I was unpacking when a German plane unloaded its bombs while on the way home. The house I was in was hit, and I was buried under the rubble. After they got me out, I had labour pains. They turned out to be false, brought on by shock, but I was taken to hospital for observation.

It was there that I lost my nerve, and I was terrified of air raids for the rest of the war. Having a new life inside one arouses feelings of protectiveness. Because the hospital was on the coast, planes were flying over all the time, and I kept diving under the bed. As soon as possible, I went back to London and the sound of anti-aircraft guns, which made me feel much safer.

Gail was born on April 25, 1943 at a nursing home in London. Her name was appropriate as there was a terrific gale blowing. At midnight, after being ignored by two taxi drivers who were also being flagged by a couple of G.I.'s—they were renowned for their generous tips—we managed to find a cabby who was willing to take me to the home.

My mother, a trained midwife, had suggested that I could cope with the early stages of labour alone. Being somewhat of a stoic and not wishing to ask for help too soon, I spent the night groaning with pain and reading the somewhat depressing *Jamaica Inn*, which I had grabbed when leaving the house.

When the nurse came in at around 7:00 a.m., she was horrified. The baby was due in about half an hour and they had to get my doctor. She explained that she had been running upstairs all night, thinking that my groans were coming from the woman next door.

It was twenty-four hours after Gail's birth that Frank came to

Gail at three years on holiday at England's
Bognor Regis.

see me. He had been playing poker with a colonel who was a tenant of ours. In the twelve years that we were together, I was never able to count on him to be there for me.

I loved my baby, but was too insecure to be a good mother. I stayed religiously with the theories of that time. The child must not be spoiled; she should wait four hours for her next meal even if she was yelling for food; picking her up when she was crying was strictly forbidden; and if she tried to suck her thumb she should wear a mitt. These rules were very hard for both of us. I couldn't bear to see Gail fighting to get her little hand, mitt and all, into her mouth.

When Gail was about eight weeks old, I joined Frank in Worthing, Sussex. In the daytime he was out and often he did not come home at night. According to him, he was taking part in nightly reconnaissance raids to France. I was very lonely and developed an abscessed tooth which did not help. He was home the night my tooth flared up, but snored loudly as I grappled with the pain and tried to quieten the screaming baby I held in my arms. The landlady was knocking on the wall. I was so desperate I wanted to kill Frank and throw Gail out the window. I went to the dentist in London the next day and felt much better. It was a painfully stressful time in my life.

In spite of these problems, I wanted a second child, and Carol was conceived nine months after Gail's birth. Soon after, Frank was sent overseas, and I heard nothing until, many months later, I was informed that he was missing and had been posted as a deserter.

Before Carol's birth in October 1944, my nerves were so bad the doctor suggested I should go to Scotland to avoid London's air raids. It was too late to book a nursing home so Auntie Margie, who knew Colonel Green, the director of Edinburgh's Royal Infirmary, arranged for me to go to their Simpson Memorial Maternity Pavilion. It was a dreadful place. The patients came from the poorest areas. I shared a side room off the large public ward with another woman and we got very upset when we heard the nurses bullying the women. One of them was quite horrible to us until Colonel Green came to visit me. "Why didn't you tell me you knew the director?" she said to me angrily. I smiled sweetly. "Would it have made you treat me differently?" I asked.

I was amused that their sanitary pads were made of sphagnum moss, which is actually very absorbent. I was not so amused when I was given one that had been sterilized and was as prickly as a thistle. I refused to use them. When I was leaving the hospital, the nurses put one on my pillow with a flower attached to remind me of them.

In the infirmary I was told that I was not providing adequate milk for Carol, but they had not detected a condition in Carol called pyloric spasms, in which a valve closes and ejects the undigested food. The baby was starving to death. As soon as we returned to London, my mother realized something was seriously wrong. Our doctor diagnosed the problem, which would automatically clear up after fourteen weeks. In the meantime, Carol was kept sedated and fed in her cot. We could not pick her up for fear she would throw up. In the raids I used to lean over the crib to protect her from the falling plaster.

Gail slept under the air-raid table in our basement kitchen. I had very little sleep as neither of the children were disturbed by the warning siren but invariably woke up, full of beans, when the all-clear sounded.

On top of all this, a day came when I spent an agonizing few hours thinking Gail had been killed. At 4:00 p.m. my sister took her in her stroller to the food office which was about four blocks from our house. A huge bomb fell close by, and I was told that the crater was so large a horse and cart had disappeared completely. I frantically followed the route Mary had taken, checking with the shop owners who knew me, and discovered that she had been seen in the vicinity minutes before the bomb fell. After a fruitless search I returned home to see everyone waving to me. Gail was at home. Her face had been severely cut from the blast. She had been taken to hospital and released; my sister was badly shaken but unharmed. I was thankful, but was haunted by the thought of those mothers who had not been so lucky. Their children were never found.

The next day an American pilot, on seeing Gail's face, asked how it had been injured. When I told him, he said, "Don't you worry, Ma'am, we'll get them for this. Now we are in the war it will soon be over." I appreciated his optimism, but couldn't share it.

With all this worry it was not surprising that I developed a life-threatening illness known as Graves' disease. I had an over-active thyroid which was causing me to lose weight and to be short of breath, and my eyes to pop out. I was not aware of all this, but a doctor friend told my mother I was very ill and must get treatment immediately. When our G.P. saw me, she was horri-fied and said I would need surgery. The best surgeon, she said, was Sir Thomas Dunhill, but he would be very expensive. I decid-ed I wanted the best if my neck was to be cut open. In an unusual move, I asked my cousin, Colonel Grant, who doted on me, if he would help.

Pat Grant was a bachelor who lived with his sister in a glorious house called Biel, near Dunbar in Scotland. He was Lord Lieutenant of Midlothian, and I had spent many holidays on his estate among the bluebells and primroses. During the war he sent us, on a week-ly basis, rabbits, hares, and game to supplement our rations.

The money was forthcoming, about two hundred pounds, and I was booked into the expensive London Clinic, which was a sharp contrast to the infirmary. The nurses told me that such luminaries as Elizabeth Taylor had been treated there. Sir Thomas was a lecherous old man. He kept commenting on my beautiful long neck, but he was a fine surgeon, and I have the neatest scar to prove it. I was frightened when I first saw it, because I mistook the ink marks, which are drawn to ensure the correct joining of the skin, for stitch marks, and they were ugly.

I was very weak when I went home, and spent a lot of time in the Square. One day I met a man who told me he had lost his wife, his children, and everything he owned in Coventry, which had been bombed continuously. I took him home for a cup of tea, and my trusting mother offered him free board and lodging until he could reorganize his life. His name was Mr. Forbes, and we called him Forty. He was very nice, but was strange in that he couldn't bear to be alone.

He started courting a single lady in our house, and when they got engaged, my mother and I became suspicious. I took his ration book to the police station and within minutes they brought me a list of crimes that he had committed. As we had feared, it included a number of cases of bigamy and he was out on parole. I felt like a heel as the police surrounded our house. He and the woman were together when he was arrested. She was heartbroken and furious with us. I felt so sorry for her.

The war ended in 1945 and Frank came home to face a court-martial. Several of my relatives held high positions in the British army. My mother reluctantly asked for their help. They were equally reluctant to use their influence with their Canadian colleagues and told my mother that they were only doing it for

Off to New Homes in Canada

Daily Sketch, December 17, 1945

Gail cuts a Christmas cake while Carol (left), in her father's arms, looks on at a party for the children of Canadian soldiers and their English brides.

me. They were successful and Frank was discharged and sent home. I was embarrassed.

My mother's next project was to buy a house in Camden Town and to move me up there with the two children. It was a horrible district. I did not know a soul and had no one with whom I could leave Gail, who was nearly four, and Carol, who was two years old. I had to take them shopping. It was a lengthy business with all the shortages and line-ups, but amusing things often happened.

When we were queuing for oranges, a rare occurrence, an obviously wealthy lady came in and bought the expensive items which were not rationed. When she came to a pineapple she said, "What is this?" "A pineapple, Madam," the shopkeeper replied. "How do you cook it?" she asked. "Well Madam," he said with a straight face, "you have to marinate it in vinegar for twenty-four hours before cooking it!" This little incident cheered us all up as we waited.

It was impossible to find the Harrington Squares that we used as diapers in those days. I had them sent by a friend from the United States. They had to be hand washed and hung on the line. Our water was heated by a coke furnace, and the rooms with coal fires. We were lucky if we could get a bag of coal a month, so we all suffered from chilblains in the cold weather. My most difficult task was to find a chamber pot for Gail. I went to all the antique stores and finished up with an aspidistra pot.

I find reliving this period extremely painful and have been making all kinds of excuses for not continuing at this point.

One evening at bedtime Carol was peering over the edge of the bath when I noticed a small protruding bone. I consulted a Swedish friend who was a physiotherapist. Her grave face told me it was serious. I contacted a specialist who had a very unsympathetic manner. After keeping us waiting for two hours, he complained about Carol dropping a barley sugar wrapper as we went into his consulting room. When he had examined her, he arranged for X-rays, and didn't want to tell me anything until he had seen them. I could not bear the suspense and begged him to tell me what he suspected. He said he thought it was tubercular bone, which would involve her being hospitalized for five or more years.

The doctor's fears were confirmed and Carol was admitted to the out-of-town branch of the Great Portland Street Orthopaedic Hospital at Stanmore. Tubercular bone (Pott's disease) is a disease caused by a dairy product from a cow with tuberculosis. The germ eats into the bone, in this case the spine, which becomes like cottage cheese and then, if not treated, collapses. Carol had three vertebrae infected, which was serious. She would have to lie on her back on an iron frame until the tuberculosis was dormant and the diseased bone had calcified. When I asked the doctor why the cows with tuberculosis were not destroyed, he explained that if they were, many people would suffer from severe malnutrition. Because of the shortage of workers on the farms, the pasteurization system had broken down.

Carol, at two years, had too much spunk for her own good. They told me at the hospital that she fought the doctors all the way and did not settle down as they had hoped. When we went to see her, she was on her back staring at the ceiling. She was learning to talk but the children were very far away from each other and it was hard for them to communicate. I noticed that she seemed terrified of losing the cuddly toys we took her. She would grab them and put them under the covers. They kept disappearing. When I spoke to the nurses about this, they were very defensive and said the children shared their toys. I was told by one nurse that some of her colleagues stole the toys to give to their own relatives.

The last straw came when I went to visit Carol and she wasn't there. In a complete panic I went to

Carol just before she was admitted to hospital with tuberculosis of the spine.

the head nurse, who said casually, "Oh, she had scarlet fever, and we sent her to the isolation hospital." I was furious that I had not been notified and set out to see Carol on the other side of London. The matron at the isolation hospital was an absolute darling and asked to see me when I got there. She told me she was concerned about Carol's emotional state. "Your child is terrified," she said, "especially of men." I asked her if she thought we could nurse Carol at home. She told me the only treatment for Carol's illness was bedrest and nourishing food. So the decision was made and I feel eternally grateful to that woman.

When Carol was diagnosed, I sent for Frank. I was sick to death of coping with everything by myself. He came and we decided, with my mother, that she would take Carol to her house and we would go to Canada to make a home for her. She needed good food and that was not available in England. I looked forward to a fresh start for all of us. I had not touched my inheritance, and, although we were limited as to what we could take out of England, we had enough to get started.

Carol's illness had been a shattering blow. My mother dealt with it silently. There was no one to whom I could speak of my pain or my feelings of guilt. Guilt, because I was sure she had contracted the disease when, a few months earlier, we had spent a week in a hotel at the seaside. Their milk was supplied in huge cans. I wanted to boil it but my mother said I was too fussy, and I had not insisted. Before we left, Carol had developed a temperature. I think, to this day, that the disease took hold at that time.

My heart was heavy at the thought of leaving my daughter even though I knew it was in her best interest. We left for Canada on the *Aquitania* in March 1947. Most of the war brides were treated as second-class citizens and were given rotten cabins on the boat. Fortunately, my mother was a friend of the president of the Cunard line and we had a first-class cabin. I was thrilled to be able to put my shoes outside the door to be cleaned. When we docked in Halifax, the people I had met were dumbfounded to see me join the line of war brides when disembarking. I felt like a traitor and was ashamed that we had travelled in such comfort.

After a long train ride, we arrived in Toronto and were met by my in-laws who came from London, Ontario. I was to have three more weeks of unhappiness.

Hansel and Gretel

OPERA IN ENGLISH

Presented by the Opera School
Royal Conservatory of Music of Toronto

•

EATON AUDITORIUM

THURSDAY AND FRIDAY, DECEMBER 18 AND 19, 1947

Hansel and Gretel, with Jean Marie Scott
and Jean Patterson, Eaton Auditorium program,
December 18 to 19, 1947.

Canada: New Beginnings

The warning of my husband's colonel came back to haunt me as I was introduced to my in-laws. Frank's father, a fire chief; his mother, an enormous woman; and his two sisters, Marion and Dorothy. Things went wrong the moment we entered the house, except for one brief moment when they were charmed by a little girl who called a bobby pin a kirby grip.

They showed us our room and said that Gail, who was almost four, would sleep with her aunt Dorothy in a room that was on the other side of the kitchen. My poor little daughter, who had travelled thousands of miles, felt very strange and insisted on staying with us. My mother-in-law was furious and made a comment about a spoiled brat, but I insisted. She angrily brought a cot into our tiny room. The crowning blow was that Gail soiled the bed, something that had not happened for years.

The next morning I faced an icy silence which was only broken by a demand that I pay thirty dollars a week for room and board. I was quite willing. I did not know that the money I had transferred to Canada through Frank's sergeant-major had all been spent. Mother had a silver tea service, Father a custom-made suit, Dorothy, the older sister, an expensive leather make-up kit, and Marion a bicycle. Apparently the family had been explaining these gifts by saying that Frank had married an heiress. That money, my Canadian army wife's allowance which I had not touched, was intended to augment the limited amount I had been allowed to take out of England. When I asked Frank for an explanation, he told me his family had expected gifts when he returned home.

The next problem related to food. Deprived of fruit for many years, I discovered grapefruit juice in the refrigerator. I drank a delicious glass, only to be told by my father-in-law that his wife had a special diet and that the juice was for her. At dinner we had fried pork kidneys while she had steak.

I reached the end of my patience when Gail became very ill with a strep throat. The doctor prescribed sulpha, but did not tell me to give her plenty of fluids. Her fever was high and she burned up. After several days without food she begged for "wormies," her name for plain boiled spaghetti. When I went to the kitchen to prepare it, I was told that if Gail couldn't eat the greasy hamburger with macaroni that was being prepared, she couldn't be very hungry and would have to go without dinner. I went out and bought spaghetti. On my return I marched into the kitchen to cook it. I was so angry that they didn't dare say a word.

Following this incident I took the old car we had bought and, leaving Frank to care for Gail, I drove to Toronto to meet my cousin, whom I had phoned from London. Charles Feilding was the dean of divinity at the University of Toronto's Trinity College. His kindly, soft-spoken greeting warmed my heart. I was pretty desperate as I knew I could not stay with my husband's family for more than a few days. He concurred and invited me to come, as soon as possible, to live on the third floor of his house in Rosedale, a beautiful area in downtown Toronto.

Greatly relieved, I returned to the Grovers' house and we told them that we would be leaving three days later. Frank was supportive although I have no idea what he said to his parents. The atmosphere was understandably chilly until we left. I was so relieved as we climbed into the car with all our belongings that I felt slap-happy. Gail and Frank seemed to share my feelings.

We arrived in Toronto and were welcomed by the Feildings. Charles' wife, Ann, was a boisterous lady from the United States.

They were complete opposites, yet they adored each other. Their daughter, Goodith, was about ten years old and we became fast friends. Geoffrey, their seven-year-old son, was his mother's boy. He would only eat shredded wheat and drink chocolate milk and had them for every meal. Once, when I was babysitting, I tried to get him to wash his hands before we ate. He was furious and went to his room in a huff. When my cousin came home, he told me my action had been quite justified, but Ann grabbed a tray and took Geoff's supper to his room.

As we got to know each other, Ann confided that she had not looked forward to receiving a relative of Charles into her home. However, she was a terrible housekeeper, and she was grateful for all the help I gave her. We became very fond of each other, and when I left she was truly sorry.

As dean, Charles was second-in-command to the provost of Trinity College, who was a bachelor. This meant that Ann had to act as hostess at official functions. She always spoke her mind, and the visit of the Bishop of London was no exception. A dinner was given in his honour at the college. I was not there but apparently Ann leaned towards the bishop and confided that she had spent the whole day looking for a bra to go with the dress she was wearing especially for him. The meal ended with Ann's comment, "Oh boy, what a meal!" Nobody minded Ann's loudness, and Charles was amused and delighted by it.

Having heard endlessly that the bishop would be in Toronto, an excited Geoffrey rushed in one day exclaiming, "I have just seen the Bishop of London riding down Yonge Street in a jeep." He had actually seen General Montgomery, "Monty," in a post-war victory parade.

I was happy with the Feildings, but anxious to get on with my life. I missed Carol and was looking for a house so that I could bring her over. I frequently sent parcels of food and toys. Everything was so plentiful. I remember being enraptured by the piles of fruit in a store. The owners were moved by my reaction, and we became friends. At Christmas, I asked them for twelve identical oranges to hang on the tree. "So it's size and shape now!" they said. "We can remember when you were thrilled just to see an orange." It hadn't taken long to get used to all this luxury, but I wanted it for Carol to speed her recovery.

To keep her occupied, I enrolled Gail in the kindergarten at Saint Mildred's Convent School. One day, when I went to fetch her, she was surrounded by a group of children and nuns. "We should be paying you for sending her here," said one of the nuns. "We are charmed by her accent." It didn't last long. Gail soon spoke like any other Canadian.

My cousin tried to hide it, but I was aware that he felt pessimistic about my chances of succeeding in Toronto's ballet world, which was already firmly established. In the fall a miracle happened. I was asked by Dr. Ettore Mazzoleni to arrange a ballet for the dream sequence of Humperdinck's opera *Hansel and Gretel*. Mazz, as he was called, was the much-loved principal of the Royal Conservatory of Music. He had heard, through an acquaintance, of my professional experience. He invited me to meet with him and Dr. Arnold Walter, who was responsible for the newly created Opera School.

They told me that an American director, Mr. Brentano, was being brought in to oversee the production, which would take place on December 18 and 19, 1947, at the Eaton Auditorium, where the National Ballet of Canada also made its debut four years later.

When I met Brentano, a confident and aggressive man, he seemed happy to work with me. My only disappointment was that he wanted me to design a ballet using singers rather than dancers. I warned him that all I could do was play a sort of chess game, moving the fourteen angels from tableau to tableau as gracefully as possible. He was satisfied and returned to the States. Then the fun began! In rehearsal, the singers were wonderful. They worked hard in spite of being out of their element, and we laughed a lot. I felt sorry for them when, on Brentano's return, he reversed himself and instructed me to use dancers instead. I, of course, was vastly relieved.

All conductors are not suitable to work with dance companies. It makes them feel constricted. Although a good artistic director will insist that dancers show respect for the music and will not allow them to take liberties with it, there are bound to be some constraints when it comes to tempo. Nickolas Goldschmidt was to conduct *Hansel and Gretel*. He came to the first rehearsal and set the tempo he wanted for the ballet. I was satisfied and my pianist used the metronome so that, when rehearsing, we would remain true to his instructions.

Near the actual date of the production "Nikki" came to a rehearsal accompanied by George Crum, the assistant conductor and chorus master. I was horrified as Goldschmidt proceeded to conduct the hapless pianist at a speed that the dancers could not possibly manage. I tried to explain that it was much too fast and he was furious. He said he was an artist. He had to do what he felt in his heart, and that varied from day to day.

George Crum came to my rescue. He argued with Goldschmidt that he had previously set a much slower tempo and that now, with the choreography in place, it was impossible for the dancers to keep up with him. He almost lost his job for supporting me, but he saved the day.

From then on, George and I had a long and lasting relationship. He was obviously someone with a true talent for conducting dance. When the National Ballet of Canada was founded, he was invited by Celia Franca to become its first conductor. He remained with the company until 1984, when he retired.

During this time I had many other concerns. I had bought a house on Tranby Avenue, a downtown street off Avenue Road. I paid five thousand dollars for it and was to sell it later to a bootlegger for nine thousand eight hundred dollars. Frank and I started painting, and I arranged for Carol to come over with my mother and sister. They came, as I had, to Halifax. I received a phone call from there. The authorities would not allow them to proceed by train unless we paid three hundred dollars to fumigate Carol's coach. I argued fruitlessly that tubercular bone, unlike consumption, was not a communicable disease. Finally I agreed to pay and waited anxiously for their arrival. As Carol was carried in on her iron frame I heard a little voice saying, "Is that my mummy?" I felt all choked up.

I had experienced great difficulty finding an orthopaedic surgeon who was willing to treat Carol at home. They wanted to hospitalize her. I was lucky enough to meet Dr. A. W. Farmer from the Sick Children's Hospital, who agreed that she would be much better with us than in an institution. He was willing to come to the house. He explained that when the tuberculosis was dormant and the bone sufficiently calcified, she would have to have surgery to fuse seven vertebrae with bone taken from her shins.

I had trouble with certain Canadian sayings such as "knock up," which in England simply meant a knock on the door as a wake-up call. The most embarrassing was when I went to buy a roast of beef. Using the English expression, I asked the butcher if he had a nice joint. "Well, my wife thinks so," he replied. As I turned the colour of beetroot, he was highly amused. I was similarly embarrassed by my poor innocent mother. I took her to the opening of *Hansel and Gretel*, which was followed by a reception. Edward Johnson, the famous singer, was there. She was in a group, apparently telling an amusing story, when I heard her say, ". . . and he was screwed." This refers to being drunk in England. There was silence as I went to her rescue.

Once we were settled in our own home, I tried to convince Frank to find a job. He had no interest in the programs offered by the Department of Veterans' Affairs, which would have given him further education or vocational training. He wanted to work as a mechanic, and, as I had been able to transfer more of my inheritance from Britain, I set him up with his own service station, hoping he would make a go of it. Some months later it burned to the ground and we used the insurance money to buy another one. When that too burned down I was not the only one to be suspicious. The fire marshal investigated and told me that, out of sympathy for me and my little ones, they would not charge Frank with arson. I found out, accidentally, that all the time I had thought Frank was working, he had been learning to fly and needed money to pay for it.

I was brought up with the idea that "you have made your bed and must lie on it." I also believed that children should never be deprived of a father simply because their mother was unhappily married. The thought also crossed my mind that it would not be good for Gail and Carol if their father went to jail.

Early in 1948 I had a call from a wealthy friend of my cousin. Her daughter and some other girls had lost their dance teacher, Jean MacPherson, who had left Toronto. She wondered if I would take over the group. The classes were held at the Jesse Ketchum Hall on Davenport Road, close to my house. I was delighted, but had a shock when I arrived for the first lesson. The students wore frilly tutus and were accustomed to a teacher who dressed as a Swan Queen. I arranged for them to wear tunics, which they

80

hated, and at the next class we settled down to work.

I was not very popular as I expected the girls to work. One of them, a judge's daughter, decided to give me a hard time. She was a natural leader and the others followed her. After a few weeks of this behaviour, I asked her mother to remove her as she created an atmosphere that I could not overcome. The world almost came to an end. Mama went to her husband, who said, "Well, there you are, my dear, the British won't put up with that sort of thing." The other mothers were delighted. They told me that this girl made life miserable for any child she disliked and they admired my courage. That was the beginning of my reputation for refusing to compromise.

I also inherited some well-trained students from an excellent teacher, Anna Verity (Mrs. Rae Purdy), when she left Toronto with her husband. Among them were Rose Marie Burns, Lorraine

photo: Erik Dzenis

Jocelyn Terell, my first ballerina, in the ballet *Death and the Maiden*, 1959/60 Company Season.

Thompson, Lorna Would, and Barbara Gray. They were wonderful, hard-working, and loyal, and danced in several of my early productions. My most talented pupil, however, was the daughter of a famous neurosurgeon, Harry Botterell, and his wife Margaret. Jocelyn Terell—she dropped the first syllable of her name—joined the National Ballet in 1957 and was cast in many important roles when she became a principal dancer. Sadly, after seven seasons, her back problems forced an early retirement. She had a spiritual quality and gave an unforgettable performance of the white girl in Walter Gore's ballet *Winter Night*, which was choreographed to Rachmaninov's Second Piano Concerto.

In March 1948, Pauline Patey arrived on our doorstep. Finding she did not know a soul in Canada except me, the immigration authorities had tracked me down through the publicity I had received from the opera. We were all thrilled to see her; she stayed for two years, helping me, and making a name for herself as a dance teacher.

We kept Carol, who had been on her back all this time, constantly stimulated with books, occupational therapy, and a flow of visitors. She lay in the window of the front room and everyone was her friend. I had a stretcher made on wheels and took her out to visit more friends. One of her favourites was the commissionaire at the Park Plaza Hotel.

In the summer we rented a house on Lake Joseph in Muskoka. The people who owned it ran Pinelands, a nearby lodge. We spent three months there and Carol's health improved.

In the fall of 1948 many things happened. I had rented the Jesse Ketchum Hall on a full-time basis and opened a school. I taught everything: ballet, tap, pre-ballet for tots, keep-fit classes for adults, and, for the last time in my life, ballroom dancing. I charged fifty cents a lesson.

Gail, now five years old, went into the first grade at Bishop Strachan School and loved it. In November Carol was to have a spinal fusion. The night before she went into hospital I was feeling very ill. I did not finish teaching until late in the evening and went home with a ghastly sore throat. I had not yet fully realized how my mother's love for me had been transferred to Carol, almost to the point of an obsession, but that night it became very clear.

My mother accused me of faking illness in order to avoid

going to the hospital with Carol. It is true that I was dreading seeing her suffer, but I would never have allowed that to stand in my way. The next morning I was covered in a rash. My mother was not speaking to me. She and my sister went to the hospital with Carol. I called the doctor, who came and told me I had a severe case of scarlet fever and must be very careful in case of complications.

I lay there stewing about Carol and wondering how she was faring. In those days relatives were not welcome with the children in hospitals and I had fought to make sure that one of us could be with her at all times. As for myself, I drank fluids and struggled with the realization that my mother couldn't care less what happened to me.

Eventually, I recovered and Carol came home. She was in a body cast with a heavy headpiece which reached to her knees. We used a cool hair dryer to get rid of crumbs but were stymied when a thermometer fell down inside the cast. I was afraid it would break, but we managed to get it out.

My worst experience with that wretched cast came when Carol developed mumps. The swelling was so severe that the sides of the headpiece were pressing against it. It was a weekend and no doctors were available, so I decided to remove the headpiece, which was causing considerable pain. All I had was a two-sided razor blade. At the neck of the cast the plaster was about four inches thick. It took hours and my thumb was shredded. Carol, however, was greatly relieved.

The following Monday they replaced the cast. Two weeks later there was a lump on Carol's neck. I called Dr. Farmer, who came immediately and wanted a biopsy as he suspected a tubercular gland. We were devastated because this would mean the disease was active and not dormant. After consultation with my mother, who believed that the lump was associated with the pressure on the swollen area, I refused to allow the biopsy and the doctor stormed out in a fury.

I phoned a friend who was also a doctor. He said he would take a look at the lump. It burst as we were taking Carol to his hospital. It was a huge abscess and not, as we had feared, a tubercular gland. Ethically, Dr. Farmer could not refuse to continue to see Carol unless we had interfered with his treatment of her back.

I wrote a sweet letter pointing this out and added that I was sure he would be glad to hear the outcome of the mumps incident. He was sulky when he returned, but he soon got over it.

In the late spring of 1949, I gave my first and last recital at Hart House Theatre. I dislike recitals intensely. They are a waste of time for the students and expensive for the parents. Yet I felt that it was expected and knew that I was in need of some exposure. It was a great success and I was amused to hear that Boris Volkoff, of whom I will speak later, was skulking in the corridor in the intermission. When asked if it was a good performance, he replied in disgust, "Too good!"

A few weeks later I came out in a rash. I had a severe case of chicken pox, which I had caught from one of my students. I had to isolate myself for Carol's sake. I was extremely nervous because I suspected I was pregnant. I thought about it long and hard. I knew there was a distinct possibility that the foetus would be damaged by the chicken pox and that I could not cope with another disabled child. I also knew that Frank, who did not have a job, was seeing a girl called Helen on a regular basis and that the chance of our marriage surviving was minimal. When my fears were confirmed, I decided to have an abortion.

In those days this was not easy. I broached the subject with my regular doctor. He treated me like a criminal and never spoke to me again. I was given the name of a less judgemental doctor who was willing to help me.

Time was of the essence, so as soon as I was out of quarantine, I went to see the woman whom he had recommended as the only safe person in Toronto. It was a simple procedure, no surgery, but she told me to walk a lot. Although the event was serious, I cannot help laughing at the thought of marching around the grounds of Queen's Park until I had covered about ten miles. Frank, who was around for once, slept on the grass until I had finished my wanderings.

This continued for a few days and I became worried when I didn't expel the foetus. I returned for a repeat of the treatment, which was immediately successful. I was alone at Tranby. Frank had gone out and my family was at Pinelands. I suffered intense labour pains until I aborted the male foetus which was, as I had feared, deformed. The doctor came as promised and said I was well enough to travel to Muskoka. Unfortunately, part of the placenta was still attached to the uterus. Two weeks later I was rushed to hospital with a severe haemorrhage and was given a D & C. Soon after, the same thing happened again, and then I was clear. During that time Frank did not attempt to visit me. I did not find out until later that Helen was staying at the lodge.

In spite of these interruptions, I was acting as a sports and social director for Mr. and Mrs. Jones, who owned the lodge. I organized water and land games for the children. In the evenings, for the adults, I ran bingos, charades, party games, and on Fridays a dance. I remember teaching them "the Lambeth Walk," which was all the rage at that time. I did not enjoy this, but my rent was reduced considerably. I believe that those holidays played a large part in Carol's recovery. By this time she was in a walking cast. When I returned to Toronto, in order to give her some companionship I hired a teacher and opened a small nursery school at the Jesse Ketchum Hall. We wheeled her there every day and she had a great time.

Although I had made every effort not to deprive my children of a father, I could no longer tolerate Frank's affair. When we returned to Toronto, I told him I wanted to end the marriage and he left. He cleared out our joint account and even took the bonds I had put aside for Carol's expenses. As she had become ill in the U.K., I could not get health insurance in Canada. I was fortunate that the house was paid for and my school was doing well.

Usually, when I felt depressed, something would happen to cheer me up. This time it was special. I was approached by Eric Christmas, a British comedian, to arrange the dances for *Mother Goose*, a pantomime which was sponsored by the New Play Society. The society's founder, Dora Mavor Moore, was a fearsome woman, a great pioneer of theatre in Toronto, but I found her very difficult. When I went to discuss my contract, she informed me that she had no intention of paying the dancers. I said they should not be expected to work for nothing and she replied, "They should do it for love." I pointed out that this was unprofessional and that I could not accept her conditions. She reluctantly agreed to pay them thirty dollars a week, and I was hired.

My first task was to hold a public audition. Having found the required number of dancers, we started rehearsals. Almost immediately Mrs. Moore and I crossed swords. She asked me to fire one of the dancers to make room for Carole Chadwick, her friend's daughter. I refused, but suggested that if she agreed to hire Carole as an extra dancer I could use a general understudy and would arrange for her to share some performances with the other girls. This was approved.

When I met Carole, I found that I could not use her as she had only studied dance for two months. Infuriated by my decision, her mother marched onstage in the middle of a rehearsal, accompanied by Mrs. Moore, and proceeded to give me a piece of her mind. Her parting shot was to tell me that I should go back where I came from as I wasn't needed in Canada. I was flabbergasted but said nothing, as I did not want to make it worse for Carole, whom I had liked immediately.

This was the beginning of a lasting friendship. Some years later, in 1963, I invited Carole to teach at the National Ballet School, where she has always given a fine grounding to the younger children. Eventually she became the ballet vice-principal and headed the Teachers' Training Program, as well as being responsible for the national auditions.

It was to be a traditional British pantomime with Eric directing it and playing the "dame." He was a superb comedian. We were both experienced and worked well together. The cast was professional and included Jack Medhurst as Priscilla the goose, Bob (Robert) Christie as the Demon Discordo, and Gladys Forrester as the Fairy Queen. Samuel Hersenhoren conducted the orchestra. The only

Robert Christie in his T.V. role in *The Road.*

86

My publicity photo for Royal
Alexandra Theatre, 1949.

serious problem was that Mrs. Moore's daughter-in-law, who made the costumes, seemed to have had no theatrical experience.

For the ballet we needed long classical dresses. I explained how they had to be made. The skirts must be in three layers of silk net, each layer requiring five yards of material. When I saw the dresses, I had a fit. The two underskirts were made of two and a half yards of a cheaper material and only the top one met my specifications. The results were comical. When the dancers moved they had the two bottom skirts clinging to their legs and the top one flowing and swirling at waist level. The rest of the costumes were simply amateurish.

There was an unholy row. I said that everything had to be scrapped and Mrs. Moore refused. Later I told Eric that I could not continue under the circumstances. He agreed, saw Mrs. Moore, and the matter was resolved. New costumes were ordered. However, after being told that I should be like a soldier who does not question the orders of his superiors, I was virtually "sent to Coventry" by Mrs. Moore and the rest of the cast. Only Bob Christie refused to be intimidated and was very kind. Eric and the dancers continued to give me their full support.

The show opened for a two-week run at the Royal Alexandra Theatre on December 26, 1949, and was a great success. At the reception—Nescafé and cookies—Mrs. Moore still refused to acknowledge me.

In the *Toronto Star* the next day, Jack Karr was enthusiastic about the production and commented on my contribution:

Betty Oliphant has staged some very pleasant dances, particularly in the first act finale—a Scottish number with kilts swinging through a sword dance—and in the second act when she turns to ballet. She has also provided an amusing bit of voodooism in a haunted castle where her young ladies are dressed completely in black, with only the palms of their hands visible, eerily in strobolite.

The following year John Wayne and Frank Shuster took over the production. It was wonderful working with them. While retaining the essence of a pantomime, which to them was a fascinating piece of theatre, they were able to modernize it. I arranged all-new routines for the dancers and was inspired by Johnny and Frank to do something much more original. With their penchant for humour, they worked with Eric Christmas on the comedy, and the results were hilarious. They brought in Johnny Dobson to do the musical arrangements and hired Henry Matthews from Montreal to conduct. We had new costumes and a few changes of cast: Jack Medhurst returned as Priscilla but Ben Lennick

The inimitable Wayne and Shuster with Mother
Goose in their T.V. production, 1957.

replaced Bob Christie, who was not available, as the demon. Other leading roles were played by Joan Fairfax, Mae Craven, and Paul Kligman as Mother Goose's son, Jack.

This production, with a cast of fifty, including nine little girls, went to His Majesty's Theatre in Montreal for the last week of December 1950 and the first week of January 1951. From there we went to the Grand Theatre in London and ran for a week. I am proud to say that this time around the dancers' salaries were increased to sixty dollars weekly.

I was with the National Ballet so did not take part in the CBC television show of *Mother Goose* which was produced by Wayne and Shuster in 1957 with Johnny and Frank playing the leading comedy parts of Mother Goose and Jack.

In the summer of 1950, between the two pantomimes, Eric Christmas and I decided to take a small revue to Muskoka. We planned to play all the hotels and lodges surrounding Pinelands. I would once again be sports director, Eric would take the show out, and we would split the money raised from the collections. I had a line of four girls, good tap dancers, who had appeared at numerous functions in Toronto, headed by Barbara West who taught in my school. They came with us to Muskoka.

The house we rented at Pinelands was big, but that year it was completely full with my family, Eric, his wife, their two children, and some of the performers. We were allowed to use the ballroom at the lodge for rehearsals, and in return, on Fridays, we performed for the guests. It was a very successful project, but not financially. I found out why when one of the cast told me that Eric stuffed a large part of the collection into his pocket before bringing it home to split with me. There was nothing I could do, no proof.

In the fall, Carol, who was now wearing a brace, went into Grade 1 at Bishop Strachan. They looked after her well, and she rested each day in the principal's office.

During rehearsals for the first pantomime, I was interviewed by a reporter from The Canadian Press, John Paterson—Pat for short. He became interested in my background and, later, in me. Although I could never have taken him seriously, it was nice to have a friend. He was crazy about me, and I heard when I remarried in 1958 that he was inconsolable on the day of the wedding.

Strangely enough, it was a visit from Pat at my house that

made me think about moving. My mother was with us the whole time. After he left, I realized that she had monopolized him for the entire evening. I rarely got a chance to speak.

A much bigger factor in my considerations was the effect my mother's preference for Carol was having on both the children. Gail was afraid of her and begged me not to take her side in arguments for fear of my mother's anger. Carol was encouraged by my mother to believe that I did not love her as much as Gail, because she looked like her father. I was able to be strong for my children if not for myself. I decided to move.

I found a large house at Sherbourne and Wellesley for thirteen thousand dollars. I told my mother I had to live alone with the children and she was furious. Frank turned up and wanted to come back. He said, and there was some truth in it, that our relationship couldn't work while my mother was living with us. His return lasted one week. Constant calls from Helen, disguised as an employee of the post office, and his absence every night convinced me that he had not come back to work at the marriage. It was well and truly over.

Frank then went to my mother who, with my sister, had bought a house on Woodlawn Avenue, and told her that I was running around with men and leaving the children alone in the house. She was only too willing to believe him and took him in. When I phoned, she was abusive. When Carol went to visit her my mother would accuse me of neglecting her—once because there was a button missing from her coat. Another time, when Carol had hurt her finger and I had kissed it better, my mother insisted that it might have been broken and I hadn't bothered to find out. Poor Carol. When I went to fetch her on that day, she was hiding in the bushes outside the house. She didn't want me to go in as she thought I would be killed. By then, I had had enough. I told my mother that Carol could not visit her if she was going to be placed in a situation where she had to choose between us. It was better for Carol after that, but my mother wouldn't speak to me and she returned the gift I sent for her birthday.

That was a very unhappy time for all of us, and writing about it has been painful. Things looked up when Celia Franca arrived in Canada.

photo: Erik Dzenis

Rehearsal of *Swan Lake* for a School performance
by professional students. Nancy Schwenker, teacher.

The National Ballet
of Canada

The first three years I spent in Canada were difficult personally and professionally.

While working with the Canadian Opera School and the *Mother Goose* pantomime and teaching master classes to raise money for the Canadian Ballet Festival, I was able to get to know most of my fellow dance teachers. To find dancers for the Opera School project, I was taken to the various dance schools to select students who were suitable to perform in the opera. The teachers weren't thrilled that a stranger had been chosen to choreograph this ballet, but they knew how few opportunities there were for their advanced students to perform, so they reluctantly agreed to allow them to work for me.

In the case of the *Mother Goose* pantomime, we held public auditions. When they were over, I was told by one of the dancers that this was the first fair audition that had taken place in Toronto in many years. She explained that in the past preference had been given to pupils of the Volkoff school. I, of course, was solely interested in finding the best dancers, and was only vaguely aware of local politics. Many of the people I chose in these auditions became founding members of the National Ballet of Canada.

A word here about Boris Volkoff. When I arrived in Canada, he was "Mr. Ballet." I was told by many people that I had very little hope of establishing myself in Toronto because no one could compete with him. Yet when I was invited to watch his class I was not impressed with his teaching or with the caustic and often humiliating remarks he made to his pupils.

I was also concerned that the thigh muscles of most of his regular students were overdeveloped. I found out the reason when I counted seventy-two *grands pliés*, or deep knee bends, in a single class.

As I became more intimate with my new colleagues, I was surprised to discover that they rarely got together to share their expertise, and operated their individual schools in isolation. The Canadian Ballet Festival was a happy exception to this state of affairs. With Mildred Wickson, a popular and successful teacher, as president, and with the support of many of the teachers I had met, we were able to start the Canadian Dance Teachers Association (C.D.T.A.) with a view to sharing ideas and raising standards.

The C.D.T.A. had regular Sunday meetings, and I gave classes frequently. It was hard to gain the trust of my fellow teachers, but I did not know how suspicious they were until a certain incident occurred.

While teaching a pointe-work class, I mentioned that to get on pointe (i.e., on your toes) one should give a little spring, pulling up the thigh muscles quickly in order to land lightly. This is not the only method but it is the one most commonly used. I felt a little stir in the room, but thought nothing of it until the visit of Ninette de Valois, the founder of the Royal Ballet. This august person was invited to give a class to our advanced students which was followed by a question period for the teachers. To my surprise, one of the teachers stood up to ask Madame de Valois if it was correct to use a slight spring when rising on pointe. She is a very forbidding person and her impatient "of course, of course" sounded like a put-down. Although I was pleased to have been proven right, I learned that I must be more understanding and take nothing for granted if I was to be of any help to my colleagues.

The first big challenge for the C.D.T.A. came when Celia Franca was invited to Toronto to explore the possibility of founding the National Ballet of Canada. First came the rumours: this famous English ballerina was in Toronto and was about to teach master classes to senior students from schools selected by Boris Volkoff and his wife Janet Baldwin. Once again I was confronted with the politics of the Toronto dance world, and I was outraged. We had a meeting, and I was chosen to contact Celia Franca to present the case for the dance teachers.

I had heard of Celia in London when she was with the Royal Ballet. She had been recommended by Ninette de Valois as artistic director for the new Canadian venture. It has been said that Celia was rebellious and showed strong leadership qualities and that de Valois, who was extremely autocratic, saw her as a potential rival and wanted to get rid of her.

When I went to see Celia she was screwing up the switchboard of the Eaton Auditorium. This job had been found for her by the promoters of the National Ballet so that she could earn her keep while assessing the situation. After we had laughed heartily about her inability to find the right key for the right hole on the switchboard, I told her of the unhappiness of the teachers who felt excluded from what could be one of the most important happenings in the history of Canadian ballet.

Celia's reaction to my story was, as I came to learn, typical. She was hurt, and therefore angry and defensive. "Why don't the teachers trust me?" she asked. "Because they don't know you," I replied, and went on to explain that the C.D.T.A. had been founded to enable the teachers, as a group, to discuss their problems and to act on them when necessary. I suggested a meeting with the teachers, and she seemed relieved. Although it sounds simple, I had a difficult time. Celia was extremely intimidating, and I was able to get a glimpse of this woman with whom I would work for many years.

The meeting with the teachers took place at my house on Sherbourne Street. We were crowded in my little sitting room, but the atmosphere was warm and friendly. Important decisions were made. The master classes would be run by the C.D.T.A. and would be open to students of all schools, providing they were sufficiently advanced.

At the same time, we agreed to raise the money for Celia to cross the country to meet teachers and look for talent. By taking responsibility for organizing these events, we took a great load off Celia's mind. She, in turn, told us of the plans for a National Ballet and promised that the auditioning process would be open to all and that Canadian dance teachers would be kept fully informed.

The burgeoning relationship with my colleagues, coupled with Celia's arrival, gave me a big boost. I was alone in a big house caring for two children. Carol was missing her grandmother very much, and the latter was very angry with me for moving out on my own. I had a daily housekeeper who had been with us at Tranby Avenue. She was constantly reminding me how foolish I had been to move to this rambling old house with two furnaces, an old-fashioned kitchen, and ghastly wallpaper.

I also had to cope with some extraordinary tenants who, in the post-war era, had to be given six months' notice. One couple gave me the most trouble. They were always drunk and screamed at each other incessantly. I was afraid they would become violent and frighten the children. Less stressful was an eccentric old lady who was a kleptomaniac. The walls of her room were lined with jars of jam and pickles which she had "acquired" from the local supermarket. The other tenants were harmless but unsavoury. I was delighted when they finally departed.

Although I had originally made the decision to move to escape the constant friction with my mother, I had another practical reason for choosing that rather unlikely property. I knew I could make two fair-sized studios on the ground floor so that I could be teaching at home in the evenings and would not have to leave the children. Eventually the alterations were completed and the school was opened.

Among the students were several young girls who were starting their professional training. Later well-known dancers, they were Victoria Bertram, Vanessa Harwood, Martine van Hamel, Nadia Potts, and Veronica Tennant. They often remind me of the days when Butterscotch, our beautiful cat, sat on the piano, which was played by dear old Mrs. Mayhew who had been the pianist at the school in London where I trained.

After our first meeting, Celia and I saw each other frequently, and I helped her find an apartment close to my house. We discovered that we had been at the Marie Rambert School in London

My Sherbourne Street studio, 1955. Pictured in the first row of students
are Nadia Potts, Vanessa Harwood, Linda Fletcher. Second row,
Victoria Bertram, Barbara Malinowski, Linda Stibbard. In the back
row are my daughter Carol, Janet Battye, and Veronica Tennant.

at the same time but in different classes. Celia had not been
allowed in the morning professional class because she was performing in the chorus at the London Hippodrome and Madame
Rambert was a ballet snob. I, on the other hand, was allowed in
that class because Madame did not know that I had also "prosti-
tuted" myself to become a competent musical comedy and tap
dancer. A few years later when I was visiting the school of Buddy
Bradley, a famous tap dancer, I found it ironic to discover that the
star of the class was Lulu Dukes, Marie Rambert's daughter. Mama
was sitting there, oozing disapproval. After the class, I said to
Lulu, "How was it?" "Ugh," she replied. "My mother! I wish she
hadn't come." Lulu was one of the stars in the original production
of *Oklahoma*.

Plans for forming the company were moving along. In July of
1951 the first National Ballet Summer School was to take place at
the St. Lawrence Hall on King Street. This historical old building,
at one time Toronto's City Hall, had not yet been renovated. In the
winter it was used as a shelter for the homeless, and we were to be
allowed to use it in the summer—after it had been fumigated—for
a fee of one dollar.

I say "we" because, after having seen me teach, Celia had asked me to help her organize this venture. I agreed and gave up plans for my own summer school to be a part of a very small faculty which consisted of the two of us, Louise Goldsmith who taught the Royal Academy system, and Lucille McClure who specialized in character dancing. The course was to last for six weeks. Applicants were to be boarded at a university residence. Although we had houseparents, I would have to deal with many of the students' problems. These, I was to discover, included homesickness and, most particularly, the fact that they felt they had been placed in a class that was too easy for them.

This feeling was understandable. The students, who came from all over North America, had often been very poorly trained, and yet they were the stars of their local schools. In the recitals they had danced such difficult roles as the Swan Queen in *Swan Lake* and Aurora in *The Sleeping Beauty*. It was my job to give them a daily class to correct their basic technique—hence their dissatisfaction. The logic of good training usually won them over. I became known far and wide as an excellent teacher, able to provide dancers with a sound technical foundation. It took me years to prove that I could also teach and coach advanced pupils.

As the founders of the embryonic National Ballet had not, as yet, raised any money, Celia was told that if the fees did not cover the costs of the Summer School, she would have to pay any loss out of her own pocket. If there was a profit, it would be used to benefit the new Company. We completed a successful six weeks with a credit of one thousand dollars. This Summer School was an annual event for many years and became so well known in North America that we cleared at least ten thousand dollars every year.

Following the Summer School, Celia set out to cross the country, looking for talented dancers who would be invited to be the founding members of the National Ballet of Canada. Many of the people who had worked with me in *Hansel and Gretel* and *Mother Goose* had already auditioned in Toronto and Celia had accepted them, but they were all girls. Very few boys studied ballet in those days, so Celia was looking for girls to add to those she already had, plus boys. She knew she would not find many of the latter who had received adequate ballet training, so they were to be sent to me. I was supposed to give them a quick intensive course so that she could put them on stage knowing at least the rudiments of ballet.

First I received a postcard from Celia saying she was sending me a twenty-three-year-old lawyer. He had received some training in interpretive dance but none in ballet. This was Grant Strate who later became resident choreographer of the National Ballet and went on to found the Dance Department at York University.

Celia's next male discovery was Howard Meadows, known to us all as Hy. He was not a very good dancer. Later, when I asked Celia why on earth she had taken him, she explained that she had to have someone who looked good when stripped to the waist for the Danse Arabe in *The Nutcracker*. But it wasn't that easy; she hadn't realized that his chest was covered with a mass of curly black hair. Added to the aesthetic problem was the fact that he would have to wear brown body make-up. Hy was not willing to shave his chest. They compromised. He agreed to trim the hair and all was well.

After a short dance career, Hy Meadows worked in the wardrobe and eventually became its head. He was passionate about caring for the National's thousands of costumes, and woe betide the dancer whom he caught eating or drinking in one of them. He died in 1994, and is sorely missed by all of us who loved him.

Celia returned from the tour. I was in the process of training her discoveries, several of whom were living at Sherbourne Street because they were broke. She had assembled her company, which included David Adams, with whom she had worked in England; his wife, Lois Smith; Lilian Jarvis; Earl Kraul; Judie Colpman; Brian McDonald, who became a well-known choreographer; his wife, Olivia Wyatt; Angela Leigh; Yves Cousineau; Oldyna Dynowska, and others. Many of these dancers were very good. I do not wish to suggest that they all needed my "crash courses" in ballet.

The National Ballet of Canada gave its first performance in the fall of 1951 at the Eaton Auditorium. I was impressed by Celia's achievement. The program was well structured, simple, and tasteful. The dancers did not have to attempt anything that was beyond them. I was totally in agreement with Celia's belief that one never allowed the audience to see any movement that had not been fully mastered in the studio. This respect that we both feel for the public has been an essential part of my professional life. I have never allowed my students to experiment on stage although they often want to add one extra pirouette or, in the case of the boys, a double *tour en l'air* when their landings are still shaky.

I have no intention of writing a history of the National Ballet. I just want to share my experiences as ballet mistress—a job that Celia offered me soon after the Company was started. Although sorely tempted, I did not accept the offer, because I could not leave my children to go on tour. However, Celia suggested that she would take an assistant on the tour if I would agree to work with her in Toronto. I was delighted, even though it would mean being with the Company from 9:30 a.m. and teaching at my own school from 4:00 p.m. to 8:30 p.m.

A word about the position of ballet mistress. She assists the artistic director, whose responsibilities include setting artistic policy; choosing repertoire, dancers, and artistic staff; inviting choreographers and supporting them in their efforts to develop their ideas with the help of the permanent staff. There are many other responsibilities and, of course, the artistic director reports to the board of directors who, at times, can be very demanding.

The duties of a ballet mistress are less global and have more to do with the nitty-gritty aspects of running a company. She gives a daily class to the dancers. In my case, it was often two classes when we divided the boys and girls, but most companies have more than one ballet mistress, plus a ballet master who usually teaches the boys. She takes a great many rehearsals, both with the *corps de ballet* and the soloists. When the company is performing, the ballet mistress is out front writing corrections which she will give to the dancers before the next performance. Scheduling, replacing sick dancers, sometimes at the last minute, and arranging photo calls and media interviews in conjunction with the publicity department are also part of the job. The life is strenuous, and the dancers need understanding and compassion, especially when they are exhausted, injured, or disappointed when the casting list goes up.

When I agreed to become ballet mistress, Celia sent me to discuss my salary with Walter Homburger, the Company manager. I have never been very commercial. When I saw his relief at my request for thirty dollars a week, I knew I hadn't asked for enough. However, it was arranged, and the press was notified. The next day I saw an announcement in the paper saying that Betty Oliphant had been appointed mistress to Walter Homburger of the National Ballet at thirty dollars a week.

I loved working with the Company and learning the classical repertoire. For financial reasons, the last few years I had spent in England had been in the world of musical comedy, but ballet was my first and only true love. It was also inspiring to work with well-known choreographers whom Celia had invited to reproduce old works or create new ones.

Antony Tudor was one of these. He and many other artists had left London for New York when the war was imminent. Those who remained thought of them as rats who had deserted a sinking ship, but I felt sympathy for them. Ballet is a very short career and would have been almost impossible to resume after the military service that was compulsory in Britain.

By the time he came to Canada, Tudor was famous, not only for his powerful works of art, but also for his caustic wit and cruel tongue when dealing with dancers. Our Company members were very young and inexperienced. Celia and I, who had known Tudor in England, were concerned that he would intimidate them, but they handled his sarcasm with a smile even though at times they were obviously close to tears.

At that time there was no union, so we worked long hours including Sundays. One of our dancers, who was very religious, came to a rehearsal one Sunday and Tudor promptly asked her if she had been to church. "Yes," she replied. "So I suppose you think you are much better than the rest of us," he said. "No, it is because I don't think I'm better than the rest of you that I went to church." Tudor subsided and I cheered silently.

When giving Company classes, I had similar problems to those of the Summer School, but it was more difficult because the dancers were older and already performing in a professional Company. Many of them confused the talent that had caused Celia to accept them with their technical ability which was sadly

photo: Joseph Ciancio

Cover of *Dance in Canada* with students
Dominique Dumais, Jennifer Fournier, and
Caroline Richardson on pointe.

lacking. For example, when Lilian Jarvis was on pointe her weight was almost entirely over her big toe. Apart from this being ugly, she was bound to develop horrible and painful bunions if it were not corrected. Going back to basics did not fit in with Lilian's image of herself as a soloist, and she was very resistant to my attempts to help her. Earl Kraul was the same. With his enormous talent he wanted the freedom to indulge himself without recognizing the need for the disciplined technique that would allow him to develop his potential. Trying to reverse this "cart before the horse" situation was a burden to me and boring, but essential for the dancers.

Because of the Company's financial situation, I felt obliged to help with fund-raising. I remember a horrible evening when I was taken to see a play at the Royal Alexandra by Eddie Goodman, a lawyer, who was at that time chairman of the board of the National Ballet. He asked me how I would feel if I were the ballet mistress of a non-existent company. I can still remember the terrible jolt I received and cannot recall one moment of the play we were watching. Although I was furious at Eddie's timing, I soon realized how desperately concerned he was.

With the help of the C.D.T.A., I got to work. We organized a car raffle which raised about eight thousand dollars the first time and continued for many years. We ran a fun fair for several years, which we enjoyed, but it was very hard work. On one occasion when the Company was stranded in the United States, I spent twenty-four hours phoning people for donations and received five thousand dollars. There were numerous times when dancers and staff turned in their salary cheques so that we could survive for one more week.

In January 1953, we moved to the Royal Alexandra Theatre, and were to remain there for ten years before going to the O'Keefe Centre. The Royal Alex, although not designed for dance, was a theatre with a great tradition. Ernest Rawley, the manager, loved the arts, and both he and Edwin DeRocher, the box office manager, had a soft spot for us.

One crucial day in the middle of the season, we realized we couldn't pay the dancers as well as the theatre rental, which had first claim on the box office receipts. We invited Ernie and Eddie for a drink after the show and armed ourselves with two bottles of Scotch. As we imbibed the whisky, Ernie was reminiscing about all the wonderful artists who had appeared in his theatre. At the appropriate time when we were close to the bottom of the second bottle, I took a deep breath and blurted out, "We don't have enough to pay the dancers this week. Would you be willing to wait for the rent?" They laughed and agreed. Actually, I believe they would have done so even if sober.

As you can see, my job involved far more than the typical duties of a ballet mistress, but I was perfectly happy. I love challenges and refuse to give up until I have achieved my goal. My administrative talents were useful to the Company, as we had periods when the general manager was away or we were in the process of replacing him.

When the Company went to the Carter Barron Amphitheatre in Washington, Celia and I were on our own and had to make many important administrative decisions. The first was regarding rain insurance. Because it was very expensive, we decided to insure only the Saturday performance as it would be the most lucrative. The deal was that if we collected two inches of rain in a particular bucket, we would be reimbursed for that evening's performance. We had a separate deal with the theatre which entailed finishing two-thirds of the performance in spite of bad weather before we could receive our share of the box office.

We had excellent weather for the first few days but on the Saturday, soon after we had started a performance of *Giselle*, the rain came. The Company continued even though the orchestra could barely see the music for smudges. The dancers were slipping all over the place, with the exception of Celia, the old pro, who was dancing the leading role with such caution that she managed to remain on her feet. I, in the meantime, was watching the bucket and willing it to reach the two-inch target. It did, and the Company completed two-thirds of the performance, so we actually made a profit.

Another amusing event occurred in Washington. A young violinist was being groomed as an occasional replacement conductor. Unfortunately, because he was not really suitable, he had failed to gain the respect of his colleagues. One night, when he was conducting the orchestra, a musician spoke to his neighbour. "How is Charlie doing?" he asked. "I don't know, I haven't looked," was the reply.

In the early days of the Company, Celia was performing regularly. On the day of a performance she was extremely nervous, and I was often the recipient of some bitchy remarks. I tried not to respond with anger, understanding the tension she was feeling; but she could be very mean, and I was naturally upset. She came to the theatre very early, allowing about five hours to prepare for her appearance. She was a perfectionist about her shoes, her make-up, her costumes, and she checked everything. Sometimes she had corrections on her mirror which I had given at her last performance, and she studied them. Giving her a warm-up class was also difficult. It was almost impossible to please her, but the results were worth it. Celia was a fine dramatic dancer, and in *Giselle* she often moved me to tears.

The dancers had a good relationship with Celia at first. They were young and for the most part inexperienced. They called her Auntie Celia, which she loved, and were very dependent. As the years passed, they gained more confidence. They wanted to discuss their careers with her and to complain if they felt they were not being given the opportunities they deserved. Depending on her mood, they sometimes received a very chilly reception and went away feeling devastated. I naturally supported her decisions but tried to make them feel more positive about themselves.

Dancers are usually dissatisfied and do not always see themselves realistically. On the other hand, their self-confidence needs boosting, and the truth does not have to be presented in a destructive way.

As for me, I had a deep friendship with Celia for many years. I adored her and admired her for her artistry both as a dancer and a director.

We often went on holiday together to Muskoka. I remember she was terrified of moths, and I had to clear her room every night. She couldn't swim, and, unlike me, she had never practised sports. She was very timid, and when we went out in a canoe, she used to sit on the bottom and usually finished up with a very wet rear end.

Celia was very fond of my children, although she often hurt their feelings. She was always nagging them to be kind to me. Nevertheless, when the Company went to Mexico, Gail came with us and stayed with Celia after I left. She had a wonderful time.

This reminds me of a funny story. When I took Gail for her shots, she nearly ruined her chances of going to Mexico. Our G.P. was a big fat man. As he prepared the needle and was ready to inject it, Gail ran behind the desk. The foolish man started to chase her and they went round and round. I was laughing so hard it was difficult to interrupt. I said sternly to Gail, "If you don't have the shots you can't go to Mexico." She calmed down immediately and our doctor, who was very angry, gave her the injections.

Mexico was gruelling for the Company. Without taking the

altitude into consideration, we had agreed to perform seven times in one week. The dancers were collapsing when they came off the stage. They greedily took great gulps of oxygen, which was available in the wings. Then, on their next cue, they went back to continue dancing.

In spite of our friendship, I had many experiences of Celia's biting tongue and am ashamed to admit that I handled them very badly. The worst was one I will never forget. I was worn out with toothache from a dry socket. This was caused by a clot of blood, which formed after an extraction, flying out while I was doing a pirouette and leaving the nerve exposed. I had been in agony for over a week, and we were rehearsing late at night with an audience of board members. Celia was dancing the role of "The Woman in His Past" from Antony Tudor's *Lilac Garden*; Jimmy Ronaldson was her partner. They were attempting a lift, and it wasn't working. She

Carol attended the 1957 performance.

suddenly screamed at me to do something about it. I made several suggestions, and eventually they mastered it.

I was staying with Celia at the time, while my children were at the lake with my mother. When I got in the taxi with Celia I broke down completely. We arrived at the house, and I was still sobbing. I told her how I felt in no uncertain terms, and I think she was scared because the worm—that's me—had never before turned. Eventually a doctor was called, and I got a shot of morphine for the pain. It was many years later, when I had psychotherapy, that I realized how I had allowed myself to be used by Celia and others.

A rather amusing postscript to this story was Celia and my mother's hatred for each other. Although I allowed both of them to treat me badly, they thought they were protecting me when they had long arguments over the phone. My mother accused Celia of killing me with overwork and said she would be responsible if I died before my time. Celia pointed out that I loved what I was doing and that even if I did die young, at least I would have been happy.

Because it was close, I sent my daughters to Branksome Hall soon after we moved to Sherbourne Street. It was a decision I regretted as they missed Bishop Strachan School very much.

Some years later Gail and I had an experience that was difficult for both of us. For three years she had worn braces on her teeth which I could ill afford. The day after they came off I sat at breakfast admiring her. At noon I had a message to go immediately to Branksome. Gail had been hit across the mouth with a baseball bat. Five teeth were damaged and she had to have a cap for the broken front tooth and root canals for the others. Poor kid, she was so self-conscious and suffered so much pain and discomfort. I felt rotten, but was relieved that the school's insurance covered the expense.

The Company was appearing at the Royal Alexandra in 1957 when my mother suffered a stroke which paralyzed her from the neck down. When I returned from a Sunday's teaching in Montreal, she berated me for not being there when it happened. By this time she rarely spoke to me. When she did, it was to criticize. She made me promise not to put her in hospital as the doctor had suggested. I found myself faced with paying for two private nurses, who took eight-hour shifts. My sister was on duty at night. I felt so sorry for my mother and agreed when she said they would never permit a dog to live in that helpless state.

Had she not died when she did a few months later, I might have been forced to break my promise, as my savings had all but disappeared. I have to confess to a profound feeling of relief— almost euphoria—when it was over: for her because she was out of her misery, and for me because our relationship had deteriorated to the point where nothing positive remained between us.

At the funeral home they were charming until I chose a simple pine coffin, their cheapest. I explained that my mother would prefer me to spend the money on the children's education. They asked coldly if I wanted to use their chapel for the service. I said I would have to discuss that with my cousin Charles Feilding, who, you may remember, was dean of divinity at Trinity College. What a transformation! They bowed and scraped and could not do enough for us. I found it despicable.

When I returned to the Company, I felt like a hypocrite. I was complimented on my courage for returning to work so soon, but I felt a huge load had been lifted from my shoulders.

A year after my mother's death, my sister was very lonely so Carol, who was thirteen, was spending a fair amount of time at her house. There was a tenant, Reginald Mawer, in the upper duplex, and he seemed taken with Carol. Mary was very kind to him; he was a bachelor and lived alone. With our family's predilection for picking up strays, she adopted him and frequently invited him for meals.

Reg was very keen on music. Although I hardly knew him, on being told by Mary that he would like to visit me and exchange records I said she could tell him to phone me. He came to Sherbourne Street regularly and I realized he was courting me. He was my age, rather pompous, and not unattractive. With the stupid idea that I would be giving my kids a father, I agreed to marry him and did so in December 1958.

The first time Celia met Reg was when he was seeing Gail and me off to Mexico. When I told her we were engaged I could tell that she thought I was making a terrible mistake, and of course she was right.

The negative side of Celia, which I have mentioned, was not the only one. She was often kind and generous and a true friend to many people. She had a great sense of humour and was always hamming things up. When Karen Kain came to her one day saying she was bored with being in the *corps de ballet*, she told her to go and learn *Swan Lake*. This was a brilliant decision made on the spur of the moment and most likely prevented Karen from giving up the career that has been so rewarding for her and so thrilling for us.

After the National Ballet School opened in 1959, Celia had more trouble with the graduates who were accepted into the Company. Like Karen, they were not afraid to speak their minds, and were unhappy with Celia's dictatorial methods. At the School their opinions were respected, and they were not brought up with the "dancers should be seen and not heard" attitude which was prevalent in her time.

Ann Ditchburn, Timothy Spain, and David Gordon were three such dancers, and Celia called them the "rebellious trio." They were somewhat scornful of the classics and pushed hard for more opportunities for Canadian choreographers, including themselves. They were given their chances, and their ballets were successful in some cases and disastrous in others. The point of my story is that they gave a press interview in which they spoke of Celia as "a black omnipotent presence." They assured me that they had also spoken of her in positive terms but, as is often the case, this was not reported. Celia was furious and forgot that she was always preaching that we should ignore the press. I had to persuade her not to fire the dancers. They, in their turn, told me with great bitterness that they would never again be able to trust the media.

When I went to devote my energies to the School, Joanne Nisbet, a dancer with the Company, took over my job as ballet mistress. However, in 1969, when things were not going too well with the Company, I was asked to return as associate director to help Celia, although she was not thrilled with the idea. At my suggestion, we formed an artistic management committee to consider and recommend artistic policy. It consisted of Celia; Grant Strate, resident choreographer; Wallace Russell, administrative director; George Crum, musical director; and me.

In that same year, when I was visiting Paris, I discovered a fine dancer for the Company. A Romanian, Sergiu Stefanschi had

Future members of the National Ballet Company? 1973.

trained from an early age in Leningrad. He was in the same class as Nureyev. I had taken two of our senior students, Andrea Davidson and Wendy Reiser, to a class with Franchetti, one of the city's best teachers.

Everybody was very impressed with our students, including Sergiu, who was taking the class. He came up to congratulate me. I was equally impressed with him. He was extremely musical, with beautiful *port de bras* and an elegant style.

Sergiu told me he was interested in joining the National Ballet of Canada. I phoned Celia, who told me to offer him a soloist's contract. I was dubious but he was not offended when I did so and accepted gladly. As soon as Celia saw him, she promoted him to principal dancer.

In 1978, when Stefanschi retired, he joined the School and ever since has been a valuable staff member.

The Company was to go to Europe for the first time in the spring of 1972, but before that happened we were all involved in a big drama which almost cost Celia her job.

Wallace Russell was secretly working behind the scenes to wrest control from Celia. He wanted to be the general director of the Company with an artistic director, not Celia, reporting to him. This has been tried in other companies but, in my opinion, has

110

never been very successful. It is based on an idea that artists always have their heads in the clouds and are unable to behave responsibly in the area of artistic management. In the Company, the policy had always been that the artistic director was the ultimate head even though she would work in tandem with her general manager as co-director.

I knew what was going on because Wally, as we called him, had approached me to help him with his plan. I felt, like many others, that it was time for a change of artistic director, but I was not going to support Wally's efforts to knife Celia in the back. She, unfortunately, had lost a lot of credibility with the board of directors, and because she trusted him, she allowed Wally to deal with them almost exclusively. This gave him the opportunity to spread his anti-Celia propaganda around. He was personable and persuasive and respected by the board.

I heard from the president that a special board meeting had been called and that Celia's job was in jeopardy. I immediately contacted the senior staff members and the dancers. Two dancers and a person from each department, usually the head, were chosen to present the views of the group to the board. The president agreed to allow them to speak, one at a time, at the meeting, but he made it clear to me that he felt they would not be able to turn things around.

I did not attend the meeting but heard about it from my colleagues. It seemed that nobody tried to deny that Celia was hard to work with and, at times, downright unreasonable, nor did they hide their dislike and mistrust of Wally. Whatever was said, it was successful. Celia remained as artistic director and Wally, hearing that his coup had failed, went to his office, emptied his briefcase on the desk, and left the building.

We were all excited about going to Europe, but were without an administrative director. This problem was solved when David Haber was loaned to us by the National Arts Centre in Ottawa. David had been the first stage manager of the Company. He and Celia were very close. He took good care of her and waited on her hand and foot. He was optimistic and cheerful, and I had no inkling at that time that this relationship would bring about the end of my long friendship with Celia.

We opened at the Coliseum in London on May 17, 1972. It

was a very important occasion for Celia. All her teachers, mentors, and colleagues were coming to see what she had achieved with this fledgling company from the "colonies." It was important for me too as many of my young pupils were making their appearance as Company members in my home town. I remember Karen Kain's mother rushing up to me in the intermission. She had heard somebody comparing Karen's performance with that of a dancer from the Royal Ballet in a detrimental way. She wanted to know if I thought Karen was dancing well. I told her to listen to the enthusiastic applause and to ignore national prejudice.

The opening gala and the season that followed were a resounding success. In the first-night intermission we met Princess Anne and Edward Heath, then the prime minister.

Erik Bruhn was with us in London to coach the dancers in Bournonville's *La Sylphide*, which he had produced for the Company. He was staying at Rudolf Nureyev's home just outside London. One night Celia and I went there for dinner after the show and were picked up at the theatre by Rudolf's driver. The house was dark and gloomy and filled with large pieces of antique furniture. An excellent dinner was served by an old Russian couple, after which we went to the living room, where Celia fell asleep, and Erik talked incessantly. He was extremely humorous in a cynical way, but had a very black side which was disturbing. We were driven to the hotel at 5:00 a.m. and to our surprise the driver demanded five pounds from each of us. I am sure, knowing Rudolf, that he paid his staff very well. Both Erik and Rudi would have been furious had they known that we had to pay for our transportation.

At the end of the London season, the Company continued to tour in Europe, and I returned to Canada. Before I left I had initiated something which turned out to be enormously beneficial to the Company.

I had been for some time on the Advisory Panel of the Canada Council, where I had met many distinguished colleagues. One of them was Gerry Eldred, who was general manager of the Manitoba Theatre Centre. One night when the meetings were over, there was a terrible blizzard and all the planes were cancelled. Gerry and I decided to take the train from Ottawa to Toronto, and we often laugh when we recall the events that followed.

photo: Andrew Oxenham

Nadia Potts was seven years old when she began
training at the National Ballet School.

It was a long journey, made worse by the bad weather. We
were both very tired from a long day of discussion but I had
decided that Gerry would be a perfect administrative director for
the Company and I set to work. My friends could tell you of my
tenaciousness and I'm sure Gerry would agree. I spent the whole
journey trying to convince him of the Company's quandary and
the need for someone of his calibre to take over. I did not hide the
fact that Celia was difficult, nor the fact that she was mistrustful
after her experience with Wally Russell. Gerry knew that the
National Ballet was an important institution with high artistic
standards, and, although he was cautious, I knew when we
arrived in Toronto that he was interested.

I passed all the information on Gerry to the ballet's new
president, Ian (Jock) McCleod. His company, McKinsey and Co.,
had been running the National Ballet in the interim. When I

returned from London, I heard that Gerry had been offered the job and would start on July 1, 1972.

This arrangement worked well until 1973 and then I made a big mistake. Celia asked me to use my influence with Gerry and the board so that David Haber could be hired as her personal assistant. I agreed, knowing how happy she had been in London. I asked her to make two promises: first, that David would not interfere with Gerry's responsibilities; second, that she would never allow him to become artistic director as he was not qualified. Of course, she agreed.

It was soon apparent that David and Celia had no intention of consulting with Gerry, and were making all kinds of plans for the Company without his knowledge.

In the latter part of the year I had a minor stroke. I was hospitalized, and it was at the Toronto General Hospital that my worst fears were realized.

One day Gerry walked in with Jock and they informed me that it would be announced by the media that day that David Haber had been appointed artistic director of the National Ballet. I remember saying to them, "You are making a terrible mistake," and they left. The nurses had a difficult time with me. I cried for hours, and it was hard for them to understand why I was so upset. Apart from knowing that this would be a disaster for the Company, I felt totally betrayed.

As I had predicted, David's appointment was a disaster. He knew nothing of the technical aspects of ballet or music. I once heard him ask the ballet mistress whether the orchestra had played well. When she confirmed that it was a good performance, he went over to congratulate the conductor. Similarly, the dancers could not respect him because he had never danced or practised any art form.

It was clear that the Company was being run from Ottawa, where Celia was living. Decisions on choice of repertoire were being made which were of great concern to all of us who cared about the future of the Company.

In March 1975, I asked John Fraser, the dance critic for the *Globe and Mail,* to announce my resignation. I chose John rather than a general press release because I trusted him to give my reasons in an objective way.

Under the heading "Oliphant resigns from National Ballet" John wrote as follows:

> Betty Oliphant, the associate artistic director of the National Ballet of Canada and principal of the National Ballet School, has resigned her position with the company citing "unresolvable" disagreements with the present artistic management as the main reason.
>
> The resignation, first revealed yesterday by the National's president Ian McCleod, brings to a head a controversy that has been building up in the company ever since the appointment of David Haber last year as sole artistic director to replace Celia Franca.

After an explanation of my concerns the article ends:

> Since the appointment of Haber, no secret has been made of the fact that Miss Franca and Miss Oliphant have had strong, often bitter, disagreements, which effectively ended a close association that had endured since the company's founding in 1951. Miss Oliphant said yesterday that she felt the company had gone "from strength to strength," but had now reached an artistic impasse because of direction.
>
> "I think that ballet companies are basically very fragile and can rest on good reputations for only a year or two before dreadful things start to happen. I've lived with the present situation as long as I could, always with the hope that things would work out. Now I see real problems and since I can't do anything to stop them, I can at least resign and state clearly why I am doing so."

In June of that year David resigned, and he left at the end of July. Celia returned to lead the Company for the New York season. In the meantime a search committee had been established to find a new artistic director, and Alexander Grant had been invited to fill that position, which he did on July 1, 1976.

At the company's twenty-fifth anniversary in November 1984 I was to receive my comeuppance from Celia. When speaking from the stage, she listed everybody who had helped her in her efforts over the years except me. I had half expected this treatment for I knew how angry she was with me, but I was hurt and my friends were furious. Erik Bruhn led me from the theatre and many people came over to express their sympathy.

The following day Celia was asked by the press why she had not mentioned me. She said she had forgotten, which she felt was a very easy thing to do.

Years later, when Celia was writing her book, she came to interview me. When she had finished, I asked her why she had broken her promise not to make David artistic director. She replied, "You were a fool if you believed me."

This well-known Peter Varley photo captures the solid cornerstone
of the National Ballet School at 105 Maitland Street.

The National Ballet School

*Ballet does not come easily to Canada; we do not have
the long tradition of folk dancing of many countries, nor
the tradition of courtly dancing of France and Italy
where ballet originated. We are introspective and self
conscious, embarrassed by self expression, even more
embarrassed at expressing ourselves with our bodies. Our
general cultural insecurity is manifest by the vital public
interest in visits by great foreign companies or artists and
the frequent lethargy shown towards equivalent
Canadian efforts: and equivalent they are. . . .*

These are the words of Michael Koerner, in 1966 the chairman
of the National Ballet School. They describe the lack of confidence in the arts in Canada that I encountered when I arrived.
Celia Franca too was constantly coming up against this attitude.
We learned that not only must we prove ourselves before expecting help and support, but even when we did, the media's acknowl-
edgement of our achievements was grudging to say the least.

The School opened in 1959. Before describing this exciting event, I want to move to our first major success which in 1966 provided the proof we needed. Michael Koerner referred to it at the end of the above quote: ". . . and finally the results of this year's Varna competition brought international recognition to the Canadian participants and also to their schooling in the art of ballet."

Martine van Hamel won the gold medal in the junior section (under twenty-one years) of the International Ballet Competition at Varna, Bulgaria. In the male section the junior gold medal was won by Mikhail Baryshnikov. Martine competed against dancers from leading ballet companies throughout the world, including

photo: Ken Bell

Martine van Hamel won a gold medal in Bulgaria in 1966. Her success established our international reputation in classical ballet training.

the Bolshoi and the Kirov. She was the unanimous choice of the panel of distinguished judges. She was also awarded the City of Varna Prize for artistic interpretation, in competition with all the entries in both the junior and senior sections.

As a result of Canada's success, we received compliments on our schooling from all over the world. Arnold Haskell, an English critic, wrote of Martine's training that it combined the best of the English and Russian schools—the beautiful legs and feet and clean technique of the former with the latter's impressive jumps, flexible backs, and generous movements of the arms and upper body.

Martine was the daughter of the Dutch consul in Toronto. She came to my school on Sherbourne Street about two years before I gave it up to become principal of the National Ballet School. She continued her training at the School and graduated in 1963. Celia Franca accepted her into the National Ballet and it was as a Company member that she went to Varna.

In many ways Martine reminds me of Karen Kain. She is taller than Karen, but lacks her beauty. Physically, Martine had an easier time than Karen because she has a more flexible body. Both had doting parents so I found them rather spoiled. They were unquestionably great talents with strong wills that generally served them well, although sometimes this caused them to make career choices that were unwise.

Martine's perception of why she left Canada, which recently she expressed to the media, is quite different from mine. She said she was not well treated. She, again like Karen, was impatient. Celia was grooming her as quickly as possible, but Martine was not getting all the roles she wanted immediately. I think she would have settled down had it not been for a crazy boyfriend. I do not use this word lightly. I, and several others, received abusive letters accusing us of not appreciating the great talent in our midst. We were informed by this boyfriend that Martine was going to New York where she would be more highly valued. When I told Martine I thought she was making a mistake, she said, "I know, but I love him."

It broke my heart when I went to New York and saw Martine in the back row of the *corps de ballet* in American Ballet Theatre's *Coppélia*. By that time I believe the man in her life was writing to the president of the United States! Finally this destructive relationship was over. Martine's career had a happy ending. She became a principal at A.B.T. and has a following of ardent fans. She has choreographed and has headed her own small company. At present she is dancing with Netherlands Dance Theatre 3, an exciting company formed by Jiri Kilian to present those dancers who have so much to offer in their mature years.

Celia Franca and I knew that a good company needs a good school to feed it. To produce the integrated fluidity of a first-class professional company, we had to engage dancers who were trained together in the same school by the same teachers, according to accepted methods and techniques. This would result in a consistent style and, consequently, a superb ensemble.

At my own school I was developing such dancers, but there was a terrible snag. Veronica Tennant explained it well when she was interviewed in the late sixties by Gloria Varley who, with photographer husband Peter Varley, published *To Be a Dancer*, the first book written on the National Ballet School:

> We came to Canada in 1955 when I was nine and I went immediately, luckily, to Betty Oliphant who had her own school on Sherbourne Street. During that time I was going to Bishop Strachan School and taking my ballet classes. It was getting impossible, absolutely impossible. After school I would run off to my ballet class—I had one every night—and then come home about ten, have dinner, and start my homework. It was really ridiculous. The only answer for anyone who seriously wants to be a ballet dancer is to go to a school that can combine the two. There were really sad cases before of girls who had to leave high school at fourteen because they couldn't keep up both.

I, as you know, was one of those sad cases, so I was enthusiastic about a school that would combine academic education and professional ballet training. But I wanted more. Aware of my own deprivations, I saw a need to emphasize two important aspects of the program. First, the education must be of such high quality that the students would not be trapped into a career in ballet, or—if they chose to have one—they would be equipped, on retirement, to follow a second career. Secondly, recognizing that ballet is a composite art, I felt that the curriculum should be enriched, stressing the related arts such as music, drama, and the visual arts, from both an historical and practical viewpoint.

My dreams were shared by Celia. There seemed to be little hope that they would ever become a reality until one day I was invited to meet John Osler, later the Honourable Mr. Justice Osler of the Supreme Court of Ontario. He was a member of the National Ballet Guild, the Company's board of directors. They asked him to be part of—and later to head—a committee to investigate the possibility of setting up a school. He had been impressed by Celia's report stressing the need for a school if the Company was ever going to amount to anything.

I was obviously a key figure in this project. With many potential Company members in my private school, I would have to give it up to participate in the founding of the National Ballet School. I was eager and willing and also, in the financial sense, very unwise.

At Sherbourne Street the talented students, who paid only five dollars a week, had classes every evening and on Saturdays. I earned my living from the three hundred students who came once or twice a week. My days were long. I was with the Company, when they were in town, from 9:30 a.m. to 3:30 p.m. From 4:00 to 7:00 p.m., I taught the amateur children, either at Sherbourne Street or, on Tuesdays, at the Willowdale Community Centre. On Thursdays I went to a church hall at Avenue Road and Eglinton.

For one year I took a teaching job at the newly opened Jewish Community Centre on Spadina Avenue at Bloor Street. I hated it because the physical conditions were terrible and the children weren't interested in ballet. For two hours' work I was paid sixty dollars, which was a great deal in those days. I remember walking around in the class saying to myself, "Betty, you are earning sixty dollars for this." It didn't help and I refused to go back the following year.

A word now about my talented students. As well as Martine van Hamel, there was Veronica Tennant. The intensity of this young girl the first day I saw her was awesome. She had some problems with her feet but her determination overcame all obstacles. Victoria Bertram came, when she was very young, to

Vanessa Harwood at age sixteen. My pupil
from age six, she was one of the first
students of the National Ballet School.

Willowdale. She was extremely serious. When, at six, as the golden butterfly in my recital, her little four- and five-year-old butterflies forgot their steps, she came offstage fuming. When I tried to comfort her by telling her she had done well, she looked at me scornfully and said, "It was terrible."

Vanessa Harwood also came to Willowdale when she was six. She was tiny and very pretty, and, when she pointed her foot, she had an instep that made me drool. When I told her that she must try to work a little harder, I received an adorable shy smile, but not much more in the way of effort. Both Vicki and Vanessa came to Sherbourne Street every day as soon as it became obvious that they wanted professional careers.

Nadia Potts was seven when she came to Sherbourne Street. She was dark like Lucy, her attractive Russian mother, and she had little pigtails. She always gave Bob, her English father, credit for her beautiful legs. Nadia had an ideal body for ballet. She worked hard and developed a strong technique. I was amused, some years later, when I used her to demonstrate in a T.V. show. She went home greatly excited to tell her mother that the make-up people had "painted out Miss Oliphant's bags" (under my eyes).

All the students I have mentioned became principal dancers, but there is always the one who got away, and that was Barbara Malinowski.

Barbara was in the same class at Sherbourne Street as the others. She was like a reincarnation of the great Russian ballerinas from the past. In fact, she was Polish. Her parents had been in a displaced persons' camp before coming to Canada. As a child Barbara had everything except, as I was to find out later, a deep commitment to ballet. With wonderful long legs, a flexible body, great big eyes, and a dancer's soul, she seemed marked for stardom. After she had moved with me to the National Ballet School, her parents' insistence on the importance of her academic education, which she did not resist, got in the way of the time she spent on ballet. She was not in residence. To get the high marks she expected from herself, Barbara had to work harder than most of her peers. As she drew closer to her graduation, I talked to her about neglecting her ballet. I pointed out that it should be a priority if it was to be her career, but I got nowhere.

At the end of each year at the National Ballet School we put on a performance in our two main studios. We had lights and a huge stage area in Studio A, and in Studio B very uncomfortable bleachers for the audience. It is well known that Karen Kain, who graduated in 1969, danced the Swan Queen in Act II of *Swan Lake* in her final performance at the School. It is not so well known that on each of three nights there were different dancers in the principal role. The other two were Linda Maybarduk and Barbara Malinowski.

The French choreographer Roland Petit, whom Karen was to work with later, was there the night that Barbara danced the Swan Queen. He sat there with tears rolling down his cheeks. When it was over, he told me that he wanted to take her to his company in Marseille, create ballets especially for her, and build her into a great star. I warned him that there was an element missing in

Barbara's make-up that might prevent him from achieving this goal. However, he didn't believe me, and she wanted to go, so I gave her my blessing. I don't know the full story of her sojourn in France, except that she married a sailor, had a son, and is now back in Toronto. One can never force these things, and probably Barbara does not regret that she never fulfilled the great promise that so many of us saw in her.

As I have said, I was willing to allow my own school to form the nucleus of the National Ballet School. Martine, Veronica, and the rest would be part of the professional program, receiving their academic education in what was to be called the Full-Time School. Where necessary, bursaries would be provided for those unable to pay the fees. My bread-and-butter students—those who came once or twice a week—would transfer to the Ballet Division of the National Ballet School. Their fees would be instrumental in making the School financially viable. This was my first big mistake.

When John Osler, in his efforts to see if a school was feasible, discussed salary with me, I underestimated, as I had with the Company, my worth. This time it was more serious as it would be all I had to live on. The net income from my school was about nine thousand dollars. I did not take into consideration the difference, in terms of income tax, between a salary and being self-employed. At Sherbourne Street, with my workplace in the same building as my residence, I had a number of deductions, including the space used for my business, all kinds of supplies, such as paper cups and toilet rolls, plus my car.

I told John that I would need a salary of nine thousand a year, not realizing that the income tax would be deducted from the top, leaving me with much less than before. When the School became a reality, I did not even consider selling my flourishing business to them, but just turned it over lock, stock, and barrel. So one could say that I was the School's first major donor.

Once John's committee had decided to recommend the School as a practical proposition, a number of people began searching actively for a building. Mrs. Herbert Agnew and Mildred Wickson found the ideal place at 111 Maitland Street. Situated just below Wellesley, between Church and Jarvis Streets, it was originally a Quaker church. We bought it for eighty-five thousand dollars from a Baptist congregation. The principal feature of the ground floor was an auditorium with a sloped floor surrounding a large baptismal tank.

I saw immediately that this huge space, with its beautiful windows, was ideal for a studio. We would of course have to have a new floor. I insisted, in spite of the fact that it would be less durable, that the floor should be made of soft wood and sprung so that the dancers' muscles would not be harmed. There was just enough space in the rest of the building for classrooms, offices, and an art studio in the basement.

Once the renovations had started, John was very strict with me about the budget, which, foolishly I thought, did not include painting the main studio. When he was away one weekend, thinking I could get away with it, I told the workmen to go ahead and paint it. When John returned, it was half finished, and he was furious. He stopped the work. I told him if we didn't do it at that time we would probably have to wait ten years—which is exactly what happened! I felt angry every time I taught a class in that half-painted studio. Usually John was very reasonable and I was good about respecting the budget, but in this case I felt he was "spoiling the ship for a ha'p'orth of tar" and he, understandably, felt annoyed that I had taken advantage of his absence.

The School was due to open in September 1959. Carman Guild, the Company's administrative director, had taken on two tasks, neither of which was completed. The first was to make sure that the residence we had rented on Jarvis Street would be altered, according to the fire marshal's requirements, in time for us to use it for the annual Summer School. Taking place in July, this would precede the opening of the new School. Carman was a great procrastinator. When I realized that—in spite of his protestations—the residence would not be ready in time, I had to rush around finding homes for the fifteen students we had booked to stay there.

Far more serious was Carman's lack of action on hiring the academic teachers, something he had insisted on doing. I became suspicious when I asked him to interview Lucy Potts, Nadia's mother. She was eminently qualified to take charge of the French program. A White Russian, born in Constantinople, and brought up in Nice, she had her French baccalaureate. She had also earned a degree in Canada.

photo: Erik Dzenis

Teaching an adage. Left to right, students Marnie Edwards,
Kerrie Szuch, John Fletcher, Annette Gadusek.

Myself and Wendy Reiser at the barre.

Carman behaved in a very odd way at Lucy's interview. She came away convinced that he would not offer her the job. She was right. I soon found out that he was in touch with the Toronto Board of Education. They had recommended a retired French teacher whom he wanted to hire. I had visions of being without teachers altogether or having a whole group of senior citizens forming the staff of the School. This was not what I wanted for our young students.

Ballet class: Lynda Okmanas, Rachel Taylor, and Huguette Griswold.

By this time it was only one month away from the scheduled opening and I had had enough. I went to John Osler and said that I would not continue unless I could be responsible, with his help, for all aspects of the School's functions. He agreed. An advertisement was put in the *Globe and Mail*, and he and I spent a whole afternoon in his office, interviewing prospective teachers.

From the thirty-odd teachers we interviewed, we were able to pick the whole academic staff. As well as Lucy Potts, whom John liked immensely, we found Mrs. Anna Haworth. We immediately put her in charge of the academic program, subject to my general direction. She had been head of the classics and English departments in a large Toronto girls' school. She had also been connected with the arts in Bermuda.

John and I made only one major mistake. We interviewed a prospective science teacher. He was weird but seemed to know his subject. It was late and we were a trifle slap-happy. We offered him the job. As he left the room John said to me, "Do you think he is crazy or just eccentric?" I voted doubtfully for eccentric. On his first day I knew it should have been crazy. I could see that the students he was interviewing were concerned. I approached them and they told me that he was asking them very personal questions. A quick phone call to John brought him up immediately to Maitland Street, and the man was fired. A few days later John helped me do the same thing with an alcoholic cook.

We settled our science problems very satisfactorily. Our senior students (Grades 9 to 12) went to nearby Jarvis Collegiate for their science classes. The teachers there were thrilled with our students' ability to work in depth. Because they were in uniform, they were nicknamed "the ladies of the chorus" by the kids from Jarvis, who thought they were nuts to be so committed to ballet. Conversely, the National Ballet School students found the Jarvis kids boring because all the girls talked about were boys and clothes.

We started with twenty-seven students, all girls unfortunately, fifteen of them in residence. We had some talented students who came regularly to the Summer School and they enrolled immediately. Others auditioned and the residence was soon full. Most of the remaining twelve day-students came from my school. One of the last students we accepted was Carmen von Richtofen. She was related to the Red Baron, the famous German flying ace. Carmen was not talented for dance, but she was extremely good at art and needed a school atmosphere like ours. We had a space and her parents could afford the fees. This was important, as we had to find bursaries for most of the people we accepted.

Hilda Sterndale-Bennett, Carman Guild's secretary, was loaned to us to help deal with the nuts and bolts of our institution. Sadly, it was a not-so-subtle attempt on Carman's part to get rid of her. She discovered this when she was due to go back to the Company and was told she wasn't needed. She was deeply hurt but I convinced her that their loss was our gain and told her how much we appreciated her. She was a tower of strength. Without her the National Ballet School would never have opened only one week later than we had planned.

When John first approached me, I was adamant about certain conditions. I had seen in Europe the problems caused when the school director was under the company director. For example, if I felt that it was in a child's best interests to remain in the School for an extra year before joining a company, I wanted to have the authority to keep her. Celia supported this. The result was an autonomous organization with its own board of directors, responsible for its own funding. I also wanted the students to be allowed the freedom to follow their careers wherever they chose and not to be obligated to join the National Ballet or even to stay in Canada. This idea was contentious, but eventually, when we received funding from the Canada Council, it supported this policy.

As with my salary demands, I made one more serious mistake. I agreed to Celia having the title of director, with me as the principal. This was Carmen's idea. He was angry with me for going over his head in hiring the academic teachers and wanted to be sure I didn't become too powerful. I thought Celia's position would be in name only, until two things happened that made me uncertain. The first was quite minor. After eight weeks I wrote a report for my own board of directors. Out of courtesy I showed it to Celia and she verbally tore it to shreds. I had twenty-four hours to rewrite the report and decided against doing so. When I presented it to the board members, they congratulated me. They liked the humour and the casual intimacy of the way I shared with them my hopes and fears.

The second incident was much more serious. Shortly after the School opened, Celia took a small group of my students to appear on T.V. in Hamilton. I prepared the show, rehearsed the dancers, and gave her a script. In a one-hour program, she took full credit for the School and did not even mention my existence. I was shocked and hurt. I did not have to protest. I received a call from a board member telling me that from now on my title would be director and principal. I have no idea what was said to Celia but I was grateful for this show of confidence.

The early part of 1959, before the School opened, should have been a happy time for me and my children, but it was marred by my husband's unpleasantness. Gail and Carol wanted me to be happy and did everything they could to get on with Reg. Because I didn't communicate adequately, I was not aware of their strong dislike for him. I should have guessed when Gail refused to call him Dad, and only gave in to please me. Later Carol told me that he reminded her of a snake. He was crazy about her, and his feelings seemed unnatural. I was horrified to discover, when I was writing this book, that Reg had, in fact, sexually abused my daughter.

The honeymoon had been a nightmare. It was the reverse of the previous one, as Reg turned out to be impotent. He had warned me that he had never had sex, which seemed strange for a man in his forties, but I suggested he talk with a doctor and thought no more about it.

What was even more upsetting was the fact that he could not contain his jealousy of my career. Reg was a snob. He wanted me to wear cashmere sweaters, preferably a twin set, a string of pearls, a pleated skirt, and pumps. This was thoroughly British, the way my aristocratic cousins dressed, but was totally unsuitable for a working woman. I soon realized that he wanted to ignore my career completely. I found this somewhat ironic, as two months after the wedding he gave up his job as a fund-raiser, and I supported him for the next twelve years.

With the opening of the National Ballet School, I would have no need for studios in my home, so I decided to sell the house on Sherbourne Street. With the proceeds I was able to put a down payment on an attractive Tudor-style house in Forest Hill. Reg, with his conservative taste, loved it, and I hoped it would make him happier. However, although we had a wonderful decorator, and Gail and Carol designed their own rooms, they were very unhappy.

Before I closed my own school, Carol had been in a class with Veronica, Vicki, Vanessa, and Barbara. She still wore a back brace. She grew to love ballet and was very talented. As she became more advanced, the doctor felt it was too much strain on her fused spine, and recommended that she discontinue her classes. I had watched Carol's emotional and physical pain since she was two. Now, I had to see her suffer a crushing blow, and my heart ached for her. To make matters worse, Reg barely hid his delight that she could not share my passion which he resented so much.

I foolishly allowed Reg to adopt my children. I had no idea that the process would turn me into an adoptive mother rather than a birth mother. Reg was a bully. He would spy on Gail and Carol to see if there were cigarette ashes in the toilet, or, when they came home with boyfriends, he would look out the window to see if they were necking. I had always trusted them and did not pry. I believed, to some extent, that what I didn't know wouldn't hurt me. I hated his suspicious mind. He became white with anger when the children rebelled at some ridiculous demand. I was often afraid of what he would do to them, and once I had to call on a neighbour to calm him down.

It was painful to see my children having such a miserable adolescence. Gail's school work suffered and she failed Grade 11 at Branksome Hall. I sent her to Thornton Hall Senior High School, where she would receive more individual attention and would not have to repeat Grade 11 in the same class as her sister. Gail was very happy there and, incidentally, was in the same class as Conrad Black, who would become an international newspaper magnate and businessman. She stayed there for Grade 12 while Carol remained at Branksome.

Both girls persuaded me to send them to North Toronto Collegiate for Grade 13. During that year Gail, who was unhappy at home, went to stay with my sister. I was not aware that Mary was on the verge of her final breakdown until Gail told me how strangely she was acting. Eventually I had to send her to the Women's College Hospital. The psychiatrist there insisted, in spite of Mary's objections and mine, that all she needed was a vacation. I reluctantly bought an airline ticket and arranged for her to visit my aunt in England. She resisted strongly, however, and the trip was postponed. Unfortunately the hospital staff still believed that a holiday would solve her problems, and I had foolishly left the ticket with them. One weekend, when I was away, the hospital staff put her on a plane with a month's supply of drugs. Mary was unconscious when she arrived, having taken all the medication. She was taken in an ambulance to a British mental institution where, as I mentioned earlier, she was permanently hospitalized. Gail returned home.

Gail in the garden of our Russell Hill Road home.

When the girls finished school, Gail was accepted at Thistletown—a treatment centre for emotionally disturbed children—where she would train to become a child-care worker. Carol, egged on by Reg who had definite ideas about suitable careers for women, decided to enrol in the nursing program at the Wellesley Hospital. She did not enjoy it, and about one year later, preferring to study for a degree, she transferred to the University of Toronto. At the same time she asked me if she could move out. I knew she couldn't stand Reg, so agreed to finance her in an apartment. Carol always wanted to be a lawyer, and I realize now that I was a fool not to encourage her to follow her dream.

In 1966, Gail married Stanley Sadava. He was Jewish but not very religious, and she was what my cousin, Charles Feilding from Trinity College, called a hazy Anglican. Because it was important to Stan's parents, we agreed to invite a rabbi to conduct the wedding ceremony at our house, and it was charming. Gail and Stan left immediately for Colorado, where he would receive his doctorate in psychology and she would work with children as a psychiatric technician (child-care worker).

My marriage ended in 1971. With Reg refusing to work, our finances became difficult. I sold my beloved new robin's-egg-blue Chevrolet so that we could keep his horrible old Pontiac. I was trying to protect his male ego! I would have filed for a divorce sooner, but Reg had a coronary and I felt I had to see him through that. The final straw came after Gail and her husband returned and brought two-year-old Kevin to visit us. When they had gone, Reg told me that he could not stand to have children around. I realized suddenly that life was intolerable. I was burying myself in my work, dreading going home, and now I was not to be allowed to enjoy my grandson.

Professionally I was much more capable than I was in my personal life. The School was a success from the very first day. From that small beginning in 1959 until I retired thirty years later we had gone from strength to strength. Our dancers were sought after by companies all over the world. They made their mark—frequently as principal dancers—in Stuttgart, Hamburg, Munich and Berlin in Germany. They were accepted in Belgium by Béjart and in both the Dutch National Ballet and Netherlands Dance Theatre in Holland. They were also accepted by artistic directors of several U.S. companies, including New York City Ballet, American Ballet Theatre, San Francisco Ballet, and Boston Ballet.

Closer to home, almost seventy percent of the members of the National Ballet Company were graduates of the School. Others who also chose to remain in Canada danced with the Royal Winnipeg Ballet and Les Grands Ballets Canadiens.

Most of the companies I have mentioned had their own schools, so we must look at what it was in the training of our students that made finding jobs so easy for them.

As a teacher, I believe I am remarkably thorough. When I gave up being solely responsible for the students' training, as I had been at Sherbourne Street, I had to employ staff members who shared my views on basic training. We refused to take shortcuts and I insisted on the classes being carefully graded. For example, if somebody came to the School later than his peers I placed him in a lower class with plenty of private coaching to help him catch up. I remember giving Luc Amyot six months of private lessons before he joined my class. He hated it but I had to make sure that he did not miss out on the basic fundamentals. So often exceptionally talented students are pushed. Their talent is used as an excuse for not providing them with a solid technique—an essential tool in the development of their full potential. Happily, Luc became a superb *danseur noble* and was the first to admit that he was glad I did not give in to his frustration.

In *To Be a Dancer*, the Varleys' book, Veronica Tennant commented on the worldwide recognition of our training:

> I went to Europe one summer on a Canada Council grant. I studied classes and I went to ballets and plays and I gained a great deal. Not only by realizing how much there is there but how much we have here. It was funny—everywhere I took a class people would come up at the end and say, "Where were you trained? I've never seen such fine training." I went to Germany, France and England. This happened in every place.

Luc's impatience with my attention to detail was not uncommon. Most came to appreciate it. They found that, by and large, their bodies were able to survive relatively long careers. Also, apart from accidents, they had fewer injuries than the numerous dancers around the world who had been forced beyond their physical limits.

When I auditioned Karen Kain in 1961, I was excited by her talent. In spite of her mother's reservations she came to the School in 1962. Residence life was very difficult for her. She was high-spirited, extremely stubborn, and unwilling to accept rules that, although I tried to keep them to the minimum, were necessary in an institution. Her mother supported her at all times. When I asked her mother for an interview because of Karen's rudeness, I explained that the final straw had been when Karen had told one of the houseparents to "fuck off." On being asked by her mother if this were true, Karen said, "Oh no, Mummy!" Mrs. Kain looked at me and said, "I have to believe my daughter." I weakly replied, "I have to believe my staff." After her mother had

Karen Kain and Frank Augustyn in *Afternoon of a Faun*.

departed, I asked Karen why she had lied. I was amused when she told me with great charm, "My mother would have been upset had she known the truth."

In that third year, apart from my own students, Karen was the first big talent to come along through the auspices of the newly created School. Unlike most of our illustrious alumni she is, and has every right to be, critical of her training. Because she has difficulty turning, she once told me that I couldn't teach pirouettes.

A dancer's subjectivity is quite acceptable. I do, however, question some of Karen's generalizations on the correct training of the body. I will be technical for a moment. There is a school of thought that believes one can flatten one's seat by contracting the buttock muscles and tilting the pelvis under (tucking under). I always warn my students that trying to get rid of something that nature intended—in this case the seat—will affect other parts of the body. I demonstrate how people who "tuck under" over-develop the front of their thighs. I also explain how, when the

hips are thrust forward, the alignment of the spine is upset, so
that on landing from a jump the upper body is thrown back.
Karen believes that my fear of "tucking under" caused me to err in
the opposite direction, thereby causing her and her peers to
develop sway-backs. In fact, there is no connection between not
tilting the pelvis under and developing a sway-back. In my comments on acrobatic dancing I discussed the causes and my abhor-
rence of the latter.

It is true that Karen's long back was hard to control, and she
compensated by arching her back. I do not really believe it was
the fault of her teachers. Anyway, Rome wasn't built in a day. As
Karen matured she was exposed to other influences against whom
she did not feel the need to rebel. She was able to pinpoint her
weaknesses, overcome them or work around them, and present to
her public the great artist she has become.

In the School's second year, two important things happened.
First, with a contribution of ten thousand dollars from our generous patron, Bobby Laidlaw, we were able to buy, for seventeen
thousand dollars, 105 Maitland Street, the house on the west side
of the church. This solved many of our problems. We moved all
the offices into the new building, thereby leaving more space for
academic classrooms. We had started with only seven of these,
which included one at the residence. We planned to have a school
that ran from grades 5 to 12, so I was short one classroom. I knew
it was a gamble but luck was on my side. Our first enrolment
included all grades except Grade 11! Acquiring the house allowed
us to have eight classrooms in the main building.

Although the extra space was a boon, the second occurrence
was far more important to me. We accepted our first two boys,
Andrew Oxenham and Howard Marcus. Following Andrew's entry
into the Company in 1964, we graduated fourteen other male students by the end of the School's first decade. These included
Timothy Spain, who had a successful career as dancer and choreographer in France, and Garry Semeniuk, whose interest lay in
the filming of dance.

It is a myth that we or other professional ballet schools are so
hungry for boys that we will accept anything in trousers. I consider this very dishonest. If students, girls or boys, do not have a
chance of a successful career on a long-term basis, it is unfair to

encourage them. I hasten to say that we only make educated guesses. In the course of the students' training so many changes can take place that it is impossible to guarantee that they will be able or even want to achieve their original goal. At least the talent and physical instrument should be suitable. If things don't work out, the academic program is there to protect all those who follow different careers.

Boys feel comfortable at the National Ballet School. They have often come from schools where their peers have teased them unmercifully for wanting to dance, and they are relieved to be among people who share their interests.

photo: Erik Dzenis

Christopher Czyzewski graduated in 1969 but
decided to pursue a different career.

When speaking to the graduating class in 1976, Veronica Tennant was describing her life as a professional dancer and telling the graduates what to expect. She covered many aspects of the career they were contemplating, and her comments on homosexuality were amusing and pertinent. Near the end of her speech she said:

> Then there are the times you are required to perform without even dancing. The interviews! . . . During the interview he [the interviewer] will probably make all kinds of oblique references about male dancers and it will be up to you to come right out, ask his question for him, and then answer it. . . .

Even while still at the School the boys were good at dealing openly with snide remarks on this subject. However, occasionally they became angry. In one case I received a call from the principal of Jarvis Collegiate, where our students studied science. To my surprise, he congratulated me because one of his boys had been punched by one of ours for making such a remark.

I have always had a special interest in teaching boys, and the School was known worldwide for the excellence of its male students. Before I retired, about eighty of them had graduated. Of the fifty or so who became principal dancers or soloists, I will list those who I believe reached the heights and will remain in the hearts of their public.

First and foremost is Frank Augustyn. He had the simplicity, the musicality, and the graceful arms that I look for in a dancer. Like Barbara Malinowski's parents, Frank's father was far more impressed with academic achievement than with his son's great talent and ability. However, his love for Frank took precedence over his feelings, and he reluctantly agreed with me that Frank, at the age of seventeen, should join the Company rather than spend another year at the School.

Early in his career Frank wrote the following: "The highest possible level of emotion combined with the highest possible level of technique makes a good performance. That is what I strive for." These words proved to me that we at the School had done our job.

photo: Peter Varley

Creative dance including a young James Kudelka (right) who in 1996
was to become artistic director of the National Ballet of Canada.

The list of male graduates in the ten years following Frank's
departure in 1971 sounds like a Who's Who of male principal
dancers.

Robert Desrosiers also graduated in 1971. As a choreographer
his imagination is limitless. He always presents himself to the
media as a rebel who caused problems for the staff at the School.
The truth is quite the opposite. He was a rebel in the best sense of
the word. He was obviously not destined for a classical ballet
career, but he respected his training as a point of departure and I
think it has served him well. He is a warm, caring man and has
shown me his love and his loyalty on many occasions.

In 1973, an extremely precocious young man named James
Kudelka graduated. The first work he choreographed was impressive. He was very young and had obviously been influenced by
Balanchine's *Concerto Barocco* but his ideas were original. When
he was twenty-one he told me a story that showed me how angry
he had been with me some years earlier when he felt I was inter-
fering with his life.

James was walking up the street near my Cabbagetown house. He was sticking a pin into a Plasticine figure which represented me. He turned the corner to see an ambulance outside my house, into which I was being carried. James explained that he was filled with guilt, although of course he was not responsible for what was in fact a minor health problem.

In 1975 Luc Amyot, Peter Ottman, and Raymond Smith were starting their successful careers, followed by David Nixon in 1976. Most of David's professional life was spent in Germany and he is highly thought of throughout Europe.

The year 1977 was to see Kevin Pugh, a dancer with superb elevation, emerge from the School. I will always remember the hysterical crowds yelling "Canada, Canada" as they surrounded our bus in Moscow after Kevin had danced in an international competition. The same year, Barry Watt graduated. He developed his career with the Dutch National Ballet where, as a principal dancer, he often partnered Jane Lord, another National Ballet School alumnus. Our dancers are well loved in Holland, and many of them have remained there throughout their professional lives. Others, including Lindsay Fischer, who also became a principal in Amsterdam, left to return to North America. Lindsay joined the New York City Ballet where he received excellent reviews.

Two artists for whom I have the utmost respect graduated with Lindsay in 1978. The first was John Alleyne, who started his career in Stuttgart. This was because the National Ballet's artistic director was too blind to see the possibilities for a black man in a classical ballet company. This changed when John was invited by Erik Bruhn, who took over the Company, to return to Canada. Since then he has gained great prestige as a dancer and choreographer and as the director of the British Columbia Ballet. The second was Jeremy Ransom. He is one of the most sensitive dancers I have known. With superb good taste he excels in many roles. His performance of Lensky in *Eugen Onegin* is one that I find extremely moving.

Soon after he graduated in 1979, Jeffrey Kirk was hired by John Neumeier, artistic director and choreographer of the Hamburg Ballet. Jeffrey became a principal dancer and John created many new ballets in which he danced leading roles. Sadly, Jeffrey, who was greatly loved both here and in Germany, died recently.

To complete the roster in the second decade was Tony Randazzo, who spent his first years in the Company and then went on to become a leading dancer with the San Francisco Ballet.

In 1981 we had a bumper crop, including Serge Lavoie, who with Martine Lamy won the prize for the best couple in Moscow, and Owen Montague, a very special talent who was a great favourite of choreographer Glen Tetley. Owen was brilliant in many roles, including the white rabbit in Tetley's *Alice*. And, finally, someone who is known to most of us—Rex Harrington. In his first year at the School I had no idea Rex would develop into such a fine dancer as well as an extraordinarily good partner.

Between 1982 and 1991, my last year at the School, the following men went on to become soloists or principal dancers: Pierre Quinn in Canada; Brendan Collins, now with the Royal Swedish Opera ballet company; Stephen Legate in San Francisco; Alexander Ritter in New York; Aaron Watkin in Britain; Johan Persson with the National in Canada; Pedro Gomez in Stuttgart; Ryan Martin with a company in Russia. There are others but they have not yet matured, and who knows how far they will go?

I had a difficult time proving that we, in Canada, could produce first-class dancers. In the fifties Peter Dwyer became a dominant force as associate director and then director in the development of the Canada Council. He was very British, a typical product of Oxford University. Until I got to know him I thought he was rather a wimp. How wrong I was. He turned out to have been one of Britain's most important spies, a colleague of William Stephenson, the author of *A Man Called Intrepid*.

The policy of the Canada Council under Dwyer was to send successful applicants in the Dance Section abroad for their basic training. When I argued that the grants should be provided for these young dancers to attend the National Ballet School, Peter Dwyer told me in no uncertain terms that we had not yet proved that our training was on a par with that given at schools such as the Royal Ballet School in England.

I respected the fact that high standards for talented Canadians were Dwyer's aim, and I agreed with his philosophy of "few but roses," but I had to persuade him that I too was dedicated to excellence. Fortunately, Martine van Hamel's success in Varna affected him profoundly. He told me that in future, individual

photo: Courtney G. McMahon

photo: Andrew Oxenham

Collage of male dancers. Clockwise from top, Andrew Oxenham, Rex Harrington, Jeremy Ransom, graduates of 1964, 1981, 1978 respectively.

photo: Andrew Oxenham

grants would only be given for students to receive basic training at our School. Then he spoiled it all by saying that this only applied to girls, and that boys could still apply to train outside Canada. Not long after, this policy was changed, and as well as supporting individuals, the Council supported the School generously and continued to do so until responsibility was recently transferred to the Department of Canadian Heritage.

The other cross I had to bear was when visitors from abroad expounded theories with which I did not agree. I remember Margot Fonteyn speaking in the lobby of the O'Keefe Centre. She told the audience that if they couldn't find a male teacher for their sons they should send them away. I believe that from the age of fifteen male students should have a male teacher. Before that age I have found that women, providing they can empathize with and enjoy teaching boys, usually do a more thorough job. The argument that a masculine style can only be achieved in students who have been exclusively taught by men is ridiculous. I know men who produce a beautiful feminine style in girls, and conversely women, including me, who are extremely successful in developing male dancers with a style that is entirely masculine.

We have had some remarkable male teachers at the School. From the Company, Glenn Gilmour—like Sergiu Stefanschi—decided to make a career of teaching when he gave up dancing. He received a Canada Council grant to train as a teacher before joining our staff.

I should say here that I deplore the practice of professional dancers becoming teachers without any pedagogic training. When approached by retiring dancers who I felt had a gift for teaching, I used to insist on them coming to the School for two years before I decided whether to take them on staff. During that time they would study anatomy and music as these related to planning exercises and working with a class pianist. They would also attend theoretical lectures in which they would learn how to structure classes, how to deal with bodies other than their own, and how to understand the damage they could do to young people if they forced them beyond their limits. Finally, by allowing them to assist experienced teachers and supervising them in practice-teaching, we were able to help them with hands-on corrections and to see whether they had a pleasant and positive approach to their students while still insisting on hard work and self-discipline.

It is a tall order to accomplish all this in two years. In Russia, they take five. They may give their pupils a more comprehensive program than ours, but it is too bureaucratic and the individual is not taken into account. For example, if their syllabus says that in the fourth year a boy must be able to execute a double *tour en l'air*, he must attempt it even if he has not yet mastered a single. This results in great frustration as the faults from the basic movement are compounded in the effort to perform the more difficult one.

I have always had an instinct for pinpointing potential teachers. A pupil who shows an interest in her fellow students and the organization of the class is more likely to become a good teacher than the somewhat egocentric and unaware student. However, it is only by results that one can discover which teachers are able to find the key to unlock the door to the minds and hearts of each and every pupil. If they have this precious gift, their students will understand and apply that which is required of them and will improve accordingly. Teachers with good personalities can give impressive and enjoyable classes with well-chosen exercises and appropriate corrections. Even so, because they do not have a good "eye" for spotting faults, these teachers' pupils will not improve. We have an ironic comment that illustrates this point: "You know she is a wonderful teacher. Isn't it strange that her pupils are so bad?"

To return to Glenn Gilmour. He came to the School, trained for two years, and has been a valuable staff member ever since. Once, when we were having Toronto auditions, the ballet staff were sitting at a long table. I had been delayed by a T.V. interview. As I approached the table I said, "This looks like the Last Supper." Glenn quickly replied, "And we sure as hell know who is Jesus Christ."

Daniel Seillier was another superb male teacher at the School. Celia wanted to take him on staff at the National Ballet but said they couldn't afford him. I didn't want to lose him so I arranged to pay half his salary so that he could teach for both organizations. He was trained at the school of the Paris Opera, whose students are known as "Les Petits Rats." He was extremely stubborn, which was both good and bad. He refused to speak English. This was a plus, as we had an excellent French program and wanted the students to be exposed to the language as much as possible. Although his ballet terminology was different from ours, I was happy to have the students learn it. According to him, it was the only correct one, coming directly from Louis XIV, the "Sun King." It could be confusing, as he refused to admit the possibility of differences in other parts of the world.

On one occasion Daniel made a student hold a piece of Kleenex between her thumb and forefinger because she was constantly sticking out the former. At the end of class she was brought over to my office because her hand was in spasm. I was concerned but they soon relaxed it at the hospital, and Daniel roared with laughter when I told him. This was not serious. My worst problem with him was his attitude to my concern that forcing turnout could lead to severe knee problems. He laughed at my shock when he pulled up his pants to show me scars from several knee operations, which he thought were a neccessary part of being a dancer.

In spite of our disagreements, Monsieur Seillier played a vital part in the development of many of our students. Karen Kain, Martine Lamy, Luc Amyot, and many others will bear witness to his excellent teaching.

In our fifth year, 1963, the School was well established, with seventy-seven pupils in the eight grades from five to twelve. In Grade 7 the boys outnumbered the girls six to five. Those who had been unsure of the quality of our academic education had been convinced of its excellence by the reports from the inspectors of the Board of Education and by the performance of our students in departmental examinations, S.A.T.s, and other indices. In that year one student, Adrianna Lawrence, who had left us in Grade 12 to pursue an academic career, earned nine first-class marks in Grade 13. She then passed the entrance examinations for Cornell University at Ithaca with marks of ninety-eight percent and eighty-five percent in English and mathematics. High academic achievement is not unusual in dancers; although lying on her back with an injury, Veronica Tennant wrote her final exams and graduated with a ninety-three percent average.

For the first five years we had no outside funding and our income came entirely from fees. If I remember correctly, our first operating budget was just over sixty-eight thousand dollars. In 1994 it was over six million dollars. Our policy was that talent and a suitable physique were the only criteria for acceptance at the School. No child was to be refused for lack of funds. Although the School *per se* was not financed, we were soon able to establish a bursary fund. The money for this fund, which was largely raised by the Women's Committee and by branches of the National Ballet Guild, included a grant from the Municipality of Metropolitan Toronto and grants to individual students from the Canada Council. We also received a major contribution from the Ontario Arts Council.

I had made a vow when I started the School that I would introduce a major improvement every year. It could be an addition to our physical plant—studios, a library, or a residence—or increases to the staff—a physiotherapist, massage therapist, or podiatrist. Eventually I became more ambitious and finished up with a theatre.

In the Varley book, John Osler speaks of my approach to expansion:

> I think we thought in terms of fifty to sixty as the sort of optimum at that time and quite early we began to realize the very skillful way in which Betty persuaded the Board that an ever-expanding policy was the only one that was ever going to work. She has a sort of step-by-step technique which is probably the one every really successful principal has adopted. She would tell the Board from time to time when things became absolutely imperative. She never encouraged negative discussion. In other words, there was never a time in the early days when we really seriously looked at anything at all comparable to the size of the operation we have now. It was a question of repairs to an additional room for another makeshift studio and then after that the possibility of perhaps acquiring an additional building on the street as it became vacant. One by one she'd disclose some of the thoughts that she had and we would do them one by one and then of course we woke up after a while to find that we were really committed to quite a large undertaking. But it's proved possible by this step-by-step method.

I always had a wonderful board. I took the trouble to share my feelings with them, not only about finances but about artistic matters. When all else failed, I let humour win the day. Once they were unhappy because I wanted to buy a house on Maitland Street to use as a boys' residence. I was dealing with a large house on Jarvis Street where the older girls were on the first and third floors and the boys, with their own facilities, were on the second floor. I heard lurid tales from the youngest girls of events that took place during the commercials when they were all together watching T.V. I thought the board would understand my concern and agree immediately to purchase the new house. I listened quietly while they argued the case at length until I became exasperated and said, "Well, if the board is willing to take responsibility for the girls becoming pregnant then so be it!" There was a roar of laughter and it was moved immediately that the boys should have a separate residence.

Eugen Valukin of the Bolshoi, teaching male students in 1977.

Russia: New Friends

Even when I was a child I had a close connection with White Russian émigrés, artists who had escaped from Russia in deathly fear of the revolution. They were my mother's friends and included Anna Pavlova's husband, Victor Dandré. One woman who had been in a labour camp had wrists of iron from having to dig trenches. I was horrified when she told me she had been given a bowl of soup containing a human finger.

My first exposure to dancers from the Soviet Union was when, in 1959, I flew with Gail and Carol to New York to see the Bolshoi Ballet. It had come to the West from behind the Iron Curtain for the first time since the Communists had taken over the country. The performance was superb and I will always remember Galina Ulanova, one of the world's greatest ballerinas. Although close to the end of her career, she was deeply moving as Juliet in Leonid Lavrovsky's somewhat boring version of *Romeo and Juliet*.

When this ballet was first produced in Moscow, Lavrovsky had collaborated with composer Sergei Prokofiev, whose beautiful score has inspired many other versions of *Romeo and Juliet*, including those of John Cranko and Kenneth MacMillan.

Friends of mine were in the audience at the Bolshoi Theatre at a performance of this newly created ballet. Like me they found it boring and commented on this at the end. "But," my friend said, "I loved the music." She felt a tap on her shoulder. "Thank you, Madame," a voice said from the seat behind. It was Prokofiev.

The next time I saw Ulanova was in 1963, when she was dancing with the Bolshoi Ballet at the O'Keefe Centre in Toronto. Lavrovsky was the artistic director of the company. I had invited him to give a master class to our senior students. He came and was delighted to meet Lucy Potts, who acted as interpreter. After Lavrovsky had taught the class, which included Veronica Tennant, Martine van Hamel, Vanessa Harwood, and Nadia Potts, he said apologetically, "I haven't taught for years. Your students are much too good. Would you mind if I brought Ulanova to teach them?" Would I mind! I was flabbergasted and honoured.

We were on tenterhooks all that day. Hoping that Ulanova would agree to come, I laid everything on and waited. At midnight I received a call to say that the great ballerina would teach class at eleven o'clock the next day. At the same time, I was told that in response to my request for someone to teach our younger students, Eugen Valukin would arrive at the School at nine o'clock.

Valukin's arrival was the beginning of a long and loving relationship. A tall, handsome young man walked into the studio that morning, and staff and students fell in love with him on sight. Somewhat arrogant, with a booming laugh, he gave an excellent class. He had no idea of time and was still teaching when Ulanova arrived with Lavrovsky. Graciously she refused to interrupt him and we took her to a nearby classroom to wait. When he finished he was mildly embarrassed at keeping her waiting, but spoke to her enthusiastically about the standard of our pupils.

Ulanova was equally enthusiastic about the older students. She gave a class that lasted over two hours. "The girls have been professionally trained. They have nice figures, very good placement, and admirable discipline," was the comment of these distinguished visitors from the Bolshoi. Ulanova was also very complimentary about the students' arms, a subject of vital importance to me. As they left, they all agreed that of the many schools in which each had taught in North America, the National Ballet School provided the best training.

Before this visit I had been fruitlessly negotiating with the Canada Council and the Department of External Affairs with a view to securing the services of a teacher from the ballet school of the Bolshoi Theatre. Looking back on these talks I am reminded of the proverb: "The Russian has three strong principles: PERHAPS, SOMEHOW AND NEVER MIND." *Perhaps* the Canadian school could have a teacher. *Somehow* there must be a way to send them a teacher. But *never mind* if we can't spare a teacher right now.

Thanks to Ulanova, who had offered to do anything she could for us, the negotiations with Madame Fourtseva of the Ministry of Culture were speeded up. Also, Ulanova stipulated on my behalf that the visiting teacher should be Eugen Valukin.

Like Caesar, Mr. Valukin came, he saw, he conquered. We were to learn to call him Gennia. He spoke no English, and his first words were step, step, step. "Bettee, I step, step, step to studio," he would say. Lucy was such a wonderful translator that he and I would have violent arguments on training without realizing that she was in the middle. I could sense that she sometimes softened the angry words that passed between us, and I asked her to translate exactly. She would be embarrassed, but he and I thrived on expressing our views on technique, which by and large were very close. The main difference was on the placement of the hips, and I was amused to find out, on my first trip to Russia, that he had incorporated much of what he had learned from us into his teaching. He was, of course, far too proud to admit it.

Gennia's visit, the first of several, was in the fall of 1963. In November he came into my office in a dreadful state. While shopping on Church Street, many people had spoken to him about something that was clearly a major event. He returned to the School to discover that President Kennedy had been shot. He told me that he had been saying "Good, good" to his informers and was shaken at the thought of how they might have reacted.

With the climate of suspicion in the U.S.S.R., it was no wonder that Valukin was nervous. The KGB kept tabs on him throughout his stay in Canada. On his second visit, he told me he had been asked to spy but had vehemently refused. When I negotiated his salary with the Soviet government, knowing that they took most of it, I kept the amount low and paid him, in cash, a large per diem. We still had to be careful, as I received calls from the

Soviet Embassy asking about his purchases. On one occasion, they wanted to know if he had bought a refrigerator!

When Gennia returned to Russia, laden with gifts for his wife, Tanya, and a T.V. set from us, I knew I was going to have a rough time balancing what he had given us with what we already had.

In spite of my excellent basic training I was always open to new ideas; however, I knew what to accept and what to reject. Some of Valukin's methods, especially his insistence on forced turnout and high extensions, were potentially damaging—more so in Canada than in the U.S.S.R. because we did not have such a wide choice of applicants. We often had to accept students who, although extremely talented, did not have the flexibility or the near perfect proportions demanded by the Russians. Even then, when I visited Russia, I found that they had more injuries and were more casual about them than I could accept.

On the other hand, Valukin was a superb teacher with a magnetic personality. He gave exhaustively of his time and knowledge. He taught the students a more formal discipline than ours. In *pas de deux* classes they learned many exciting lifts that we had never attempted, and for selected students he created dances which they found both challenging and inspiring.

My problems arose from the fact that the ballet teachers, with one exception, were besotted with Valukin. Margaret Saul was the exception. She left the School because she was convinced that I had accepted his methods one hundred percent and she saw that as a betrayal of the valuable principles I had learned from the Cecchetti system. She was wrong but her fears were understandable.

The staff went overboard and I saw some very dangerous things happening as they struggled to emulate Valukin and embrace all his ideas. It took about a year for their own sound knowledge of training to make them realize that some of the things they were doing did not work. They learned the truth of the Russian saying "Great is Holy Russia but the sun shines elsewhere too." We came out of this difficult time with gratitude for what we had learned but with a more balanced approach to our teaching. When Valukin returned in 1964 and 1965, this more objective attitude continued.

Karen Bowes, now chair of the Dance Department of York

University, was at the School at that time. She was in Ulanova's class and studied with Valukin. In *To Be a Dancer*, written after she became a National Ballet principal dancer, she summed up my attitude to new ideas:

> Even in her teaching, I've noticed she hasn't set herself a standard and stuck by that standard no matter what. She's continually absorbing things from other teachers and from other methods, and that, I think, is what makes the School so great. It's not staid. It hasn't steeped itself in a tradition that is dying. She takes the best of whatever she sees and applies it, assimilates it. She doesn't impose it; she absorbs it somehow, and somehow all those children get the best of everything.

I had been invited by my new Russian friends to visit the school and the company in Moscow. In March 1965, Lucy Potts and I set out. It was an important journey for her. Although her parents were from Russia, she had never been there. In her youth she had been educated in Germany as well as in France. She was fluent not only in Russian, French, and German, but also in English, having taught in an English school in return for her board and lodging. During the Second World War, before coming to Canada, she had translated for Reuters the speeches of Hitler, Goering, Stalin, and others.

This visit was equally important to me, not only because I wanted to study the training of the superb Russian dancers I had seen, but also because of my background with my beloved teacher Tamara Karsavina and my memories of Anna Pavlova. I was aware that their school in St. Petersburg, later Leningrad, differed widely in matters of artistic taste from the one in Moscow, and I planned, while I was in the country, to visit it, as it was generally considered to be superior.

Lucy and I arrived safely in Moscow and were enthusiastically greeted by Gennia. He took us to the old Metropole Hotel which was close to the magnificent Bolshoi Theatre and not far from the school. The hotel had not yet been renovated so there were numerous problems. There were no plugs in the baths or the washbasins, and when I ran water into the latter, it poured all over my feet as the pipe was not connected. Lucy was extremely nervous that our room might be bugged so we had a hilarious time looking for some evidence that this was so.

There was a huge dining room, but the waiters were not interested in serving us. After an hour, they would come to take our order, but insisted that nothing on the menu was available. We suspected that this was because they could not be bothered to go to the kitchen. We ate whatever they chose to bring us. Sometimes it was a bowl of borsch or a cucumber and yogurt salad, but we lived mostly on black bread, caviar (which at that time was cheap and plentiful), and delicious ice cream.

I enjoyed the vodka and the brandy and was taught many useful tricks by Valukin and his friends. The vodka must always be downed in one fell swoop. Then, to prevent me from getting drunk, they would make me eat a piece of black bread spread with very hot mustard. They laughed when my eyes watered as they poured the next glass. The slice of raw lemon I had to eat after a glass of brandy had the same effect.

Everybody was amazed at Lucy's remarkable fluency in Russian. They were also fascinated by her knowledge of words that were no longer in use. She is attractive and friendly, only a little younger than I, but something happened that made me feel ancient and almost got her into trouble.

The Metropole was a hotel where men went to pick up girls. One night in the dining room Lucy struck up a conversation with a man at an adjoining table who had obviously been admiring her. At first I was not concerned, but as the conversation continued, I felt that he would not be easy to get rid of when we went upstairs. I was trying to convey this to Lucy when he asked her, "Who is this woman? Is she your *duenna*?"

We spent every day at the Bolshoi school. The building was full of history. To reach it we had to go through an old courtyard. I am thankful that I was there before they moved to the new sterile building out in the suburbs, which I saw when I returned.

We were warmly welcomed by all the staff, including the *babushkas* (grandmothers) who supervised the cloakrooms. I quickly learned to say *do svidania* (goodbye) but could never master the word for hello. Although in time I was able to get the gist of the conversations, the only other words I mastered were *spasiba* (thank you), *nyet* (no), *da* (yes), and *bolshoi* (big). On special occasions I could rise to *bolshoi spasiba*. I have to admit to being very nervous when I was out by myself. I could not read the street signs, and nobody would have understood my request for directions.

The director gave us the run of the school and even arranged for us to have lunch in the cafeteria. The children, like ballet children all over the world, were charming. The girls at the Bolshoi, in their old-fashioned pinafore dresses, would give us a little curtsy whenever we met; the boys would bow. Regarding the latter, I was told that the hardships of the war had affected the children's development and that the school was having trouble finding boys with suitable physiques. In spite of this, I have seen some fine male dancers who were produced in that period.

Valukin arranged which classes we saw and was not afraid to tell us what he thought of the teachers. They ranged from excellent to poor. In each of the several beginners' classes they had the same teacher for two years. I found them all very good. The next four years were crucial, as the students had only one teacher. In the last two years, they went to a teacher who gave them the final touches. I saw many talented children being given inferior training in those middle four years, when they should have been developing a solid technical foundation.

I was distressed to see that the students' places in class were never changed. In a class of twelve, divided into rows of three, the best child was centre front, the second best on the right, the third on the left, and so on. The children at the back were ignored. I must say these last children were not very good, and I doubt that we would have accepted them in Canada. When I asked what would become of them, I was told by amused staff members that they would land up in small companies in places like Minsk.

We became friendly with some of the teachers and were invited to their homes. Their living quarters were very cramped, and they often had to share kitchens and washroom facilities with other families. Gennia and Tanya had only one room, and the dining-room table had to be moved according to whether they were eating or sleeping. Their hospitality was such that we felt as if we were dining in a palace.

Eventually the staff of the Bolshoi school had their own apartments in a new complex. On one of my later visits, when I went to meet Mr. Ford, the Canadian ambassador, I saw Valukin dancing on his balcony which overlooked the embassy steps. I waved and did a little jig, much to the amusement of the maid who was holding the door open for us.

There were many highlights on that first trip to the Soviet Union: the friendships we made; the rehearsals and performances we saw, thanks to the generosity of Alexander Tomsky, the director of the Bolshoi Ballet; and the visit to Leningrad (St. Petersburg), where we stayed at the Astoria, an historic old hotel.

In Leningrad, at the Kirov school, we watched a class given by Alexander Pushkin, famous for his teaching of male dancers. We gave him a message from his pupil, Rudolf Nureyev, and his face lit up. In this class we noticed another student, Mikhail Baryshnikov, who had not yet defected.

In the girls' classes at the Kirov, I was deeply impressed with their lovely arm movements and classical style. Their training was more tasteful and, therefore, more artistic than that of the Bolshoi school. This carried through to the performances of the company at the Kirov (Maryinsky) Theatre. Although technically strong, the dancers abstained from the showy circus approach that I had seen in Moscow and which our present-day North American audiences love so much. Many of us will remember the beauty of the Kirov Ballet's performance of *Les Sylphides* when they visited Toronto.

On our return to Moscow, we watched the company taking class with Asaf Messerer. Like Pushkin, he was a renowned male teacher and was the uncle of prima ballerina Maya Plisetskaya, who has appeared many times in the West.

It was in Messerer's class that I saw the influence of Enrico Cecchetti. Many of the exercises were identical to those I had learned when I studied the Cecchetti method. There is no doubt that the post-revolution training has deteriorated considerably from that given by the older teachers such as Pushkin and Messerer and the relatively few women from that period whose classes I observed.

During our six-week stay in the country, we had visited many interesting places, including the Kremlin Museum and the palace of Prince Sheremetiev, in which the salon could ingeniously be transformed into a theatre. Also, in the lovely city of Leningrad, I could have spent a month at the Hermitage Museum, but we were only there for three days.

When we went to Red Square with Valukin, I was told off by the police for running in the vicinity of Lenin's tomb. They found it disrespectful. When we went in to see their hero, Gennia was the one to disgrace himself. He burst into laughter and irreverently declared, "He has shrunk." We concluded that they had done a poor embalming job on poor old Lenin.

Before leaving for Canada, I was invited to teach the graduating class of the Bolshoi school. This invitation arose from a discussion I had with staff members on how to teach *chaînés* (spins across the room). They teach them facing the corner; I feel one gets a better effect if they are taken sideways to the corner. They asked me to demonstrate and then said, "Oh! You do them so well you must have learned them our way." This is typical of their attitude, as I had discovered in my arguments with Valukin.

When I walked into the room I was very nervous. The whole staff had made themselves available to observe my class. At the barre I gave some exercises for warming up the feet. In them, the students had to press up to a pointe, using all the parts of the foot, especially the metatarsus. They lowered in the same way. This was new to them. At the end of the barre work they approached their teachers and asked why they didn't do this, as they found it very helpful.

I have to empathize with the Russians' blunt approach to each other as I have often been faulted for being too honest. At times, however, it can be cruel, as I discovered while watching an end-of-year examination of a *pas de deux* class. The purpose was to assess the students, who would be asked to leave if they were given a mark of less than three out of five. An experienced teacher was crucified by his colleagues because some of his students did not successfully execute all the lifts that were required. He pointed out that the rehearsal, which I had seen, had been perfect, but they said that wasn't good enough.

The pianists were equally straightforward. If the class didn't end on time, they walked out, so I made sure that I finished promptly. I concluded that the students were superb at balance and control in the slow *adagio* movements, and, of course, the Russians are famous for their high jumps. But where I found them sadly lacking was in steps that required small, quick movements. They had not heard of some of them and could not get their feet around them. This also applied to their beaten steps (*batterie*) such as *entrechats quatre*, *six*, and *royale*.

At that time the Russian attempts at contemporary choreography were unimpressive. Valukin craftily arranged for us to go to hear the Red Army Chorus so that we could not see a new ballet of which he was ashamed. He laughed heartily when we fooled him by seeing it in Leningrad. The choreography was a combination of *Swan Lake*—except that the swans were seagulls—and *West Side Story*. The scenario was full of propaganda. The British police, representing imperialism, had their own special musical theme of heavy chords to accompany their brutality. The hero, a fisherman, was shipwrecked on an island and thrown into jail. He was saved by the young Communist pioneers wearing red kerchiefs. The message was that with the right beliefs one can survive anything.

In June 1969, my tenth year as director and principal of the School and my second as associate director of the Company, I was invited to return to Moscow as a guest of honour at the First International Ballet Competition. I was accompanied by Lucy Potts, Celia Franca, Mary McDonald, who was the Company pianist, and three dancers I had trained: Karen Bowes, Vanessa Harwood, and Barbara Malinowski.

We were greeted at the airport by welcoming officials with armfuls of flowers. They included Irene, the interpreter who was assigned to me for the duration of the competition. These officials, who have an enormous respect for their artists, were a little disconcerted to find several of our friends from the Bolshoi hugging and kissing Lucy and me. We had to work hard to make them feel they were not redundant.

For me this visit was not as enjoyable as the first. As an official guest, I missed the freedom and the intimacy with my colleagues from the dance community. There were seven of us, and even with two interpreters, Irene and Lucy, it was quite strenuous.

The dancers' reactions were interesting. They all found the service excruciatingly slow in restaurants and suffered from the lack of fresh fruit and vegetables. Karen, who has a highly developed social conscience, was very depressed by the way people lived. She decided that she loved decadence if that meant the comfort and luxury of North American life. It is hard to say how Barbara felt, as she was in love most of the time we were there with a very nice young dancer from the Bolshoi who was introduced to her by one of the teachers. When Barbara left Moscow the tears were streaming down her cheeks as she held his flowers and carried his photo in her purse. Vanessa thoroughly enjoyed herself. She is full of fun, and her fashionable miniskirts were a source of constant interest to the Muscovites.

Irene arranged for the people who came with me to attend all the functions that were laid on for the official guests. We spent many hours watching the competition. As we expected, Mikhail Baryshnikov won the Grand Prix in the male section. His dramatic talent, added to his superb dancing, was evident in the final round. On our free days we visited science exhibits—lots of propaganda— museums, and art galleries. I arranged for the dancers, who were getting itchy feet from observing rather than taking part in the competition, to take classes with the Bolshoi company. This was a great privilege. Their teacher, Semyonova, a retired prima ballerina, complimented them on their work and they were thrilled.

Before returning home we went to Leningrad. On arrival at the hotel there was some confusion about our rooms. In that slow-moving, bureaucratic country we could easily have been out on the street, so I was relieved when a flushed Irene appeared to tell us that all was well. I was curious as to how she had managed to fix things. "I told them that you lunched with Brezhnev yesterday," she said proudly!

Unfortunately Irene was not allowed to take us sightseeing in Leningrad. I was very comfortable with her, as she had been a translator at the Soviet Embassy in Denmark. She had a great respect for Westerners and never forced her politics on us.

We were assigned a local guide. As our small group rattled around in a large bus, we listened to the party line *ad infinitum*. We heard that at 9:45 p.m. on October 25, 1917 (November 7 on the new calendar), the *Aurora* had sailed up the Neva River to signal the start of the revolution. As we boarded the bus after a rest stop, our guide wheeled around, pointing her finger at us like a schoolteacher testing her pupils. "When," she asked, "did the *Aurora* sail up the Neva to start the revolution?" Celia, with a downward flick of her wrist, replied, "You tell us, dear," and we all giggled.

On returning to the hotel, I greeted Irene with relief. I told her that there was no way we were going to spend another day with that dreadful woman. She laughed and somehow arranged to take us herself the following day.

Back in Moscow, we were preparing for our departure. I was horrified when Celia told me that Joe Lewis, our publicity director, had asked her to smuggle out some film for Boris Shapiro, a well-known press photographer. Boris had come to the country on a visitor's visa to avoid the paranoia that the Soviets felt towards the press. An airline had commissioned him to take some photographs of Moscow. He asked Joe for help because he knew that the authorities would be suspicious of his camera and would search him at the airport.

Celia agreed to take the film, as Joe was not going directly to Canada. We would be on the same plane as Boris and were to hand over the film to him after takeoff. I objected strongly; I told Celia that she was risking jail. Not only that, but my ongoing valuable relationship with the Soviets would be in jeopardy. She refused to listen to me so I phoned Mr. Ford, the Canadian ambassador, and asked him to speak to her. I could see her go pale as they spoke, and he obviously got his message across, as she gave the film back to Joe Lewis.

This story has a sad ending. To our surprise, when we were on the plane, Boris asked us for his film. We told him that we assumed Joe had taken it. When, on his return to Canada, I asked Joe where the film was, he said he had thrown it away in Moscow. Poor Boris! All his work was wasted.

Mr. Ford was a wonderful man. He was on very good terms with the Soviets and had a superb collection of their underground art. He was trusted, which was rare for a Western diplomat in the U.S.S.R., and was called upon by many of the other embassies to help with the numerous problems they faced.

The Fords entertained us several times, and it was always very informal. Mrs. Ford was Algerian and had a great sense of humour. They were renovating the embassy, and she told us of her difficulty with the plumbers, who paid no attention to her requests. Knowing how impressed the Russians were with any bureaucratic document, she manufactured a certificate stating that she was a qualified plumber. From that moment on she had no further trouble.

My next visit to Moscow was as a member of the jury for the Third International Ballet Competition in June 1977. At the second one in 1973, which I did not attend, Karen Kain and Frank Augustyn were given the prize for the best *pas de deux*, and Karen won a silver medal in the female section.

On my arrival at about midnight, I was met by the organizers of the competition. My luggage, which I had last seen in London, had not arrived. Having given a description of it to a bored employee at the airport, I was taken to the hotel. A colleague lent me a nightie and I fell into bed.

The next morning we were given our badges, documents, and two hundred roubles. Everybody expressed sympathy for my dilemma and some amusement that they were going to see me in the same suit for two weeks. I was assigned a very gentle young man called Oleg as an interpreter. He followed me about like a puppy and was quite useless. On the third day, he became very concerned and decided that he would take me to buy a whole new wardrobe at GUM, the famous—or infamous—department store. I tried to hide my horror at the idea of being outfitted at GUM and explained that I would have difficulty in finding my size, that I was not easy to fit, and that anyway we wouldn't have time as we were due at the Bolshoi Theatre in one hour.

By that time I was desperate and dragged Oleg to the British Airways office. They were not responsible for my loss but they volunteered to help, knowing that I would get no satisfaction from Aeroflot, with whom the authorities had arranged my travel. That afternoon they phoned to say my luggage had been found. Meanwhile, knowing that Oleg would be unable to handle the translation at the competition, I had asked for a replacement and was given another Irene. She was efficient and strong-minded. After a hair-raising taxi ride to the airport and a frustrating wait for the lady in the lost-luggage area to release my suitcase, we got back to the hotel just in time for me to change my clothes for the official reception that opened the competition.

The chairman of the jury was Yuri Grigorovich, artistic director of the Bolshoi Ballet. On the first day there were thirty judges, most of whom were either from behind the Iron Curtain or from countries friendly with the U.S.S.R. Those of us from the English-speaking countries included Robert Joffrey, U.S.A.; Nadia

Nerina, U.K.; Garth Welch, Australia; Ivor Kramer, Sweden; and several others. On the third day of the first round, four more judges, who had arrived late, were added.

I should explain that marks from one to twelve were given; these were added and then divided by the number of judges, unless a jury member had marked three above or three below the average, in which case the mark was disqualified. Eight points qualified a dancer to move on. The first- and second-round points were combined to decide on the finalists.

It became obvious on the first day that the Muscovites, who with their friends comprised approximately two-thirds of the jury, had already decided that a dancer from Moscow named Alla Mikhaltchenko was going to win the Grand Prix in the female section. The rivalry between Moscow and Leningrad was well known, but we discovered that one also existed between Moscow and Kiev.

In the first round the judges from the West marked very strictly, but were in close agreement. The hardest marker was Bob Joffrey, who allowed only twenty-two people into the semifinals and did not give eleven points to anybody. I gave eleven points to two people and passed twenty-five into the second round.

When the results came out we found, as we expected, that Alla was first, but to our consternation, a marvellous dancer from Kiev, Nina Semizorova, was eighth. We decided, although it was against our principles, to try to balance the marks in the second round. As a result, Nina came first. In the finals the jury decided that nobody was worthy of the Grand Prix, but Alla and Nina shared the gold medal.

A similar situation occurred in the male section. Thanks in part to us, an Australian and Muscovite shared the gold medal.

We were powerless to do anything about the prize-winning concert that was attended by Leonid Brezhnev. The only person allowed to dance her best number was Alla Mikhaltchenko, who was the star of the show. Nina Semizorova had to perform one of her weaker *pas de deux* and the Australian could not do his contemporary piece, which had brought the house down. So Mr. Brezhnev and his colleagues saw what they were supposed to see—that Moscow produces the greatest dancers in the world.

Having said all this, I should express the joy I felt at being in a country where dancers are treated as very special people. Citizens of Russia from every walk of life love ballet. For the competition, they were lined up hours before the theatre opened. As an audience, their knowledge and discernment, their enthusiasm for the best—regardless of nationality—their empathy with a slip or a fall, their tolerance and courtesy towards something inferior, created a wonderfully warm atmosphere.

I was to experience this warmth even more when I returned in 1981, not only as a jury member, but with six competitors from Canada. Kim Glasco and Kevin Pugh from the National Ballet of Canada were to compete in the senior group (twenty to twenty-eight years). Entered in the junior section (sixteen to nineteen years) were Sabina Allemann, Martine Lamy, Owen Montague, and Serge Lavoie from the National Ballet School.

photo: Andrew Oxenham

Kevin Pugh and Kim Glasco,
senior silver medallists, Moscow, 1981.

165

We were accompanied by Alexander Grant, artistic director of the Company, who was an honoured guest; pianists Mary McDonald and Janis Nielson; plus Jean Geddis. Jean, a former graduate and long a staff member of the School, was an invaluable member of our group. As teacher, coach, wardrobe mistress, and organizer of everything from rehearsals—in three different places at once—to trying to find food for the dancers, she was calm, supportive and, even when exhausted, available to the dancers.

Our success was beyond my wildest dreams:

FOURTH MOSCOW INTERNATIONAL BALLET COMPETITION

From Canada
Toronto Daily Star – June 17th, 1981
William Littler reporting from Moscow:

ALL OUR DANCERS PASS MOSCOW'S FIRST HURDLE
"We made it," yelped Martine Lamy, as she heard the announcement last night from the stage of the Bolshoi Theatre that all six Canadian competitors in the Fourth Moscow International Ballet Competition had qualified for the second round.

The announcement came around midnight Moscow time as a bleary-eyed collection of 102 dancers from 23 countries was summoned back to be told who had survived the five-day marathon that constituted the first round of the world's most important ballet competition.

From the U.S.S.R.
TASS – Moscow, June 20th, 1981:

CANADIANS ARE A SUCCESS
All Canadian dancers taking part in the second round of the Moscow Ballet Contest have shown their programs. . . . The audience and the experts were unanimous in their opinion that their performances were the highlight of the competition. They danced gracefully and emotionally showing great skill.

From New York
Dance News – September 1981:

ANNOUNCING THE RESULTS . . .

Kevin Pugh of the National Ballet of Canada received a silver medal for his impressive mastery of a broad vocabulary, fine theatrical sense and strong partnering of colleague and fellow silver medallist Kim Glasco. Canadians Owen Montague and Martine Lamy garnered silver and bronze medals respectively in the junior division, making a fine showing for their country with awards won by four of its six participants.

From England
The Dancing Times – August 1981
Mary Clarke reporting from London:

A BRITISH VIEW

The Russian Ministry of Culture sent an invitation through the British Council for four guests from this country to observe part of the competition.

One of them, Bridget Espinosa, kept a diary of her trip which concludes: "A wonderful experience that makes me feel quite a different person from having experienced it." It was also reported that she was tremendously impressed with the Canadians whom she described as "amazing" and she spoke a little wistfully about "the strength of the young dancers she had seen compared with standards here."

Somewhat childishly, I was thrilled that countries like Britain and Russia, whose representatives had often suggested to me that our students should go to them for the finishing touches, finally realized that Canada could do it on its own. As a people we are modest and tend to accept condescension from others. It was satisfying to know that in ballet at least we are among the best.

Our dancers were exceptionally young. Martine was only sixteen; Kevin Pugh, the old man of our party, was bowed under the weight of his twenty-one years. I had taken Martine for the experience and had warned her not to expect too much. To my amazement, she danced flawlessly—three demanding *pas de deux* and a contemporary piece. In addition to her medal, she won—with her partner Serge Lavoie—the prize for the best duo in the junior section.

Owen Montague, the silver medallist, was also honoured with a prize rarely given outside the U.S.S.R., namely, the Moscow Academy Award for Excellence. It was given by the head of that institution, Madame Golovkina. In the jury room, when asked by the East German judge why Owen was being favoured over his dancer, she reprimanded him sharply, saying that Owen was infinitely superior to his pupil.

I do not believe that established artists should compete in these affairs, but to see the young people grow as the result of this gruelling and stressful experience, to see them dancing on the Bolshoi stage accompanied by—in the third round—the massive Bolshoi orchestra made it all seem worthwhile.

photo: Andrew Oxenham

Owen Montague, junior silver medallist, Moscow, 1981.

Something took place with the conductor of the orchestra which could never have happened in Canada. He did not know the music of the St. Petersburg version of the solo from the *Giselle* peasant *pas de deux* which Martine would dance in the third round. I was told that she must learn another version, which we knew would not suit her as well. On hearing this, she burst into tears. Immediately the conductor sent for the librarian and gave him our piano copy of the music. I could not believe my ears when I was told that Martine's appearance would be postponed by one day and that her music would be orchestrated. Such kindness and respect for a young dancer!

It was an arduous task acting as a jury member and, at the same time, attending rehearsals and dealing with the dancers' problems.

A typical day would start at 6:00 a.m. with our request for *chai* (tea) from the key-lady who sat in state guarding the key to our rooms. This was obtained by presenting a card which was also needed to enter our hotel, the Russia. I would drink the *chai*, if it came, while struggling to review the marks I had given the previous day and preparing my notes for the forthcoming day. Having done my exercises, I would get dressed and find my way to the buffet—at the end of an interminable corridor—to line up for a breakfast of black bread and yogurt.

After breakfast I would set out on another long hike—this time from the North Wing to the East Wing—to meet the dancers. Rehearsals were held either at the theatre or at the new Bolshoi school, which was served by a fleet of buses whose schedule was constantly changed without our knowledge. It was much easier when we discovered we could order a taxi from the key-lady the night before, so we were no longer dependent on the buses.

During the first few days the dancers, especially the boys, were weak from hunger, as they could not get a decent meal. Eventually we found out that we could order a more substantial meal for them to have in the restaurant at 4:00 p.m. This consisted of a beef steak, very small, with a large helping of home-fried potatoes. The boys had two servings, or for a change they would have chicken croquettes.

From the rehearsal, I would dash to the theatre to serve on the jury from 12:00 noon to 2:30 p.m. Then, having grabbed a bite to eat in the canteen, I went to another rehearsal. Before returning to adjudicate from 7:00 p.m. to 9:30 p.m., I was either preparing papers, helping Jean to get hold of some materials to replace Martine's headdress and armbands, which had been left in Toronto, or trying to charm the shoe-man from the Bolshoi company wardrobe into giving me some shoes for the boys who were slipping badly in the rehearsal rooms and on the stage. The soles of Russian shoes are made of elk, which is a much rougher leather then ours. I also spent several days pulling strings so that Bill Littler would be allowed to spend at least one day backstage at the Bolshoi Theatre. That was like storming the Bastille.

When my day's work was completed, my colleagues—most of whom did not have competitors with them—and I would make a beeline for the hotel restaurant where, after the usual long wait to be served, we would eat smoked fish and cucumber salad and revive ourselves with vodka.

There was, fortunately, some relief from this hectic pace. Between rounds we had free days. Mr. Ford was no longer there and the current ambassador was on vacation, but the Canadian Embassy staff were wonderful and on several occasions invited us to their homes, where they had prepared sumptuous meals. It gave me great pleasure to see them basking in the glory of our success. They were being complimented by all their fellow diplomats, especially the Russians. They had never expected us to be so good and were obviously very proud.

I have experienced Canadians' lack of confidence in themselves many times. That is why our talented performers have to become successful abroad before they are fully accepted in Canada. Yet, we have produced, in every field, artists who are second to none in the world.

Life became much easier when Eugen Valukin turned up on the fifth day, having been on a trip outside Moscow. We were able to rehearse in the old school building which now housed the ballet section of the Institute of Theatre Arts. Valukin, as dean of ballet, was responsible for a five-year teacher training program.

Gennia took rehearsals for us. He inspired the dancers and lifted their spirits. He had wonderful taste and simplified the *pas de deux* danced by Kim and Kevin. These had been crammed with tricks by their coach in Toronto with a view to impressing the judges. At one point Alexander Grant told me he was unhappy with Valukin rehearsing his dancers. When I asked him why, he said that they might forget he was their artistic director. I pointed out that Gennia knew what the jury was looking for, but if he wished he could take over Kim and Kevin's rehearsals and my students would continue with Valukin. He reluctantly declined.

Nothing was too much trouble for Gennia. He used his influence as a member of the Bolshoi Ballet to arrange massages for our dancers and helped himself to armfuls of company shoes for the boys. All the time his infectious laugh rang out, full of love and warmth and pride in his Canadian friends.

It is hard to describe my feelings as I waited in the jury room for the results. When two of the most revered ballerinas, Ulanova and Semyonova, congratulated me in the jury room, along with many of my fellow jury members, I began to get excited and realized we might win something. The congratulations were always for the things that are most important to me—musicality, elegance, good schooling, lack of affectation—in a word, artistry.

On the last night of the competition, which ended at 10:00 p.m., we knew that the jury's deliberations would go on all night. Bob Joffrey and I had spent very little of the four hundred roubles we had received as an honorarium. At about 3.00 a.m. we sent out reluctant interpreters out for champagne. We smuggled it in and I whispered to Bob, "Do you know how to open it?" He looked at me scornfully. "Of course. I was a waiter." As we ran down the room placing the bottles on the table, some jurors looked shocked, as if they thought we were not treating the occasion with due deference. Thirst and exhaustion prevailed, however, and they were soon all drinking it gratefully.

My last contact with Bob before he died was a letter he sent on the School's twenty-fifth anniversary:

> For these twenty-five years the National Ballet School has distinguished itself as one of the best schools in the Americas. A pioneer in the training of classical dancers, the School has made an impressive contribution to the development of ballet in Canada and all of North America. Above all, the proof of any school is in its alumni: we applaud and are grateful for the many fine dancers trained by this academy dedicated to the great classical tradition. My special congratulations to Betty Oliphant for this achievement.

While in Moscow, I inadvertently created a situation that was blown up to ridiculous proportions. A diamond ring, which had belonged to my mother, was stolen from my hotel room. Its insured value was six thousand dollars. I had to report it in order to present proof, in writing, to my insurance company in Canada that my claim was valid.

The investigation started with two ordinary policemen who searched my room and took endless photographs. This process was repeated several times by officials who became progressively more important. Not understanding insurance, they were convinced that if they put anything in writing they would have to pay me the full amount.

Irene tried hard to convince them of the facts, but to no avail. I was aware of the sensitivity felt by the Soviets and was anxious that the key-lady would not be blamed, as they kept asking if I suspected her. By the time the matter was taken to the Minister of Culture I decided to give up and settled for an affidavit from our embassy, which turned out to be quite satisfactory.

For the last ten days of our visit, while I was dealing with the problem of my ring, I was also engaged in an ongoing battle with

photo: Barry Gray

Canadian winners of the 1981 Moscow competition arriving home. Left to right, Kevin Pugh, Mary McDonald (principal pianist, NBC), Martine Lamy, Sabina Allemann, me, Kim Glasco.

the authorities about our return trip. They were determined to send us to Montreal by Aeroflot, which only flew on Mondays, three days after the competition ended. That was painful enough as we were in the middle of a heat wave (95°F) and were desperate to get home. To add insult to injury, they were not willing to pay hard currency for Air Canada to take us from Montreal to Toronto. Finally they issued a ticket for me but not for the rest of the group. I refused it and insisted that the others must be booked with me on the same plane. Eventually their tickets were produced, but in the meantime mine had been lost.

To add to our anxiety our visas had expired and we had to give up our passports in order to have them renewed. For the first time I experienced the fear that I knew existed in Communist societies. I had been aware of it when I was dealing with the police about my ring and they wanted me to point the finger at some hapless citizen.

As important guests we were treated royally, but once the competition was over we had no one to whom we could turn for help. The competition officials had disappeared from the hotel and Irene was nowhere to be seen. After three miserable days, she turned up to take us to the airport. Even then I was nervous as the immigration officer stared at my passport suspiciously. He pointed out that my name was shown as Nancy Elizabeth, whereas I had signed Betty Oliphant. It was hard to persuade him that Betty was short for Elizabeth but he reluctantly allowed me through.

It was a relief to be back in Toronto, but we did not receive the expected celebration of our dancers' success. Instead, the media's emphasis was on criticism directed at me by the *Globe and Mail* and Actors' Equity. Apparently the confidentiality of the jury room had been violated and it had been reported that I had not voted for a certain Canadian choreographer to win the prize for choreography. The jury found that nobody deserved the award and it was not given. I pointed out that I was only one of thirty-four jurors and expressed surprise that I should be expected to vote for something that I found inferior.

My protests were in vain. Sadly, I once again experienced an example of Canadians' inability to enjoy success without tarnishing it.

Erik Bruhn and Rudolf Nureyev, 1965.

Defectors

The first time I saw Rudolf Nureyev—I call him Rudi—was on
stage after his dramatic defection in 1961 in Paris. I was
excited by his animal magnetism, by his technique—mastered in
three years versus the eight years that the Kirov school usually
takes to train a dancer—and, most importantly, by his beautiful
style with its soft flowing arm movements.

I was also shocked by his bad manners on stage. Traditionally,
the classical *grand pas de deux* opens with the *pas de deux*, followed by the male solo and the female solo, and the dancers finish
together with the coda. At this first performance, after the ballerina had exited I saw Rudi going into the wings instead of taking
his place for his solo. Then the audience had to wait and wait
until he returned. People backstage told me he was putting resin
on his feet—to prevent slipping—and taking deep breaths. I had
experienced male arrogance in Russians, but had never seen it
transferred to the stage.

On another occasion, when I saw him in an open-air theatre
in Europe, he was obviously angry with his partner. The *pas de
deux* finished with him lifting her onto his shoulder. As we were
expecting them to take their calls, he lowered her, dumped her on

175

the floor, and walked off the stage. I was not surprised when my friends who had studied with him in St. Petersburg told me he had been called "the savage."

In time I came to know and understand Rudi very well. The first occasion was during his trip to Toronto to visit Erik Bruhn, the renowned Danish dancer who was performing in the ballet *La Sylphide* with the National Ballet of Canada. Rudi had seen Erik dance in Russia and recognized in him an artist even greater than himself. After his defection he had contacted Erik and had gone to Denmark to work and study with him. At that time they became lovers.

While Rudi was in Toronto watching Erik perform, he appeared to me to become very restless. He had never danced the role of James in *La Sylphide* and obviously longed to do so. Despite his admiration for Erik, who was the definitive James, Rudi was fiercely competitive. The part of James, the kilted Scotsman who fell in love with a sylph on the eve of his wedding, appealed to Rudi's romantic Slavic nature, and the choreography was a wonderful showpiece for his magnificent jumps.

Rudi's wish came true. Erik was generous by nature, so Celia Franca and I were not surprised when he suddenly "developed a bad knee." He interrupted our discussion as to who in the Company should replace him by looking up and saying slyly, "What about Rudick? He knows it." Rudick was Erik's pet name for Rudolf. Celia and I looked at each other quizzically. This would certainly solve our problem and would assure us of a full house.

At the performance that night the audience went mad and gave Nureyev sixteen curtain calls—not because it was such a great performance of the character of James but because it was superbly danced by a man who was front-page news at the time and who excited the audience with his athleticism and sensuality. We felt sad because his characterization was light-years away from Erik's and his dancing was lacking the perfectionism and clean technique that made Erik the greatest classicist of his day.

After this performance, I found Erik very thoughtful. The next day his knee had miraculously recovered and he pronounced himself able to dance that night. He gave the performance of his life. He also received a standing ovation, but it was obvious that he had to work much harder for it than Rudi, who had been put on a pedestal by the public and the media. Erik and other great Western artists have often commented bitterly on how much more recognition they would have gained had they been defectors.

This first short introduction to Nureyev made me aware that he was a complex human being, brilliant and passionate about his work, but also paranoid, arrogant, and ruthless. As I grew to know him better, I discovered his fantastic sense of humour. I became very fond of him, although I realized how difficult he found it to trust me, or anyone else for that matter.

My relationship with Rudi continued to develop when he arrived to work with the National Ballet over a period of two years. He came to the company for two reasons: to mount his version of *Sleeping Beauty* and to perform with us. This involved partnering our young ballerinas, most of whom had been trained by me either at my private school or later at the National Ballet School. He did so much for these youngsters and for the Company and was responsible for moving us into the big league, which culminated in our first appearance at the Metropolitan Opera House in New York.

None of this happened without many trials and tribulations.

The Company's association with Rudolf Nureyev was initiated by New York impresario Sol Hurok, who invited us to tour the United States with the Russian star in 1972. Celia was against the idea as she knew Rudi would insist on dancing all of the leading male roles. She was concerned about the effect this would have on our male dancers, especially Frank Augustyn. In the end we persuaded her that the financial benefits plus the prolonged on-stage exposure for the dancers would make the project worthwhile.

Nureyev's production of *Sleeping Beauty* was a lavish affair. It was supposed to cost two hundred and fifty thousand dollars but thanks to Nicholas Georgiadis, the designer Rudi had insisted on using, it ended up costing over four hundred thousand dollars. My friends often tease me when I see the dead stag being carried on a pole across the stage in the hunting scene because I sigh and say, "Can you believe that brief moment cost five hundred dollars?"

On many occasions the Company's board of directors wanted to cancel the production, because Rudi threatened to walk out every time we asked him to curtail the designer's extravagances. Each time, the general manager, Celia and I managed to persuade the board that we had already spent so much that it was better to proceed.

Finally the opening day arrived at the National Arts Centre in Ottawa. By this time Celia and Rudolf were not speaking to each other and I, as associate director, was the go-between. At the dress rehearsal it became clear that the production was going to run for over three hours. This would be a disaster for the Company because we would go into overtime for musicians, stage crew, and other union members.

I was sent to Rudi's dressing room to ask him to shorten the show by ten minutes. Celia particularly wanted him to cut the *pas de cinq* in the third act. It was original choreography by Nureyev and bore no relation to the ballet as it was conceived by Petipa. It was a clumsy piece of work and did nothing for the production. I was nervous when I saw Rudi and talked inanities until he asked me what the old bitch wanted. I told him and he replied angrily that the *pas de cinq* would not be cut if we wanted him to allow the production to go on. In desperation I asked him what we could do to save the Company from going bankrupt, so he laughed and said, "Just tell the orchestra to play the whole thing faster." What we finally did was cut the intermissions, which made it very hard for the dancers, who had to change costumes, and the stage crew, who had to make huge set changes. The show finished two minutes before the deadline and the *pas de cinq* is in the production to this day.

Celia was never happy with Nureyev's *Sleeping Beauty*. In *Dance Canada* Max Wyman writes:

> She found the production tasteless and the choreography "stinking." And she didn't like the effect Nureyev had on the dancers. "If screaming and shouting and swearing is good, then he was good but . . . there's a difference between temper and temperament. He considers he was of great artistic assistance to the company, in my opinion he was not.

I heartily disagree with Celia's statement, as do most of the dancers. Rudi chose Frank Augustyn to dance the Bluebird with

Karen Kain and then groomed him to take over the role of the prince. The principal female dancers will all attest to his professionalism in dance if not always in his behaviour. His passion for his vocation was so moving that many people were touched by it.

Two more incidents that I remember about *Sleeping Beauty* tickled my funny bone. Rudolf's paranoia led him to believe that the stagehands were conspiring against him. He was convinced that they were only too anxious to kill him by dropping some heavy object from the fly tower or that they would sabotage the lighting so that he would not be given the prominence that was his due. One night, at the crucial moment when the prince is about to wake the princess with a kiss, there was no spotlight on Rudi as he stood by the bed. He looked up, making angry gestures until the spot appeared, and then proceeded with the kiss. On another occasion, a ten-year-old boy from the School who was a page in the production told me proudly that Mr. Nureyev had spoken to him on stage. I asked if Rudi had been nice to him and he replied, "He told me to fuck off."

I think I was something of a mother figure to Rudi. I often dined with him at Barberian's Steakhouse in Toronto. Afterwards, in his usual mischievous way, he would try to persuade me to go to his hotel to see some pornographic films. We talked a lot about his mother, whom he loved dearly. The authorities were so angry with him that they would not allow him to visit her in spite of a petition signed by dancers from all over the world. It was not until 1987, when his mother was dying, that a classmate, Oleg Vinogradov, now artistic director of the Kirov Ballet, obtained permission for him to return home to see her.

There were times when Rudi was very serious and his zany sense of humour was not in evidence. This happened when he was in Toronto dancing with the Royal Ballet. He and his partner Margot Fonteyn will be remembered for *Marguerite and Armand*, the passionate *pas de deux* created especially for them by Sir Frederick Ashton.

After the performance at the O'Keefe Centre, he was picked up by the police for dancing down the centre of Yonge Street, and charged with being drunk and disorderly. After being rescued by the manager of the Royal Ballet, he sat in the taxi in gloomy silence. "What is wrong, Rudolf?" the manager asked. "Everything is all right now." Rudi roused himself. "I am trying to—what you call it—keep the stiff British upper lip," he replied.

The last time I saw Rudi was after his performance in *The King and I* at the O'Keefe Centre. He was really pleased to see me, and when I told him I thought he had done a good job, I was amazed at his humility when he said, "It could be a lot better."

The world owes a lot to Rudolf Nureyev. With his passion and dedication to dance he reached many members of the public who previously had been unaware of the existence of the art of classical ballet.

The second defection, that of Mikhail Baryshnikov, was much closer to home. To describe it, I would like to quote the opening paragraph from John Fraser's book *Private View*:

> On June 27th 1974 Mikhail Baryshnikov was dancing with a visiting Soviet ballet troupe in Canada, at the end of a week of performances at Toronto's O'Keefe Centre. Shortly after 11:00 p.m., instead of boarding a bus to go to a post-performance party with his Soviet colleagues, he bolted through a crowd of well-wishers and headed for an automobile, parked near the theatre, in which he was whisked away from his Soviet past and into a world of great expectations and beckoning horizons. Defection seems such a corrosive and negative word for what was, in effect, the most positive act of the young dancer's life, an act that was joyously received in the West. Yet defection it was, and for several days—as he hid out at a country estate in the middle of an Ontario forest—his fate became the focus of front-page news across the world.

Misha—as we call him—had many friends at the School and the Company. They rallied around when they knew what he intended to do. One of them, Sergiu Stefanschi, a teacher on my staff, discovered that he and Misha had much in common as they had both trained at the Kirov school—although at different times—under Alexander Pushkin. Through Sergiu I learned that it had become common knowledge at the National Ballet that Misha was going to defect after the final performance on Saturday night, so I went along in fear and trepidation.

Photo: Erik Dzenis

Misha Baryshnikov.

It is hard to convey the tension of that evening. Although a member of the Kirov Ballet, Baryshnikov was appearing in Toronto with the Bolshoi Ballet. His partner was Struchkova, a Bolshoi ballerina who was getting rather long in the tooth. Misha had obviously been added to the roster to bring in the crowds. Although his behaviour on stage was totally professional, it was obvious to me that he was not particularly happy with the partnership and of course he was about to take an enormous risk. If the KGB, who always accompanied the dancers, were to prevent his escape he would be punished severely—probably by not being allowed to dance anywhere except in the U.S.S.R. for the rest of his career.

As the performance ended with enthusiastic applause, an incident happened which made those of us who knew what Misha was intending to do realize how much the strain was getting to him. Many people threw flowers onto the stage. As Baryshnikov and another male dancer bent down to pick them up to give to the ballerina they bumped heads. The other dancer laughed uproariously, as did the rest of the company, but Misha did not even crack a smile. I was worried that this would make the powers-that-be suspicious. However, the Russians are notoriously temperamental and his colleagues may have thought that he was unhappy with the way he had danced or, even more likely, with his partner.

The actual defection took place successfully that night, despite a number of incidents that made the performance end half an hour late. This delay must have been particularly nerve-wracking for Tim Stewart. He had been asked by Jim Peterson, who organized the whole affair, to drive the getaway car and was waiting near the O'Keefe Centre. I remember asking Tim whether they had kept the engine running while they waited. He said that they had not, since that would have given rise to suspicion. To this day, I wonder what would have happened if the car had not started. But of course it did and the rest is history.

After Misha was back in circulation with permission to stay in Canada, I came to know him very well. I heard from his friends that he was very lonely and still in shock. Celia Franca, who could have helped him enormously, was so embittered after her experience with Nureyev that, when I asked for her help, she told me that all the Russians were the same and she could do nothing except invite him to dance with the Company at Ontario Place. She expected him to do this for nothing out of gratitude for the support he had received from many Torontonians.

I decided to invite Misha, with some of his friends, to my house. I wanted to do something special and discovered that he played the Spanish guitar. I asked a Spanish guitarist whom I knew what price I should pay for a good guitar. He felt that however much I paid I would not get a quality instrument, but offered to sell me his own, which was custom-made in Spain. Although Baryshnikov spoke very little English, he was obviously overwhelmed with my gift. I have a poignant memory of him walking around my living room strumming softly to himself.

While in Toronto, Misha was concerned about keeping in shape, so he came to the National Ballet School to take a class with our senior boys. They happened to be an extraordinarily talented group. Erik Bruhn was teaching the class, and Misha told him that even in the Soviet Union he had never seen a class of boys so well trained and with so much potential.

I tell this story because Misha made a gesture that showed his respect for our achievements at the School. Having agreed to dance with the Company at Ontario Place with Veronica Tennant as his partner, he demanded a fee of two thousand dollars. This confirmed Celia's opinion that he was "another Nureyev," without gratitude and thinking only of himself. She grumbled mightily and told me how foolish I had been to befriend him. After the performance, which was superb, he was given a cheque that he promptly donated to the National Ballet School. When we had cashed it, the bank allowed us to keep it and we had it framed.

Mikhail Baryshnikov and Veronica Tennant in Bournonville's *La Sylphide* staged by Erik Bruhn, 1974.

Our friendship over the years has been mutually beneficial. On one occasion—after he had become very famous and consequently very busy—I phoned him in New York for a piece of music that was unattainable in North America, and it was in my hands the next day. At another time I was able to be helpful by providing some young boys from the School for his television production of the *Nutcracker*, which was made in Toronto.

On the occasion of the School's twenty-fifth anniversary celebration, he sent the following letter:

Dear Betty,

I salute you today for the great work you have done in founding and nurturing one of the world's most prestigious academies of dance. Your leadership has always stood as an inspiration for those dedicated to the highest standard. But beyond those professional achievements, your graciousness and warmth have enriched the lives of your students and guests in an unforgettable way. You are a special woman and your school is a testament to your unique spirit.

Mikhail Baryshnikov
Artistic Director
American Ballet Theatre

My mother used to quote to me a fifteenth-century proverb that "comparisons are odious." This stayed in my mind along with the remark that she could see a little green goblin on my shoulder when I was jealous. In spite of her warning, I would like to comment on some of the differences I saw in Nureyev and Baryshnikov's performances.

The former lost, quite quickly, the fluidity and soft panther-like movements that had impressed me so much when I first saw him. His arms became stiff and his dancing somewhat stilted. What never changed was his extraordinary charisma. Even when he should no longer have been performing, he was able to stir an audience with his personality, so that they forgave the obvious deterioration of his physical ability.

Baryshnikov is another story and was in my opinion the

better dancer. His training at the Kirov school had been longer and he had emerged as a fine classical dancer, albeit, at least in his compatriots' eyes, hampered by his height. He was frustrated with their short-sightedness in ruling that he was too short to be allowed to dance some of the major classical roles, such as Prince Signified in *Swan Lake*.

It has always been important to me that a dancer has dramatic talent, and I found Misha stronger than Rudi in this area. It is not absolutely essential; there are many great dancers who cannot make the mad scene in the ballet *Giselle* believable. Even so, I feel there is greater emotional depth in the performance of dancers with dramatic ability even when they are not dancing a dramatic role.

On my first two visits to the Soviet Union, mention of Rudolf Nureyev produced a stony silence. One day when Lucy and I went up to the Bolshoi school library, a young dancer, making sure he was not overheard, asked us about the great man. "Is he making a lot of money?" was the question. When we confirmed that Rudi was extremely wealthy, he sighed and went back to his books.

Something similar happened when I was on the jury in 1977. We were taken to see a film which included many famous dancers when they had been in their final years at the school. The commentator proudly named each one until a superb male dancer appeared upon the screen. There was silence; it was Mikhail Baryshnikov. We looked at each other in amazement. It seemed so childish to refuse to mention his name when we obviously knew who he was, but the proud Russians had been hurt and embarrassed and this was how they reacted.

During my last visit to the Soviet Union I saw signs, in the museum of the Kirov school, that Rudolf Nureyev and Mikhail Baryshnikov, who had been obliterated from the records, were being restored to their rightful place in the history of the Kirov Ballet. In the post-revolution era they will be remembered as two of the most important artists ever to graduate from the famous school in Leningrad (St. Petersburg).

Although she did not have to defect to leave the Ukraine, I must mention ballerina Galina Samsova, whose contribution to ballet in Canada was brief but important. She came to Toronto in the spring of 1961 as the wife of Alex Ursuliak, a Canadian

Ukrainian from Edmonton. In 1957 Alex had been given a scholarship from a local dance group to study dance in Kiev. Galina was one of his teachers, and when they fell in love and married she was given permission to return to Canada with him.

Soon after she arrived I heard that Galina was to dance in Boris Volkoff's school recital. I went to see her and was bowled over. She was a superb dancer and I rushed off to tell Celia that she should invite her to join the Company. Celia was more cautious than I, but once she had seen Galina dance she agreed with me wholeheartedly.

Before Alex got a part-time job as a translator and Galina joined the Company, they were very hard up. They had paid Volkoff for rehearsals, rental of costume, and music arrangements, which I found most unusual. I was horrified to hear that on Christmas morning the milkman had arrived and, realizing that they were without food, had taken them home for Christmas dinner.

While in Toronto Galina gave a great deal to the National Ballet as a principal dancer and to the School as a guest teacher. She had an extremely flexible back, and from watching her teach I understood more clearly the importance of developing strong muscles to support that flexibility. The only sad thing was that Veronica Tennant, who was in her final years at the School, was determined to be as supple as Galina and wrecked her own back in the process.

In 1963 Galina left Canada for Europe and immediately became famous when she won the Medaille d'or in Paris as best female dancer. Nureyev was the winner of the same award in the male section. Following this success Galina was invited to join London's Festival Ballet, where she remained until 1975. She is now directing the Scottish Ballet after spending many years as a principal dancer and coach with the highly regarded second company of the Royal Ballet.

Having been a valuable member of my staff for several years, Alex, who was eventually separated from Galina, also went to Europe, first to London Festival Ballet, then as assistant director to the Vienna State Opera, and finally to the Stuttgart Ballet as ballet master and character artist.

I met Alex again when we were on the jury for a competition

—the Prix de Lausanne—in Switzerland. By that time he had become director of Stuttgart's John Cranko School. We started negotiations for an exchange between our schools which finally took place after I had retired.

Some people may remember when Alexander Goudonov, who died recently, defected in New York. His wife sat for many hours in a plane on the tarmac wrestling with the decision as to whether to stay with her husband or return to Moscow. I met him soon after, and he was shattered that she had not remained with him in the West. I learned later that while on the plane she had been bribed by the Soviet authorities with offers of promotion and the chance to dance leading roles in the Bolshoi Ballet, of which she was a fairly insignificant member. None of these things came to pass.

The famous ballerina Natalia Makarova was also a big loss to the Soviets when she decided to follow the example of her compatriots. Most of these artists had the same motive for leaving their mother country, which they loved with a passion.

They had already seen companies such as Balanchine's New York City Ballet and the Joffrey Ballet, which had visited the U.S.S.R. They saw the trends in contemporary choreography and realized that there was a whole new world to explore in their beloved art form. They longed for a chance to stretch themselves artistically. Once they had emerged from behind the Iron Curtain they were exposed to dancers and ballet companies all over the world.

I knew Makarova through her work with the National Ballet of Canada. Erik Bruhn was the artistic director for three years before his tragic death from lung cancer. He invited Makarova as a guest artist to dance *Giselle* and the leading role of Tatiana in *Eugen Onegin*. In both of these ballets she displayed great dramatic ability.

Erik also commissioned Makarova to produce the ballet *Bayaderka* (*La Bayadère*) for the Company, and she allowed Sergiu Stefanschi, with whom she had been associated in Leningrad, to stage her production of *Paquita* for the National.

I had nothing to do with these defections but I did play an important role in helping well-known Romanian ballerina Magdalena Popa leave her country.

In between the International Ballet Competitions held at four-year intervals in Moscow, others took place in three different venues under the same auspices: Varna, Bulgaria, where Martine van Hamel won her gold medal; Tokyo (eventually moved to Helsinki); and in the United States.

Magdalena—we call her Magda—and I had been on many juries together, but because we had no common language we could only communicate with nods and smiles. The year after our success in Moscow, she and I met again as fellow jurors, this time for the competition that was held in Jackson, Mississippi.

Near the end of the session, I was surprised to receive a phone call asking if Magda and her interpreter could come to see me in my hotel room. When they arrived she told me that she would like to go to Canada. Although she was an international star, she had been informed by the Romanian authorities that on her return from the United States she would never be allowed to leave the country again. It was only because of intense pressure from the United States that at the last minute they had given her permission to adjudicate in Jackson. They protected themselves by refusing to permit her husband, Amatto Checiulescu, the director of the Bucharest Opera Ballet, to accompany her.

Magdalena's family, consisting of her husband, her parents, and her six-year-old daughter, was being punished because her brother-in-law had defected to West Germany. Their passports had been taken away. When the authorities decided to allow her to go to Mississippi, her husband urged her to take the opportunity to find a future elsewhere for all of them.

I discovered more about this dancer's illustrious career as I got to know her. Following in the footsteps of Sergiu Stefanschi, her compatriot, who went to Leningrad in 1954, Magdalena had been sent one year later to study at the Kirov school. Nureyev arrived at the school that same year although he was seventeen and she was thirteen. She remained there until she graduated in 1960. During that time, while still a student, she won the silver medal at the Festival de la Jeunesse in Vienna.

In 1964 Magdalena and Sergiu Stefanschi, dancing together, each won a silver medal in the Varna competition. As a result, they were invited to dance the leading roles in *Giselle* and *Swan Lake* on a two-month tour of the U.S.S.R. This was followed one year later by her greatest success. At the Festival de Champs Elysées in Paris she danced *Giselle* with the Bucharest Opera Ballet and she won the Etoile d'or for the best interpretation—a great honour, the European equivalent of an Oscar.

The day Magdalena came to my room I asked her why she had chosen Canada. She said that she had been very impressed with our dancers and liked my attitude in the jury room, particularly, I was amused to hear, when I had spoken up against giving the choreographic prize.

Magda had commitments in the United States for three weeks after the competition ended, and then she would have to go home. Time was of the essence so I immediately went into action.

The first step was to see if the National Ballet would offer her a job as a ballet mistress. She would have liked to dance, but that was not feasible. I spoke to Alexander Grant, the Company's artistic director, and Robert Johnston, the general manager. They agreed to give her a contract. This was all-important for my approach to the Canadian authorities.

I knew I did not have time to go through the usual channels to get permission for Magdalena to become a landed immigrant. I had a brainwave and called Kenneth Taylor, the Canadian ambassador in New York. It was he who saved a number of Americans by hiding them in the Canadian Embassy in Iran. I decided that he was not the type to be bogged down by red tape, and I was right.

Ken Taylor had heard of me and was immediately sympathetic to our cause. In a very short time he had arranged for a Minister's permit which would allow Magda to enter Canada. I went home and on July 20, 1982, Bill Poole, the National Ballet School's administrative director, went to New York to fetch her. It so happened that it was her birthday.

It is hard to imagine the feelings of someone who has left not only her country, but her husband, her child, and her parents. Magdalena had no way of knowing if she would ever see her family again.

In Toronto I had arranged for her to stay in an apartment belonging to a teacher who was out of the country. When we went there, it took only one look at her face to show me how afraid she was of being alone. "You don't want to stay here, do you?" I asked.

"Would you rather come home with me?" Relief flooded her face as she nodded.

Magdalena and I became fast friends, and we consumed a lot of red wine in the process. My heart ached for her when she spoke to Amatto and her little girl on the phone. I was determined to bring them to Canada. I sent her to Ottawa to plead her case. I knew that if they met her our government officials would be moved by her situation. They were wonderful to her and promised to help in any way they could.

The whole affair was very delicate. Magdalena did not want to anger her government by calling her departure a defection. She was formerly a national treasure, and her international status made the authorities wary of any kind of repercussions resulting from their treatment of her. While in Ottawa she went to the Romanian Embassy. Following the advice of our immigration officials who accompanied her, she explained that she was merely visiting Canada for a prolonged period. This face-saving device satisfied her countrymen although they knew very well that she would never return to her native land.

Eventually Magda's husband and daughter Ama arrived, but their luggage did not. It appeared that it had never left Romania. So with no worldly possessions and obviously in shock from the strain of the past few months, Amatto was reunited with his wife.

Some months later Magda's parents arrived. I gave Amatto a job teaching at the School, and the family, with great courage, started building a new life.

At the conference "Expectations," St. Lawrence Centre, 1979.

Dark Days

I have read many autobiographies. I love getting to know somebody through his or her life story, but I am often disappointed because I sense a desire on the part of some authors to hide relevant facts about themselves and others. They seem fearful of causing controversy and wary of appearing less than perfect. This concern creates a lack of balance in their writing and usually results in a superficial story.

I found Margaret Thatcher's book, *The Downing Street Years*, a horrendous example of an autobiography in which the writer's self-adulation and lack of humility made the work unbelievable.

With this in mind I was determined, when I decided to write my own story, to tell the truth, good and bad, as I perceive it. I realize, of course, that I am bound to be subjective.

I had no trouble with my decision until before starting this chapter, when I had to do a lot of soul-searching. Did I want to reveal some of my most personal feelings? Could I bear to relive a painful period of my life? I asked myself those questions and concluded that I owed it to my readers to present an honest account of my life. Besides, it might even be helpful to those who have suffered a depression.

In 1967 my life was pretty bleak. I was unhappily married, Gail had gone to the United States, and Carol was living in her own apartment while attending university. So I was delighted when I received an invitation from Erik Bruhn, director of the Royal Swedish Opera ballet company, to reorganize their school.

It was not easy. When I arrived in Sweden, two things happened that worked against me. The first was a letter posted on the notice board by Erik, who had been admitted to hospital with an ulcer; in it, he announced my visit, and warned the staff that they should pay attention to my views as many changes would be made when I left.

The second incident was my meeting with Nureyev, who was rehearsing his version of *Nutcracker* on the stage of the Opera House. He greeted me warmly and said, "What are you doing here?" and then continued contemptuously, "It's like pouring water into a bucket with a hole in it." As I saw the reaction of the staff and dancers I groaned inwardly.

I had taken a fourteen-year-old student, Wendy Reiser, with me to demonstrate the results of our training and the methods we used. Everyone was impressed with her technique and her talent, and they paid her many compliments. We had a great time together. She was thrilled to be in Europe, but was even more excited at being able to meet and talk with Rudolf.

In spite of the difficult start, we finally won over the Swedes. I set up a new curriculum and chose, with Erik, a new school director, retiring dancer Gosta Svalberg. I had regular meetings with the staff, and, so that they could see how I applied my theories, when they were free they observed the daily class that I gave to a group of young students. When I left they were full of gratitude and told me they had shipped a complete set of Orrefors glasses to Canada for me.

Wendy is a perfect example of the success of the School's combined program. After graduation she joined the National Ballet and some years later became a soloist. Sidelined with an injury and somewhat disenchanted with the life of a dancer, she went back to school and after one year was accepted at three major universities. She is now a doctor, and works closely with the Dancers' Transition Centre—an organization that helps retired artists move into a second career.

After my return, many of the Swedish teachers came to Canada for further training and I sent our teachers over to help them. I lost one, Jean Geddis, who stayed over there as teacher and ballet mistress. When I remonstrated with Erik for stealing Jean away from me, he laughed heartily and told me I could easily spare one of our many good teachers.

During my last week in Sweden I had received a phone call from Lucy Potts with news that I had never expected to hear again in my life: Carol had a recurrence of tuberculosis. Needless to say, I was desperate to get home to be with Carol and to know more details. Reg met me at the airport and, in his usual unkind way, seemed pleased to be the bearer of bad news. I was thankful that I had been forewarned by Lucy, who had been kind and sympathetic.

When I arrived at the hospital, I found the situation was serious. For several months Carol, who was in great pain, had been going to the emergency department at the Toronto General Hospital, begging them to admit her. They refused, saying they could find nothing wrong. On her last visit she refused to leave unless she was given some help. She was seen by a resident, Dr. Alan Gross, who admitted her and ordered X rays. It turned out that the psoas muscle—in Carol's back—was full of tubercular pus. I find it incredible that, knowing her history, they had not suspected something of the sort earlier.

Carol was facing two major operations. The first was open chest surgery. They cleaned out the psoas muscle and patched up the old fusion with bone from two of her ribs. When Carol was six, I had been told by a doctor that she had suffered more pain than the average person could expect in a lifetime. Once again I watched Carol, now a young woman, go through hell, and I could do nothing.

When she was well enough, I took Carol to Barbados to build her up for the next operation. While there she met a young man, David Roach, and they were inseparable. David invited Carol to return to stay with Peggy-Ann, his sister, and her husband after the next operation. She told me recently that I knew then that she and David intended to marry. I have no recollection of this, but have to admit that I was not communicating well with Carol at that time.

The second round of surgery was equally terrible. A third rib and some hipbone were used to repair another part of her spine. Poor Carol was on an electric circular contraption so that she could be turned without being lifted. She was traumatized by all her suffering, and one night at the hospital, when I was told that visiting hours were over, I was loath to leave as she was clearly suicidal. When I left Carol's room, my heart leaped with joy as I met Dr. Carol Reed walking down the corridor. She was also an orthopaedic resident, and I had found her sensitive and sympathetic. She went into Carol's room and came out after an hour to tell me all was well. I asked her what she had done and she said, "I broke the rules and let her walk to the window so that she could see there is a life out there." Since then both Alan Gross and Carol Reed have reached the top of their professions and I am eternally grateful to them. Carol was finally well enough to go to Barbados.

It was now 1968. Although I was supposed to have known, I remember my surprise when I received a call from Carol saying that she and David were going to be married and would I please send down some white gloves. I had mixed feelings as to the timing of this union. For one thing, I had so little notice that I couldn't be there, and this was upsetting. My main concern, however, was whether Carol, who had been very depressed with all that she had endured, was well enough to make such an important decision. But, as we all know, mothers can do nothing in these situations and shouldn't try.

In August 1971, some months after Reg and I had finally parted company, Carol's son Jonathan was born. He was a beautiful baby and I visited them frequently.

I was fifty-two and the National Ballet School was twelve years old. I became more and more aware that all was not well. As I entered the third and final phase of my life I felt empty and unfulfilled. Although I still loved teaching, I had been doing less and less of it because of the heavy, and often boring, administrative load I carried.

When my marriage ended I had been lucky enough to find a house for sale, at a reasonable price, on Amelia Street in Toronto's Cabbagetown. I was alone since Reg had gone and my daughters were married. I knew a great many people, as I discovered when I was in hospital and received one hundred and fifty gifts of flowers, but I felt isolated and lonely. I had no taste for life and was exhausted—trapped by my success and the increasing demands of my job. I sensed that in order to change I would have to remove the blinkers that had allowed me to pursue one goal at the expense of everything else, but I didn't know how to go about it. I became very upset.

The situation was not helped by my poor physical health. I was menopausal and suffered constant severe back pain. I had undergone three operations within the space of a year. The third, when my gall bladder was removed, had been very painful. Also, I was so neglected in the hospital that I became hysterical and in desperation phoned Gail in St. Catharines, where she was now living. It didn't help when the surgeon marched into my room and gave me hell for phoning her.

On looking back, I realize that whatever caused the final break, my depression was long-standing, the result of years of repression, emotional deprivation, and exploitation by those who claimed and believed that they loved me—I call them my "heavies."

The first indication was probably when, at Wigmore Street, I had the agonizing pain in my head and the doctor warned my mother that I needed help. At that time I could not see that I had been conditioned to within an inch of my life. I did not know who I was, only who I was expected to be, nor how I felt, only how I was expected to feel.

I can only describe my inner turmoil after I left the hospital by saying that my thoughts could never come to rest. It was as if I had a butterfly in my head that was not allowed to alight. I had to keep it moving. I had no understanding of how hard it was for that butterfly not to be able to rest. For me peace and tranquillity were just words. I now know that everything that came into my head was too painful to dwell upon, hence my inability to cope with being alone.

When I had spent six weeks convalescing at home and was preparing to return to work, it became obvious to me that I was in deep trouble. I cried a great deal. It was as if all the tears I had not spilled since childhood were being released. I had lost confidence in my ability to teach. I sat down one day to prepare a class. After staring at a blank page for several hours I was in a panic. Nothing would come.

I am very self-disciplined and accustomed to being in control, so it was terrifying when I was unable to force myself to be productive. I could neither eat nor sleep. I tried in vain to concentrate on reading to while away the long nights. The butterfly in my head turned into a frantic rat running around mindlessly.

One day I made a great effort to go to the School. Once there I was stuck in my office. I could not leave because I was too upset and did not want my colleagues to see me in such bad shape. As I had in the bombing, but in a different way, I had lost my nerve. I could no longer rely on my strict British upbringing to see me through. I felt like a turtle without its shell, vulnerable and helpless.

My heart goes out to all those who suffer in this way. Until it happened to me I thought I was invincible. I had no idea that it was possible for a successful and presumably intelligent person to feel so useless. I had been taught to believe that one is the master of one's own fate and that any demonstration of weakness, such as not being able to cope, is a character flaw. While I berated myself I could hear my mother's voice when I failed to perform some physical feat: "You are so feeble, so feeble."

By the time I decided to seek help I was in a terrible state. I spoke to a psychologist I knew, who said my symptoms were classic. He told me that I needed psychotherapy and recommended Dr. Stanley Greben, one of the best psychiatrists in Canada.

I had heard of Dr. G., as I will call him, through a pupil of mine—later a National Ballet principal dancer—who had been helped enormously by him when she had suffered severe emotional problems. I had also met him briefly in a professional capacity when, as founder and chief of the psychiatry department at Mount Sinai Hospital, he came to the School to help me initiate a counselling and support program for our students. Little did I think that I would ever become his patient.

On November 1, 1972, I went to his office for an assessment at which he would decide whether he felt that we could work together. He sets great store on the match between patient and therapist. As for me, my only concern was whether he would take me. I believe, however, that had he not been the right person for me, I would have known it intuitively.

Towards the end of the interview he told me gently that I was a martyr. I saw that as a criticism and protested, quite truthfully, that I didn't feel like one. He said it was amazing that I was not aware of it, nor did I appear to feel hard-done-by.

When our time was up, Dr. G. told me that he would take me through my life. I wondered how he could do that. I felt I remembered little of my life, and what I did remember seemed boring and insignificant. It was, however, a great relief to know that as his patient I would no longer be alone in dealing with my confusion.

I had no idea how hard and painful psychotherapy was going to be. As memories emerged from my unconscious and the therapist helped me to understand my relationships and my own poor self-image, I was filled with regrets. Why, oh why, I asked myself, had I not sought help earlier instead of when my life was almost over? I am still struggling to accept that therapy is better late than never and that wallowing in self-pity is unproductive and destructive.

It was with some trepidation that I went to the first session after my assessment. While there, and each week that followed, I saw a young woman whose appointment preceded mine. She was remote and preoccupied as she left the office. I empathized with her because I felt that we shared, for whatever reasons, deep feelings of distress.

It did not take me long to understand the neurotic pattern of self-sacrifice that had been part of my behaviour for many years. I had thrived on my penchant for putting the needs of others before my own. This was my immature and idealistic way of making myself feel worthy. I had to be needed so I put myself in the position of being used and abused.

I had many years of therapy and was able to see how, in a subtle way, the therapist kept extending to me little branches of hope.

For example, I told him I had lost my ability to teach as well as my sense of humour, both of which had sustained me since adolescence. I felt comforted when he remarked kindly and seriously, but with his own dry sense of humour, that it was hardly likely I would permanently lose talents and traits that had been part of me for a considerable time.

On another occasion, when I was leaving, he said, "One day I am going to see you smile. I'm looking forward to that and to the time when you are not so upset and we can really talk." I knew that he was telling me that there was a light at the end of the tunnel and was surprised to feel a glimmer of hope. Unfortunately I was only able to retain it for a few seconds before my negative feelings returned.

I learned that in this way a psychiatrist, with endless patience, works to create a base of support from which a patient can climb out of the deep dark abyss into which she has fallen.

One important and revealing session was when I found out, in my mid-fifties, that I was still a child.

Dr. G. was carefully attempting to draw me out. With respect for my grey hairs and not wanting to offend or frighten me, he was trying to point out that my feelings at that particular moment were those of a child. I not only recognized it immediately but went a step further. I said very slowly, "I don't think I'm just being a child now, I think I've always been a child."

He rarely showed emotion. In fact, it was often difficult to take his silences and neutral attitude when I was struggling to verbalize my muddled thoughts. But this time he was clearly pleased at my discovery, and it felt good to share a sense of achievement.

"Share!" The first time I heard that word I squirmed with embarrassment and then dismissed it as psychiatric jargon. Perhaps it made me feel afraid of anyone getting too close. Anyway, I now believe that it is a beautiful word and an essential ingredient in any worthwhile relationship.

As soon as I started therapy, Dr. Greben suggested an anti-depressant. I resisted strongly. I was afraid of the effect it would have and despised myself for needing one. He understood my fears, but persuaded me that it would help. He prescribed Elavil.

Before receiving the prescription I was asked if I ever felt like killing myself. I replied indignantly that I was far too responsible to consider such an act, a remark that turned out to be completely untrue. It was part of my upbringing to respond in that way. I had been taught that it was a cowardly way out of one's problems. Dr. G. gravely approved my sensible reaction and I am sure that we both felt we were perfectly safe.

Almost immediately I made my first suicide attempt—fifty

Elavil on top of a fair amount of liquor. Why? Because of a phone call in which I was attacked by two people from the National Ballet with whom I had worked for twenty-two years. I was told to remove myself from any further artistic association with the organization, but to remain on the board as I was useful in raising money. In fact, they could have no influence on my employment with the Company.

Feeling desperately hurt, I phoned Dr. Greben, who was very generous at allowing phone calls. This time he was not pleased, and he reprimanded me for reacting so badly.

That was it! I felt betrayed by someone whom I was just learning to trust. I took the pills with a sense of relief that this was the end of my pain.

I phoned him again, probably to punish him, and he told me to go and make myself vomit. I made a half-hearted attempt but the phone interrupted me. "Have you tried to vomit?" he asked. "Yes," I said, but didn't explain that it hadn't worked. I took the phone off the hook and went to bed.

Immediately, it seemed, the doorbell rang. In reality, it was eight hours later. He had tried to phone and had become concerned so had sent an ambulance. I was right out of it. After telling the men to wait, I wandered around picking up some totally unsuitable clothes including a sunsuit, and climbed into the ambulance.

I woke up again at the Wellesley Hospital, having had my stomach pumped. They told me that Dr. G. had called. I sent him a message saying, "Please don't be mad at me." He replied and the doctor passed it on: "Tell her she sounds more like her old self." I was greatly relieved to find that he was not going to abandon me.

The next time I saw him I was nervous about how he would be. I felt cold and removed. He could have lost me, but he said so simply, "I didn't understand how angry you were with me," that my coldness partially dissolved. "Wouldn't you have been mad if someone couldn't understand how hurtful it was to be attacked by so-called friends?" I asked. He nodded and I knew he was telling me he was wrong. He had misjudged how to handle me and as a teacher I related to that.

That was the first time I recognized anger in myself and then only when it was pointed out. Not only that, but it was reassuring to find someone who could admit that he was wrong. It felt like a new experience, the real beginning of trust, at least on my part. I did notice, however, that I was not offered any more anti-depressants.

I do not want to dwell on the several suicide attempts I made because I am not proud of all the trouble I caused, but there was one that had its amusing side, although I did not see it at the time.

Late in 1973 I suffered a stroke. I was still in poor emotional shape and Dr. G. came frequently to the hospital. In a way it was a relief to get away from the stress that I had imposed upon myself by my efforts to hide from my colleagues my feelings of inadequacy.

After my discharge from the hospital, I was at home with a friend about whom I cared deeply. We had both had too much to drink and began to argue. After making some very cruel remarks, he left.

As usual, I couldn't handle conflict so I swallowed a big hand-ful of Entrophen—thickly covered aspirin—which I was taking as a blood thinner. Then I got scared and went to Mount Sinai Hospital. Once there, I was treated with contempt by the resident doctor in charge of Emergency. "Madam," he said, "you are far too rational to have taken an overdose."

I usually put on a good front and didn't care that the doctor was deceived by it. He was hungry and anxious to go out for a pizza. The nurse who was pumping my stomach refused to go with him. She said, "I think I'd better stay and finish this." I opened my eyes as he shrugged and left. Hours later, when he found out that my psychiatrist was chief of the department—I had been too proud to tell him—he changed his tune. Dr. Greben came in early the next morning and sent me home. He laughed heartily when I told him later that I had played second fiddle to a pizza.

In those early days of psychotherapy I did a great deal of act-ing out, and it was very hard on my children and my close friends. It was like a delayed adolescence—very delayed! I drank too much, didn't give a damn about being responsible, and was cop-ping out all over the place.

My suicide attempts were evidence of my sense of defeat and the feeling that life was meaningless, but there was also my anger. As a child I was told that it was wrong to express anger, and I unconsciously repressed those "bad" feelings. I never blew my top

photo: Jeannette Edissi-Collins

Watching a rehearsal in the studio: I continued to function, c. 1976.

and was not aware that I dealt with my rage by becoming cold, withdrawn, and often bitchy.

All this time I was functioning at the School and hiding behind my physical difficulties. Dr. G. wanted me to let him tell the board of directors what I was going through, but I was afraid that they would lose confidence in me. Although in these days there is far more understanding of people with emotional problems—it can happen to the best of us—there are those who consider it a weakness, and I couldn't risk that.

It would have been much easier for my therapist, family, and friends if I had agreed to go into a hospital. The idea of seclusion and freedom from responsibility appealed to me, but it meant working with the staff psychiatrists, and I couldn't face, even for a short while, a change of therapist. The effort of trying to convey my feelings to a stranger had cost me too much the first time and could not be repeated.

I told my therapist that if I had to go to hospital I would not be able to communicate. In spite of the strain I was putting on him, he gave me a choice and respected my decision to stay on the outside.

As the years passed and the two steps forward, one step backward process of psychotherapy continued, I experienced many valuable insights.

When I expressed to the therapist my fear that I was acting out to gain attention, he said, "Maybe you need attention." When I complained that I didn't like feeling so lonely, it helped when he responded with, "You don't have to like it; you only have to tolerate it."

I read many books on psychotherapy and became anxious about a remark made by an author. In the next session I presented my fear that I was not progressing. He pointed out that I saw myself as a failure in almost everything except teaching, and now I was seeing myself as a failure in therapy. "Throw away the books," he said in frustration. "They confuse you."

I knew instinctively that I could be manipulative, although the word was not part of my vocabulary. I told Dr. G. that I was afraid of playing games with him. Not deliberately—I could control that—but unwittingly. He teased me and explained that even at my "playingest" I was transparently honest. I was apparently sending him all kinds of messages to make sure that he knew I was trying it on. I was intrigued by the notion of unspoken messages and became much more sensitive to them in my pupils.

I see psychotherapy as a long and painful journey, but also as a voyage of discovery. The outcome is determined by a number of things, most importantly the chemistry between doctor and patient and the latter's potential for change and growth. It demands a lot of hard conscious thinking, but it also involves the emergence of deeply buried feelings, revelations about oneself that are startling and unexpected. It is difficult to comprehend the process while it is happening. "Know thyself" is the name of the game, maturity the result.

A good psychotherapist is like a sensitive musician trying to draw from his instrument—the patient—all that he believes it is capable of producing. Of course he has techniques, but they are secondary to his creative and intuitive skills and can be abandoned or adjusted to obtain the best results.

For the patient it is a lonely journey. Psychotherapists, unlike over-protective parents, are wise enough to let their patients suffer pain when it is necessary. They give them lots of room to grow, but are always available.

In those agonizing moments when I felt totally alone, unable to bear any more, and anxious to turn back—an impossible feat, by the way—Dr. Greben was immediately aware of my need and moved in to give me the strength to continue my journey.

Over the years I emerged from my depression stronger and with an increased understanding of myself and others. I had always had a good rapport with my students, but now I was more attuned to the ways in which they dealt with their problems. These could range from outright rudeness to withdrawal. I became a better boss. Some staff members described me as more mellow. Mainly I think I worked harder to alleviate the enormous stress that the young people impose on themselves and their bodies.

To accomplish this I concentrated on improving the existing School health program with Dr. Greben—now Stan—in the role of a colleague rather than as my psychiatrist.

Marian Horosko, associate editor of *Dance Magazine*, when commenting on this program many years later, wrote:

> Live in schools often provide counselling if needed. Exemplary in this caring attitude is the contribution of Stanley E. Greben, M.D., to the National Ballet School of Canada in Toronto. In the mid-1960s, Greben began informal consultations with the students of the academic-plus-professional dance school. Now, the school incorporates a multifaceted co-operative of several professional counsellors. In a report on his findings Greben points out that factors of stress in a live-in school are "homesickness, the high-level double requirements for academics and dance, competition with peers and colleagues, the awareness of the body as the artist's only instrument and the possibility of slow psychological sexual development in a near-monastic environment."

In the early days I had to take a lot of flak for my attempts to introduce professional counselling to the students.

As well as having a social worker on staff to advise on day-to-day problems, we had a team of eight consulting psychiatrists who each met with a class—Grades 5 to 12—six to eight times a year. This was not group therapy, but an opportunity for the students to discuss informally matters that troubled them. These could range from homesickness to envy of their peers who had won coveted roles in the school performance. The older ones had to cope with career choices and the transition from school to professional life. All had trouble with the famous "they." That included those of us who were in authority and who made "stupid rules" and were often "unfair."

These sessions were totally confidential. If there were specific complaints, the counsellors would advise the children on how to go about approaching us in order to bring about change. Most important was that the students had a forum in which they could speak privately of their hopes and fears.

Students Deborah Todd and Barry Watt rehearsing
Les Patineurs for a performance in the mid-seventies.

We also brought in experts to give educational lectures: on drugs in the sixties, on sexual issues, on cults when we had a problem with EST, and later on AIDS.

Our psychiatric consultants were highly respected members of their profession. Two of them who remained at the School for many years were Dr. Clive Chamberlain, formerly clinical director of the Thistletown Regional Centre, and Dr. Richard Meen. The former was fantastic with the younger ones and so relaxed. I loved to see a small boy poke him and say "Hi," and to watch Clive poke him and say "Hi" right back.

Dick Meen was a friend and counsellor to the older boys. One day a very talented young man who was about to leave the School came into my office and said, "I think I'm a homosexual." I replied, "So what!" and he looked vastly relieved. However, it was Dr. Meen who met with him and helped him with questions about his sexual identity.

Clive Chamberlain, Richard Meen, and other psychiatrists took turns screening the children who were auditioning in the summer. They tried to determine whether the child was sufficiently mature to cope with being away from home and whether, at least for the moment, the love of ballet stemmed from the child and not from ambitious parents.

Competition for entrance to the School was fierce. We auditioned close to a thousand children across Canada. Approximately one hundred of them were selected to come to Toronto in July for a month of further screening. Finally thirty to forty young people were invited to attend the full-time school in September.

Before accepting a student, we pointed out to the parents that the academic program was such that students would never be trapped into a ballet career should it turn out that they were not suited to it or had lost their desire to dance.

This reminds me of a twelve-year-old who had been sent to my office. I was trying to discover why she was consistently rude and uncooperative in her ballet classes. She was clearly unhappy, but reluctant to explore her feelings. We pinpointed a few minor problems and I tried to help her find a way to deal with them without creating an atmosphere that would make it difficult for her, her teachers, and her peers. However, I was not satisfied. There seemed to be something she was afraid to bring up.

Suddenly she burst into tears and said, "I wish the teachers would stop asking me if I want to be a dancer when I grow up." When I suggested that she could tell them she was not sure, she said, "But then they'll get mad at me and I'll be kicked out." I told her not to worry about her ambivalent feelings, that we did not want her to feel obliged to make a premature career decision. But I added that, while she was at the School, we expected her to put forward her best effort. She was greatly relieved and as a result her behaviour improved noticeably.

This youngster eventually decided to give up ballet since it was too much work. As for me, the incident served to remind me that many gifted students lack the desire, the drive, and the determination to be successful. We must respect their right to choose a less arduous career and help them deal with the feeling of failure that often accompanies their decision.

At first my approach to mental health at the School met with strong opposition, occasionally from the parents, in which case we explained that no student was forced to attend any meetings with the counsellors. More frequently, it was our own staff and some members of the media who expressed their criticism of me in no uncertain terms. I was accused by one teacher of turning growing pains into psychiatric problems. She did not answer when I asked her who should decide which was which.

Gradually the program gained acceptance. I felt vindicated when, after the tragic suicide, in 1986, of Patrick Bissell—the superb premier dancer from American Ballet Theatre—a Toronto journalist who had once been opposed to my efforts said on the radio, "Patrick Bissell might not have died had he been a student at the National Ballet School." Patrick, it turned out, had suffered from the age of ten with alcohol and drug problems for which he had received little help when he was at a professional ballet school.

As a result of the general class sessions, many of our students became more open to accepting help. But I sometimes encountered resistance when I suggested counselling to pupils about whom we were concerned. "I am not mental," was the customary reaction. "Do you think I'm mental?" I would reply. Their eyes would open wide. "Oh no!" they would say. They seemed relieved when I told them of my own psychotherapy. I went on to explain that it was a process in which they would learn more about themselves and their feelings and that it would help them in their lives and in their careers.

Students did not always agree with my recommendation to seek help, nor did the parents. I never tried to force it, but planted a seed which in some cases took years to flower and in others did not even take root.

In Karen Kain's case, I had suggested counselling before she left the School, but she had refused. As she explains in her book, it was not until she was well established in her career that she became aware she was depressed. One night I went backstage after a performance in which she had danced beautifully. She was in her dressing room, and, when I asked her how she felt, I was startled to hear that she was thinking of giving up dancing. She was grateful when I offered to find someone to help her with her feelings of sadness.

In ballet the artist's instrument is his or her body, and often the desire for perfection becomes an obsession. It is advantageous to have long limbs, a short torso, a long neck, good proportions, and harmonious features. Also, a well-arched foot is important in boys, but even more so in girls. I hasten to say, however, that many wonderful dancers have made do with less through corrective exercises, clever make-up, and boundless determination.

Thinness is the currently acceptable aesthetic image. Thus, the attitudes and conditions in a professional ballet school may predispose the students to eating disorders—anorexia nervosa, bulimia, or both.

Among our consultants, we had therapists who specialized in treating eating disorders as well as a nutritionist who worked with all the students so that they did not starve themselves while attempting to remain slim.

When it came to anorexia, which I encountered more often than bulimia, I learned that it is a profound illness which should not be dealt with by well-meaning amateurs. We had ballet teachers who told the students when they thought they were getting fat, and houseparents who gave lectures on proper eating habits to those who, typically, were in a state of denial about their excessive thinness.

I am ashamed to say that when the School first started we had

Summer picnic of 1988—fun time.

weekly weighing sessions. My motives were good. I wanted to help those pupils who had weight problems by supporting them in controlling their weight, but it was a grave mistake, one that I quickly discontinued.

As I became more educated in the causes and treatment of eating disorders I asked the staff to refrain, in the tricky years of puberty, from making any comments about an individual's weight. A child who was clearly in trouble—it is not hard to tell—was sent immediately to a professional therapist for help. In the early days it was considered necessary for therapy to take place at home where the parents could be involved. Later it was possible for the student to remain with us while undergoing treatment. The most severe cases were treated in hospital. Even then, we remained supportive, and if they had to go away we always welcomed them back.

In light of this policy I was amazed to hear that Evelyn Hart—Winnipeg's prima ballerina—has said that after being sent home from the School in order to have treatment for anorexia, I had refused to take her back. I, of course, could not wait for such a talented student to return. I did understand, however, the anger her parents and possibly Evelyn felt towards me for having insisted on her seeing a specialist. This, I presume, was the reason for their decision to send her to the Royal Winnipeg school. It was our loss. Evelyn went on to receive superb training in Winnipeg from David Moroni, the director of the school, and his staff.

I am happy to say that, now we know how to handle it, we rarely have to deal with students who have serious eating disorders.

As a result of my increased knowledge of myself and the students under my care, I was constantly aware of their vulnerability. Ballet tends to draw youngsters who are obsessive by nature. Their search for perfection makes them self-critical to an inordinate degree.

I am reminded of Veronica Tennant, who gave a wonderful performance in the *Nutcracker*. Everything worked. The dancers, the orchestra, and the audience were united. With Veronica leading them, we enjoyed a magical experience. She came off the stage thrilled and excited and told me she was going out to dinner to celebrate. A few days later, in the same ballet, everything seemed to go wrong and Veronica was sad and dejected. She was blaming herself for giving a poor performance. "I shouldn't have gone out to celebrate," she said. She seemed to feel guilty for having indulged herself, and my heart ached for her.

Critic and author Penelope Doob understands these feelings well. She writes:

> Dance people, with their ingrained perfectionism, too seldom pause for a well-earned moment of triumph: the missed pirouette rankles even as flowers cascade from the balcony during the tenth curtain call. Rigorous self-criticism is what the aristocratic arts are all about, even in the "I'm okay—you're okay" '70s, but ceaseless evaluation makes those rare moments of celebration all the more treasured.

The ephemeral nature of ballet means that we live for the present. Neither film nor video can ever capture the beauty of a live performance. Dancers are only as good as their last appearance.

They need help with their frustration and with the lack of self-confidence that, if they cannot meet their unrealistic expectations of themselves, causes them to feel defeated.

An interesting article by Stan Greben in the magazine *Humane Medicine* concludes:

> Artists are often afraid of psychotherapeutic involvement, fearing that conflicts provide the energy that fuels their creativity. This is so if what is taken to be "artistic drive" is based on neurotic needs, but true artistic and creative drive is not diminished by treatment. If affected at all, it will be increased because the person has fewer neurotic conflicts, inhibitions and preoccupations. No evidence has been seen that creative drive arises from inner conflict. Creative drive is a force in its own right, and many times we have seen it set free in those who are truly talented through a good psychotherapeutic experience.

And the years shall not dim. One of my favourite boys' classes, 1988.
Left to right, Ian Thatcher, Ryan Martin, Richard Landry,
Aaron Watkins, Frederic Massé, Jay Brooker, Philip Lau,
Anders Tulinius, assistant teacher Mary Ross.

Fruits of My Labours

My mandate when I founded the National Ballet School was to produce classical dancers of international calibre, and we have been successful. I think most serious artists will agree that a solid classical technical base is vital before they can be free to experiment with more contemporary ideas.

Russian dancers like Baryshnikov are so well grounded that they can move easily and swiftly into different dance forms—modern dance, for example—even though these forms have played no part in their initial training.

Freedom grows out of discipline. Of course, this does not apply only to ballet. Take Schoenberg, for instance, or Picasso.

Peter Brinson, the scholarly British writer on ballet, used the painter to emphasize this point when he wrote:

> Dance the classics well and all things are possible. Master the classics, as Picasso did in his sphere, and they offer you a base for invention, creation, all the more revolutionary artistic departures, because they require a mastery of technique which is the beginning of communication.

For the past few decades there has been a severe falling away from this belief. Many people are too impatient and wish to short-circuit the process. They do not agree that innovation can come from exacting classical training; they prefer to claim that it is hindered by it.

Even the believers often want to move too quickly. Instead of accepting that a student should thoroughly master one technique before moving to another, they give token homage to the idea by combining them both.

In my thirty years as artistic director of the National Ballet School, the dance curriculum, combined with a comprehensive academic education, resulted in an extremely demanding program.

As well as their daily technique class, our students had to study, at least twice a week, dance forms related to classical ballet. For the younger ones, it was eurhythmics, creative dance, and pre-character (polkas, waltzes, gallops, etc.). The older pupils took classes in variations and repertoire (classical), *pas de deux* (girls and boys together), and character dance (an adaptation of folk dance for the theatre as exemplified by the mazurka and czardas in *Swan Lake*). In addition, because of its style and rhythm, I introduced a strong program in Spanish dance.

Time was of the essence. Our students were in their formative years. When they were overloaded, they became exhausted and consequently suffered injuries or were sick.

After several attempts—only with the most senior students—I found that adding classes in modern dance, although the technique includes many sound principles, defeated rather than helped our efforts to produce the finest classical dancers.

I am happy to say, however, that our graduates had no problems when they chose to move away from classical dance. They were offered contracts by the directors of contemporary companies all over the world. In choreography, the work of Robert Desrosiers can hardly be called classical, but his training has served him well.

Choreography is the foremost medium for artistic expression in dance. It became clear to me that although dancers in their early years lack the knowledge and experience to be true choreographers, there are usually signs of a gift that may develop. I liked to encourage those students, but preferred to wait until they expressed a desire to create something. I found it a waste of time to hold regular workshops. So many students see choreography as simple—a matter of stringing steps together—and lack any spark of creative inventiveness. It seemed unproductive to put the School's resources at their disposal.

We had an exciting year in 1968 when a group of nine students asked me if they could organize a workshop. I supported them wholeheartedly because they presented me with thoughtful individual scenarios plus a well-organized plan.

The workshop took place on March 28 and 29 in Toronto's Unitarian Church auditorium. A panel of judges, drawn from the fields of dance, music, drama, and the visual arts, gave helpful advice to the choreographers. They also chose five ballets which were presented in May at the university's MacMillan Theatre.

Following this performance, I received a letter from John Osler, the School's chairman, and here it is in part:

> In the first place, it was impossible to remember that these were students. Practically all the time the level of the performance was highly professional.
>
> In the second and most important place, it seems to me that if nothing else ever came out of the Ballet School the evidence of last evening is sufficient to prove to everyone that you have trained and produced a highly creative group of young artists whose work need never take second place to that of anyone in the field.
>
> In rather different ways I think you and I have always thought about the same sort of standards and have both believed that if a good foundation was made available in both education and training, the specific content would take care of itself. Last night seemed to me to be a demonstration par excellence of the fact that a thorough classical training will equip people to do original work in the contemporary as well as the classical field.
>
> In nearly everything that was done last evening the concept of innovation within a rigid discipline was very much in evidence and completely justified the emphasis on classical training.

The one big obstacle to achieving our goal of producing first-class, classically trained dancers was the reluctance of parents to send their children away to school at the age of ten (academically the School started in Grade 5). Coming from Britain, where boarding school is quite acceptable, I had a hard time understanding why parents would stand in the way of children who obviously cared deeply for dance and wanted a chance to develop their talent.

I was totally sympathetic, however, to the student who, although accepted at the School's auditions, had reservations about leaving home. Usually the shoe was on the other foot: the children wanted desperately to come, but the parents hoped to have their cake and eat it too. They insisted that it was possible to come to the School a few years later and still have a professional career in dance. "Not true," I told them, and explained why.

Traditionally, in professional ballet schools, a period of eight or nine years is considered necessary to produce the level of performance that I am discussing. The training must start when the body is still malleable. The best results can rarely be obtained if the student comes to us as a physically mature young person.

Apart from this most important aspect of starting early, there are other advantages. The younger students feel unhurried. They easily learn that the acquisition of a strong and accurate technique is accomplished by mastering each basic movement before moving on to the next. The fourteen-year-olds are bored by this rigid attention to detail and impatient to get moving. Woe betide them if they have skipped the fundamentals because, however talented, they may never reach their full potential. They will be more prone to injury and, consequently, to shorter careers.

To emphasize my point, I made it very difficult to join the School after Grade 7 (twelve years of age). Even those students had to be in a separate class to compensate for the two years they had missed. As time passed, the fear of not being accepted, as well as our rapidly growing reputation for creating a happy family atmosphere, made parents more willing to trust us with their children at the appropriate age. They—especially the fathers—were also influenced by the high standards of our enriched academic curriculum.

Three young people, two from Grade 5 and one from Grade 6, recently wrote how they feel about the School:

"Miraculous things can happen to anyone here and the best thing of all is the teachers are one hundred percent behind us."

"What makes NBS different from other schools is that they really treat you like you're family and they have a dance and school education program in one."

"I wouldn't mind a little more ice-cream a little more often. I don't want to change anything else because the rest of the School is totally awesome."

In some countries, particularly the United States, there are schools in which a shorter training is considered adequate and the results are quite effective. I use the word "effective" in a somewhat derogatory sense, agreeing with writer Lawrence Durrell that "the effective in art rapes the emotion of your audience without nourishing its true values."

The future is in the hands of teachers such as Deborah Bowes and Luc Amyot.

Each professional school develops its own distinctive style based on the national characteristics of its students combined with the background and beliefs of its artistic director. When working with students and dancers from another country, the former must be taken into account or disaster will occur.

An example of this took place in Denmark. I heard about it when I was there reorganizing the ballet school of the Royal Danish Opera. To appreciate it, one must understand the cool, somewhat dour and sardonic nature of the Danes and the flamboyant, temperamental behaviour of the Russians.

A teacher came from the Bolshoi Theatre in Moscow to produce *Swan Lake* for the Danish Ballet. Her style was exaggerated compared, for example, to the English school as exemplified by the dancers of the Royal Ballet. But because it was true and came from her heart as well as her training, it suited her.

The clean style of the Danes, greatly influenced by their choreographer, August Bournonville, is not unlike that of the English although in my view it is more aristocratic.

For three weeks the Russian teacher stood with her back to the Danish dancers and demonstrated the choreography of *Swan Lake*. Then she turned round to see what she had accomplished. Being a sensitive and artistic person, she was horrified at the result of her efforts. The Danes were dancing with the arched backs and fanciful arms that they had copied faithfully from the Russian. In the Bournonville style the arms are used in a much more simple way, with great attention paid to form and line. The dancers were trying to emulate the Bolshoi style that was totally unsuited to them.

The Russian teacher spent the rest of her visit trying to modify what she had done so that the Danes looked more like themselves. Still, I am sure that everybody gained from the experience. Probably the Danish dancers absorbed a little, but not too much, of the Russian style and the teacher learned to be more careful when crossing national borders.

I always insisted that the style of the students trained at the National Ballet School should be pure and simple without affectation or mannerisms. It is this, I believe, that has made our graduates so sought-after by directors and choreographers in other countries. As well as producing dancers with this basic uncluttered style, we also made them aware of, and open to, the different styles of the various choreographers with whom they would work.

To accomplish this, I made sure that, in the School's annual performances, our pupils danced the works of the great classicists—Petipa, Fokine, Bournonville, and others. As well, I invited established contemporary choreographers to stage either their previously performed works or new ones that they created especially for us. To complete the experience, I commissioned staff members and up-and-coming young choreographers to compose ballets for our students.

When Eugen Valukin was visiting us, he told me that although the School produced students with its own distinctive style, he found that each one of them was more individual than the graduates of his school, the Bolshoi.

It is rare for a Russian to admit that a foreign school could have something that they lack, but Valukin was honest and clearly puzzled. I believe that he was correct, mainly because our training is not as bureaucratic as theirs, and also because we start out with a less uniform group in terms of talent and body types. This forces us to assess carefully the personalities and physiques of the students and to adjust the training to develop the potential of each one.

Most of us in the dance profession can distinguish the styles of different schools. Once, when a dancer was auditioning for the Company, I was in a quandary. I said to her, "You look as if you trained in England and yet you have something of the Russian style." She laughed. "I am a product of the Royal Ballet School," she replied, "but I have just spent six months studying in Russia."

On another occasion—when I was working with the National Ballet—we had invited a ballerina from New York City Ballet as a guest artist. She was to dance the sylph in Bournonville's *La Sylphide* and a leading role in Fokine's *Les Sylphides*. As our coach was struggling to explain the difference between the style of each choreographer, our visitor became very impatient. "Why do I have to worry about style?" she asked with a strong New York accent. "Why can't I just daaance?"

I have spoken at great length about style, but it is of vital importance. To conclude, here are reviews from two highly acclaimed critics who attended our twenty-fifth anniversary performance on November 21, 1984. They confirm that we, at the National Ballet School, have succeeded in producing dancers with their own Canadian style.

Anna Kisselgoff, dance critic for the *New York Times*, wrote:

> The evening opened with nearly an all-student cast in August Bournonville's famous 19th-century classroom-ballet scene, *Konservatoriet*. There can be no greater tribute to Betty Oliphant, the School's artistic director and founder, than the standard of this performance—in quality, integrity, style and strength. . . . This was simply the most poetic performance one has seen of the ballet.

Writing in the *Financial Times* of London, Clement Crisp summed up his impressions as follows:

> The program ended with Rudi van Dantzig's *Four Last Songs* . . . and then came the cheers. These were, of course, for Miss Oliphant and her staff; but they were equally for the frankness and harmony of style with which her School has endowed its graduates. They are dancers of which a nation must be proud.

Five years earlier, in 1979, we had celebrated twenty years of the School's existence. By this time, seven years after the onset of my depression, I was much stronger and able to plan an ambitious program. It consisted of a two-day conference, held on February 19 and 20 at the St. Lawrence Centre for the Arts, followed by a performance on February 21 at the O'Keefe Centre.

The title of the conference was "Expectations." It was chaired by Vincent Tovell, executive director of Arts, Music & Sciences for CBC TV. My plan was to bring together major artists in the field of dance to explore the "expectations" of dancers, choreographers, artistic directors, and teachers.

The roster of twenty-nine internationally known panellists included Sir Frederick Ashton (Britain); Erik Bruhn (Denmark); Robert Joffrey (U.S.A.); John Neumeier (Germany); Arnold Spohr (Canada); Gosta Svalberg (Sweden); and Rudi van Dantzig (The

The cast of Rudi van Dantzig's *Four Last Songs* danced at the twenty-fifth anniversary performance of NBS, 1984. Left to right, Jeremy Ransom, Karyn Tessmer, Rex Harrington, Martine Lamy, Lindsay Fischer, Kim Lightheart, Raymond Smith, Sabina Allemann, Serge Lavoie.

Netherlands). As one panellist remarked, "It was truly one of the Wonders of the World to experience gathered together under one roof so many of the greatest artists in the world today."

We had four panels: one for artistic directors to discuss their "expectations" of dancers; one for teachers on their "expectations" of students; one for choreographers to find out what they "expected" from the dancers they chose; and finally a panel of dancers who spoke freely of their "expectations" of all the above. On this last panel were three of our graduates: Frank Augustyn, Martine van Hamel, and Veronica Tennant.

During the question period, the comments of the four hundred and seventy-five delegates, many of whom came from Europe, as well as the United States and Canada, were insightful and enthusiastic. One of them summed up what seemed to be the general feeling in this way: ". . . as to what it [the conference] achieved, I do not have to tell you that we have all returned to our separate places, enriched and stimulated by the interchange of ideas."

An important event at the conference was the lecture/demonstration *Flamenco en Route*, given by Antonio Robledo, well-known Spanish composer, with his wife Susana. I spent a lot of time helping Antonio prepare his lecture on the development of flamenco dance. His English was not great and we got the giggles because his favourite expression was "quite almost." My friend Donald Urquhart—who always helped me with my speeches—coached Antonio on his delivery. Our joint efforts resulted in a stimulating lecture which concluded with a moving performance by Susana that was received enthusiastically.

For the performance on the last night, Susana had choreographed the ballet *Obsésion*, using thirteen of our dancers and flamenco singer Enrique Morente. She had asked me to find the money to bring him from Spain. It was worth every penny. The depth and poignancy of his voice created a magical atmosphere in both the demonstration and the performance.

I had first met Susana and Antonio when they were at Mudra, the school created by Maurice Béjart in Brussels. I had heard about them from Judy Edwards, the staff member responsible for national and character dance at the School who, when on a leave of absence, had studied with Susana. I was terribly excited at Mudra when I saw Antonio teaching *palmas* (clapping), and then accompanying Susana's class in the fundamentals of Spanish dance.

I promptly invited them to teach in Canada at the 1972 Summer School. From then until I retired they came regularly for approximately ten weeks every winter. They inspired love and confidence and brought out positive aspects of the students' personalities, as well as developing, to a much greater degree than we do in ballet, their sense of rhythm.

The highlight of Susana and Antonio's work at the School came in April 1984, when the film *Flamenco at 5:15* received an Oscar at the Academy Awards presentations for the Best Documentary Short Subject.

An amusing series of events preceded this achievement. Cynthia Scott arrived from the National Film Board to research a film on ballet training. She walked through the main studio in the late afternoon—at 5:15—and saw Susana's class with the students in their jeans. She came to my office filled with enthusiasm, but with some trepidation. She wanted to change her plans and make the film on Susana and Antonio and their work at the School. I

Antonio Robledo and Susana,
from *Flamenco at 5:15*.

soon convinced her that I was not disappointed and gave her my full support.

When Cynthia approached Susana and Antonio, however, they were very unhappy. It was near the end of their visit and they felt tired. They told her I would never agree to give up the time and were horrified to hear that I had already consented. Susana came to me with a woebegone face and said, "Do we have to do it?" I insisted and told her of the reputation of the Film Board. "It will be worth it," I said. We often laugh about how thrilled they were when, in Zurich, they were woken up in the middle of the night to hear the good news. Since then the film has been shown all over the world.

On the last night of the twentieth anniversary celebration, students and graduates shared the stage at the O'Keefe Centre for the performance. At 4:00 p.m. on the day of the show we discovered that we were to have an unexpected visitor.

Clare Piller, who later masterminded our twenty-fifth anniversary production, and finally the opening of the Betty
Oliphant Theatre, was attending to last-minute details when she
received a message. Prime Minister Pierre Trudeau was coming to
the performance. Although we were delighted, the news necessi-
tated a number of changes, particularly with regard to the carefully planned seating. However, Clare is a genius at organization,
and when Trudeau arrived, somewhat late, everything went
smoothly. He seemed to enjoy himself and stayed late at the
post-performance party.

On the occasion of the twentieth anniversary Pierre
Trudeau wrote:

> I share the high regard for Ms. Oliphant's splendid
> achievements: it is hard to think of many others who have
> equalled her contribution to Canadian excellence and inter-
> national renown in the arts. Indeed, Betty's influence around
> the world through the National Ballet School and through
> her teaching visits abroad rate her as a Canadian ambassador
> of the first rank.

> The Right Honourable Pierre E. Trudeau

In 1982 we went to Ottawa to give a performance in honour
of the Canada Council's twenty-fifth anniversary. For eighteen
years—since we had received the first grant given to us by Peter
Dwyer—the School had been supported by the Council. They
demanded high standards and we were constantly evaluated to
see that these were maintained.

In the early days I had been on a jury for the Theatre and
Dance Section of the Canada Council under Jean Roberts. The
two disciplines were combined, and I was the only dance representative. We had to decide on individual awards for artists, and
the number of applicants was formidable. Arguments were fierce,
especially when we could not agree on what qualified as art.

In the case of an eighteen-year-old magician, Doug Henning,
the discussion as to whether or not he was practising a true art
form waxed hot and heavy. Thankfully, we agreed that the level of
his skill was such that he warranted an arts grant.

Jean Roberts was one of the finest people I have known and was highly respected for her professionalism. When she left the Council she recommended that dance should be separated from theatre. This was done, and Monique Michaud, Jean's assistant, headed the newly formed Dance Section.

At that time the criterion of excellence was on its way out. The age of democratization and diffusion had arrived. But this was not the case with Madame Michaud. Trained by Peter Dwyer and assisted by Barbara Laskin, who later became head of the section, Monique ran her office with firmness and compassion. She was a fighter and she upheld her standards despite abuse and criticism from a small group of malcontents who belonged to the new order.

At the end of our performance at the National Arts Centre, Monique came on stage, and I presented her with a scroll and a gold school ring with our logo. I wanted to express our love and gratitude for her unremitting efforts to make life easier for all of us.

Monique was not the only one who had to fight for standards. In the fifties many people who believed in excellence came to Canada from Britain. Among them were Tyrone Guthrie, Alec Guinness, Irene Worth and designer Tanya Moiseiwitsch at Stratford; Peter Dwyer; architect Peter Dickenson who, by the time he died at thirty-five, had designed many major modern buildings in Canada, and Celia Franca, who was uncompromising in her efforts to build a first-class ballet company. Even earlier—in the late thirties—Gweneth Lloyd had started what became the Royal Winnipeg Ballet and John Grierson had created the National Film Board.

The Canadian aversion to invaders from overseas did not develop until the National Ballet School was well established. By that time I was accepted as a native of this country. We were funded by the federal, provincial, and municipal governments, as well as having a scholarship committee and numerous private donors.

Our success both artistically and financially engendered a certain amount of jealousy. I usually tried to ignore it but Michael Crabb, while reviewing our 1980 performance on the CBC-FM program *Stereo Morning*, commented on it:

> It's no secret in the Canadian dance world that people are jealous of the National Ballet School. . . . But why all the

227

jealousy? It's a complex question. Some people don't feel training ballet dancers warrants the kind of share of limited funds it gets. Most of them also tend to assume the School exists for the Company, the National Ballet itself. Certainly a large proportion of the National's dancers have come from the School, but it is an independent institution and aims to equip dancers for any ballet company, in Canada and beyond. Then, also, it has to do with values. The School is old-fashioned. It thinks discipline, an artistic discipline, is necessary and acceptable. That goes for competition and the elitism which accompanies it—excellence is what the National Ballet School aims for and, compared with similar schools elsewhere, it's doing very nicely, thank you.

For the first twenty years I was the only person responsible for every aspect of the School's operations. I had wonderful people helping me, but I needed someone with whom I could share the administrative load.

The 1979/80 season had been a nightmare because at the same time as we were working on the anniversary celebration we were coping with the building of a new studio/residence which was funded jointly by the federal and provincial governments.

For several years the board of directors and I had been involved in the planning of this extension, and a request for a capital grant was being considered by both levels of government. As usual the wheels were turning slowly.

When I went away for a week's vacation, the province's commitment was in place, and I had just been informed that the project was about to be approved by the "feds." When I returned I discovered that a member of the board had phoned the federal government to cancel our application as there was a possibility that the School was going to move.

With the federal government's help, we had been looking at the feasibility of moving the School, and several sites had been suggested. I was reluctant to leave the old church with its beautiful windows. For the day students, we were easy to reach from all directions. Also, the cosmopolitan atmosphere of our downtown location and our proximity to the Company convinced me that we should stay where we were.

photo: Jeannette Edissi-Collins

Dr. Vincent Bladen and I examine the model of the proposed
expansion, which nearly didn't happen (1979). Vincent was for
many years a patron and strong supporter of my efforts.

However, we had to consider all options. It was this and the
board members' honesty that brought about that disastrous call to
the Secretary of State's office where our application was being
processed.

In my absence the directors had been discussing the site of the
beautiful house that had been left to us by Bobby Laidlaw, who
had died some years earlier. There had been talk of moving the
School there. They felt it was wrong to accept money to improve
the Maitland Street property until this matter had been decided.

When I returned and heard what had happened, I was dumbfounded. It seemed as if years of planning and negotiating had
been wasted. I knew that our chances of moving were negligible. I
believed the old adage "a bird in the hand . . ." and did not want
to lose the opportunity to acquire the extra residential and studio
space that we needed so desperately.

Happily, when I phoned Ottawa, they had done nothing. They

told me they couldn't believe that we were cancelling our request when it was almost certain that it would be granted. They said they had waited for me to confirm that this was really what I wanted.

The building was finally completed and was opened on May 9, 1980. In the meantime, two things had happened that made my life much easier.

In September 1979, Gerry Eldred left the Company and came to the School as co-director. He took over responsibility for all our administrative and financial affairs, including the supervision of the academic department. I felt I had died and gone to heaven.

A few months later Shirley Porter became my executive secretary, and she is still at the School. She is wonderful: efficient, tactful, and caring. I had thought of presenting her name in a competition for the perfect secretary, but unfortunately missed the deadline.

With the advent of Gerry I was able, without being in a constant state of exhaustion, to devote more time to teaching and rehearsing and to working with the artistic staff.

In a magazine article Urjo Kareda had once called me a "dragon lady," and I believe his opinion was shared by others. When the board of directors agreed to my request to share my responsibilities, they seemed to feel that they were creating a two-headed monster—that I could never work in tandem with someone else. How wrong they were! Gerry and I had a happy and productive partnership, although it only lasted a little more than two years.

I would have been completely shattered when Gerry told me he was leaving the School to become general manager at the Stratford Festival had I not known one other person with whom I felt I could work comfortably, namely Bill Poole.

Gerry felt equally strongly that Bill was the right person so the wheels were set in motion and I soon had a new co-director. Bill came in December to spend some time with Gerry, who, on January 1, 1982, went to Stratford to face his exciting new challenge.

One of the first things Bill had to cope with was my absence for five weeks when I went to Egypt and Israel. In Egypt, Madame Ami, who had been a fellow jury member in Moscow, sent two of her colleagues to meet me at the airport. From that moment I was looked after throughout the trip, except for the eight days I spent sailing down the Nile. They provided me with a car, driver, and interpreter during my stay in Cairo. They saw me off at Luxor and met me when I arrived at Aswan. The next day they put me on the plane for Israel. Such kindness reminded me of the closeness of the ballet community all over the world. Wherever I went—Russia, Denmark, London, Paris—I always found friends who did everything they could to make my visit enjoyable.

My next big trip was in the fall of 1985. At the twenty-fifth anniversary performance I had been presented with a cheque for twelve thousand dollars. This came about thanks to the directors, led by June Flavelle-Barrett, Jocelyn Allen, and many generous friends. It was to enable me to take an extended holiday.

I was due to leave for Tibet in September but broke my ankle, so had to cancel that part of the trip. Soon after the cast was removed, I set off to join my friend Margaret Leung in Hong Kong, although my ankle was still very swollen. We had met in Toronto. She was a scholar and had gone to Asia to continue her studies in the Mandarin and Cantonese languages.

After spending some time in Hong Kong, where I accepted two pupils of local teacher Jean Wong for the National Ballet School, we went to Thailand and Malaysia, then to China for three weeks.

Since my mother was born in China and had told me so much about her love for that country, I had always been determined to go there. In the end, I found it disappointing. It did not create the warm feelings I experienced years later when I went to India. However, it is a beautiful country. I will always remember the Great Wall, the terracotta warriors and horses at the tomb of Qin Shi Huang in Xi'ang (Sian), the beautiful stone figures at the Ming tombs and elsewhere, and, most impressively, passing through the three spectacular gorges as we sailed up the Yangtze River (Chang Jiang).

In Beijing, after a severe attack of food poisoning, I spent a very pleasant week at their ballet school. I was greeted warmly by the staff, and once again I felt grateful to be in a profession where one can travel thousands of miles—to Moscow, to Japan, to Chile, to Korea—and finish up in a studio with mirrors and barres, a teacher, a pianist, and students with the same commitment and dedication to their art that our students have in Canada.

Speaking of mirrors, dance teachers are passionate on the pros and cons of the use of the mirror in the training of a dancer. In almost every ballet school in the world the walls are lined with mirrors. At the National Ballet School there are blinds that can be pulled down to hide the mirrors.

I feel strongly that, except for specific purposes, such as checking one's hip placement, arm positions, and line, a mirror should not be used. When I teach I insist on the pupils holding their heads correctly with a good sense of eye direction. This is impossible if they are always turning their heads to squint at themselves in the mirror. So I pull down the blinds and make the front of the room sideways to the mirrors.

I am in the minority but not alone in my conviction that using mirrors is counter-productive. Usually retired dancers are the worst culprits. When they become teachers, they nearly always teach facing the mirror. I believe this is because they need to see themselves while demonstrating. They are accustomed to being in the limelight and find it difficult to efface themselves for the benefit of the students.

My feelings are shared by two well-known dancers who have written insightfully on this subject—Gelsey Kirkland in her book *Dancing on my Grave,* and the late Erik Bruhn.

In a chapter headed "Breaking the Mirror," Kirkland writes:

> The dancer is trained to watch, to enter the world of the mirror until it is no longer necessary to even look. To the extent that a dancer becomes a complacent reflection, he or she does not learn how to test beauty, how to discover its inner life. In this way, the mirror can trap the dancer's soul, ultimately breaking the creative spirit. Such a dancer is created but does not know how to create. . . .

Erik's view is that of a teacher:

> In the classroom I also try to curb the dancer's tendency to be just looking in the mirror. I've seen people all over the world staring in the mirror and I wonder what they see (I

think they're seeing things!). I personally hated to look in the mirror, because what I saw stopped me from realizing my dream about how I should look. Only with something blocking my view could I have a vision of myself, work at it and try to carry it out by believing in it. I see dancers trying to create the vision from the image in the mirror, rather than from inside and I would like to provoke a kind of inner vision in each individual.

The two people whom I have quoted worked together at American Ballet Theatre. When Erik died in 1986 Gelsey Kirkland wrote:

> He was one of those rare dancers who attain a kind of immortality on the stage. The truth he brought into dance was not something that came to an end with a particular performance, nor would it end with his life.

This brings me to the difference between an artist and a technician. In this day and age one can win fame with the height of a jump. It is much rarer than it was to see ballet elevated to an art. A good definition of art is that it depends on "the level of the craft and the quality of the inspiration." The same applies to the line that should be drawn between professionalism and amateurism.

Once, when I was on the Canada Council Advisory Arts Panel, I was making the point that we should be supporting professionals rather than amateurs. Even if the former were only at the beginning of their careers, I suggested that to receive a grant an applicant should not simply have a dream, but should be able to show some proof that he or she was able to develop that dream. I wanted the difference between the professional and the amateur to be recognized.

By that time, unlike in my early years with the Council, the established groups were denigrated and there was a movement to subsidize so-called "creativity." One of the young people on the panel said, "Really, Betty, everyone knows that the amateur becomes the professional." Therein lay the crux of our disagreement. I believe that ten-year-olds can be professional in their

photo: J. Perrson

No computers at NBS in my day. In 1993
Lori McMullen teaches Eric Gauthier.

hearts and vice versa—that they can also be dilettantes who will never be able to dedicate themselves to the demands of a vocation.

I was seventy years old when I realized that I was getting tired and could not go on and on. I knew that the time had come for me to step down. My dream had become a reality. I set out in 1959 to create the ideal school: a place where young dancers would be treated as individuals and could have all the things I didn't have.

Apart from the practical consideration of doing what was best for my children, I had other reasons, when I came to Canada, for concentrating on a teaching career. In spite of the fact that I was a good performer with a very strong technique, I knew that I would never be a really great dancer. Being of the school that believes good teachers are born not made, and knowing that I have this gift, I felt that, as a first-rate teacher, I could contribute more than I would have done as a mediocre dancer.

On looking back, I am conscious of the fact that my life was absolute hell. My only real pleasure was teaching. I particularly enjoyed the "serious" students, those who were going to become professionals. A class lasting one and a half hours would fly by, leaving me feeling happy and refreshed.

The period between the end of psychotherapy and my retirement—approximately ten years—was the best time of my life. Because I had learned to know myself, and thus gained confidence, I was more comfortable dealing with my problems and those of others.

During this time both Gail and Carol were divorced. Gail is now a successful teacher in St. Catharines, most recently at Heritage College. Her results are excellent and her students think highly of her. She has a superb sense of humour and uses it, as I do, to make a point. I felt proud when Gail told me the other day that one of her bosses had asked her to change a course that she gave, in a way that she felt would be detrimental. She had refused and said if she couldn't do it properly she didn't want to do it at all. When asked why, she blurted out, "Because my mother would kill me." It gives me a nice warm feeling to know that Gail has inherited my gift for teaching and my respect for high standards.

After Carol had worked hard with her husband for several years to establish companies in the Barbados tourist industry, her marriage broke up and she returned to Toronto. She attended university to finish her degree while Jonathan went to day care and later to elementary school. In Grade 1 he complained of being bored. On hearing this, his teacher was angry and said that he didn't know the meaning of the word. When she challenged him, he said, "It means not having enough interesting things to do." In Grade 3, Carol transferred him to Rose Avenue School, where Donald Urquhart, my close friend and a superb educator, was principal. From that moment on Jonathan thrived academically.

Carol's second husband, Keith Walker, is a psychologist. They met many years ago when they were both employed by the Addiction Research Foundation. It is a happy relationship, and Keith is so good to me I consider myself blessed. They had their own business but the recession forced them to close it. Keith now works at Lyndhurst Hospital, a rehabilitation facility for people with spinal cord injuries, and Carol has a job with Metropolitan Toronto's Community and Social Services Division.

In all my years of running the School I never expected to be publicly honoured, so I was pleased and excited when, in 1973, I was notified that I was to become an Officer of the Order of Canada. At the ceremony we sat in alphabetical order so I had musicians Boyd Neel and Oscar Peterson on either side of me. When I am nervous, I tend to crack jokes. Boyd was not amused at what he saw as my irreverence, but Oscar egged me on and we had a great time laughing silently to relieve the tension. Some weeks later we were together again to meet the Queen and Prince Philip. This time I smiled to myself as I noted the Prince's expression when I mentioned to Her Majesty that I had known her dance teacher in London. Obviously horrified at the idea of a conversation about ballet, he made a beeline for Oscar, with whom he talked happily for some minutes.

Twelve years later I returned to Rideau Hall to be invested with the highest honour, the Companion of the Order of Canada. I felt quite at home when the aide to Governor-General Jeanne Sauvé whispered to me, "Welcome back."

Governor-General Jeanne Sauvé honouring me as
a Companion of the Order of Canada, 1985.

In 1978, I received Honorary Doctor of Law degrees from both Brock and Queen's Universities. In that same year I was awarded the prestigious Molson Prize. Given to two artists each year, it carried with it a cheque for twenty thousand tax-free dollars. My partner in crime was painter Michael Snow. We both felt that we were expected to spend the money on some high-class artistic project, so we were quite shamefaced when we confided in each other how we would use it. "I'm going to take my family on a vacation," said Michael in a low voice. "I'm going to have a new kitchen," I replied.

For an artist, a present of cash is comparable to winning a lottery. I was ashamed of myself the following year when I felt envious of the Molson Prize winners. The cash prize had been increased to fifty thousand dollars!

I had been nervous when I gave my convocation speech at Queen's University, but was less so in 1980, when I was given an honorary doctorate by the University of Toronto. My comments on high standards and excellence and my fear that our society is threatened by a trend toward "the ease of mediocrity" were received with enthusiasm.

In April 1990, I was one of the first two women—and only the third Canadian—to be presented with the Order of Napoleon by the Maison Courvoisier in France. Courvoisier is known as "the Emperor's brandy" since Courvoisier was the sole provider of cognac to Napoleon Bonaparte.

The award named after this great man dates back to 1912. Every other year, committees in countries all over the world present to the judges in France the names of people who, in their words, "like the Emperor, are distinguished by the quality and excellence of their deeds and outstanding accomplishment in their field."

Imagine my delight when I heard I had been selected and was invited, with a friend, to fly first-class to Paris, where we would spend the night. The next day, we would continue our journey to Courvoisier's magnificent château in the small town of Jarnac near Cognac.

On receiving the invitation, I phoned Donald Urquhart to see if he could come with me. He is the ideal companion and we always have fun together, so I was happy when he accepted

Order of Napoleon, Paris, April 1990.

immediately. Next, I went to Options of Bloor Street—my favourite clothing store—to find something to wear at the ceremony. The first outfit I tried on was perfect, so I knew my trip was blessed.

Before we left, a reception was given in my honour by Courvoisier. My friend Monique Michaud, who has a long-standing crush on Bonaparte, came from Ottawa sporting a hat similar to that of her hero, who was there—in the person of an actor—and who gave a most convincing speech.

Donald and I travelled on Air France with Martyne Simard, a lovely woman who, as Courvoisier's national public relations representative, was there to take care of us. She treated us to a sumptuous dinner in Paris, and the next day we left for Jarnac. Our plane was delayed, but when we finally arrived we were greeted by Ivar Braastad, director of public relations. I was then taken to a palatial room that was decorated in blue—my favourite colour. It was all very impressive, but I especially enjoyed finding a flask of expensive cognac on my dressing table.

When I went downstairs, I met my fellow recipients: Edward Heath, former prime minister of Great Britain, and a charming woman, Madame Lucette Michaux-Chevry from Guadeloupe, who had been Ministre de la Francophonie in the government of Jacques Chirac. We were the first women ever to receive the order.

After a magnificent banquet with numerous courses, each one accompanied by a different rare wine, I tried to persuade Mr. Heath, who is a brilliant pianist, to play for a singsong. He refused in his pompous way, and a few minutes later his aide announced in a loud voice, "Mr. Heath will now retire." The next morning Mr. Heath complained that our vocal efforts had disturbed him. Hoping to discover that he had a sense of humour, I pointed out that we would have sounded much better if he had been at the piano. He was not amused. At the end of this wonderful evening, I fell into bed, but not without having a small snifter of brandy.

The ceremony was the next morning. The representatives of Courvoisier, headed by the Grand Master of the Order, wore magnificent red velvet cloaks embroidered with gold thread. We wore the same in a brilliant jade green. One by one we went on-stage where a tribute was read, and we were given a handsome copy of an admiral's baton in green embossed leather with the Emperor's eagle in brass. It contained a scroll confirming that we were now "commandeurs" of the Order of Napoleon.

On many important occasions I have been supported by two wonderful people, Dinah Christie and Tom Kneebone. Not the least of these was when, in 1990, I received the Toronto Arts Foundation Lifetime Achievement Award. I was in very good company, as writer Morley Callaghan also won the award that year.

When asked to name my presenters for the ceremony, I had no hesitation in naming Tom and Dinah. Not only are they loving friends but they are creative and humorous entertainers. At both my seventieth and seventy-fifth birthday parties, they composed songs especially for me and sang them to an appreciative

Dinah Christie and Tom Kneebone presenting my Toronto
Arts Foundation Lifetime Achievement Award, 1990.

audience. At the awards presentation they spoke so amusingly
and warmly about me that I was close to tears.

I have been given awards and honours by a number of other
institutions, including the Diplôme d'honneur from the Canadian
Conference of the Arts; an Honorary Doctorate of Letters at York
University; the National Dance Award from the Canadian Dance
Teachers Association; and a Paul Harris Fellowship from Rotary
International. In 1985 I was named Distinguished Educator of the
Ontario Institute for Studies in Education for outstanding contri-
bution to education in the Province of Ontario.

In spite of my success, both before and after the birth of the
National Ballet School, I was constantly fighting an uphill battle.
It was really tough in the physical sense, in the sense of responsi-
bility, and even in the financial sense. It was a terrible struggle and
I doubt if I could ever do it again. I was only able to keep going
because of my deep love for ballet.

What I regret, however, is that I neglected "me" in order to
make it happen. And I realize now that my children could have
been better off. As a purist and self-confessed perfectionist, I can
only say that I couldn't help it. I was driven to make something
work.

Yes, it has been very hard, but I feel really lucky and grateful. It could have been hard and turned out badly. Instead, it has been hard and turned out well, and that makes a big difference!

I returned to the School for the thirty-fifth anniversary, which brought former and present staff together, 1995.

Left to right, back row, Carole Wagland, Jane Smith, Ted Johnson, Pauline Newlands, Gillian Bartlett, Stephen Johnson. Fourth row, Karen McDowell, Bob Sirman, Denise Schultze, Sergiu Stefanschi, Lucy Potts, Shirley Porter-Johnson, Beverley Miller, Reginald Amatto. Third row, Mandira Mazumder, Elisabeth Wojtowicz, Rosalie Brake, Elizabeth Keeble, Marjorie Clarkson, Susan Wall, Rosalind Goss, Glenn Gilmour, Trevor McLain. Second row, Jannie Berggren, Mary Goodhew, Carina Bomers, Elizabeth Yeigh, Pat Goss. Front row, Laurel Toto, Deborah Bowes, Carole Chadwick, Betty Oliphant, Mora Oxley, Mary Ann West.

My dream theatre opened in October 1988.

The House That Betty Built

There are rare moments in one's life when one is filled with a deep sense of joy, suspended in time, with nothing to mar one's happiness. That is how I felt as I stood on the stage of the Betty Oliphant Theatre on Monday, October 17, 1988.

We had just completed the first of six performances to mark the official opening of the R. A. Laidlaw Centre which consists of a teacher training building, Ivey House, and a stage training facility, the Betty Oliphant Theatre.

Leading up to the opening was a hectic time for key members of the staff. Bill Poole, the administrative director, had dealt from the beginning with the architects on behalf of the board. He had lots of headaches, mainly to do with cutting costs. I wanted the theatre to be perfect so I was mildly disappointed that I had to settle for less expensive carpeting and a few other savings.

Two people with whom I had worked for years, Mary Ann West, production manager, and Marjorie Clarkson, schedule coordinator, had their work cut out organizing the performance which would be stage-managed by Carol Beevers. Since 1972 Carol had been responsible for the smooth running of all our public appearances. Finally, Pat Goss, our superb art teacher who had been with me for many

photo: Peter Varley

R. A. (Bobby) Laidlaw, our great benefactor, with Ann Ditchburn.

years, was making sure that the students' work would be displayed on the walls of the theatre's many rooms and corridors.

R. A. Laidlaw (Bobby) was a beloved patron of the School who bequeathed his house to us. When he died we sold it for 1.3 million dollars and bought the land on Jarvis Street on which the Centre would eventually stand. You can imagine my frustration at a dinner one night when I sat next to the man to whom we sold it and discovered he had received thirteen million for it shortly after he bought it from us. I couldn't help thinking how we could have spent the money.

I had spent many happy hours at Bobby's house on Jackes Avenue, and he loved coming to the School to see the children—many of whom he sponsored. He was a connoisseur of Scotch whisky and had a cellar that would have been the envy of any true Scotsman. In this connection I am reminded of an amusing incident. My husband, Reg, and I had been invited to dine at the Laidlaws', but as I was ill I couldn't go. Reg went alone, and after dinner, he was taken downstairs as Bobby wanted to send home some Scotch for me. A barrel of 1914 Haig and Haig was opened, and Reg was told to tip it while Bobby held a container under the spout. After a few moments Reg asked if the whisky was going in. Bobby, who didn't see too well, said, "No, but keep pouring."

After the opening, we received a letter that ended as follows: "I suppose the theatre is a luxury but the School has really earned it and deserves every square inch." While appreciating the compliment, I cannot agree that the theatre is a luxury. Before the week of performances that marked the official opening, we had already presented our junior students on stage in their year-end class demonstrations. It was amazing to see how they reacted: they became performers.

Until October 17 our use of the theatre was a cloak-and-dagger affair. We were afraid that if word leaked out that it was in operation, there might be premature publicity which would detract from our official opening.

During that time Cleve Horne was painting a portrait of me to be placed in the foyer of the theatre. Sitting for him had been an easy experience. His wife talked with me throughout, and he told me later that she had touched many facets of my personality, especially when she got me going on the subject of children's feet being ruined by putting them on pointe before they were ready. I was pleased with the result. It was an honest likeness and did not try to flatter me.

Finally, the need for secrecy was over and the great day arrived. The theatre, both in appearance and function, was everything I had hoped for. This venerable mansion at 404 Jarvis Street looked from the outside much as it had in the days of Queen Victoria. Its interior had been transformed into a state-of-the-art performing facility.

In a competition we had chosen the architects, A. J. Diamond & Partner, because we were impressed by Jack Diamond's superb presentation and his obvious enthusiasm for the project. He and his staff were helped enormously by Dieter Penzhorn, the National Ballet Company's director of production planning.

Before telling you more about the ballets that were performed that night, I would like to share some of the feelings I had. Even with the best staff in the world, which I was lucky enough to have, an artistic director stands or falls alone with every decision that she makes. Because our performances to date have earned us an excellent reputation, I doubt if anyone is aware of my fear of failure each time I conceive a new project. In commissioning four original works from our graduate choreographers I took a big risk in terms of presenting a balanced program. But I sensed that the originality of each of the choreographers would produce a diverse program and hoped that it would be a fascinating one. The only limit I set was that a ballet could last no longer than half an hour. So they were free to choose their music, designer, and, in consultation with me, the dancers they wished to use—this only because we had to share the load and obviously one dancer could not perform in four ballets. We could have fallen flat on our faces. Instead, we were successful beyond my most extravagant dreams.

Hence my euphoria as I stood on the stage that first night.

photo: Rick Eglinton, Toronto Star Syndicate

Betty and her boys. Choreographers for the official opening of the Betty Oliphant Theatre, October 17, 1988. From upper left clockwise, David Allan, John Alleyne, James Kudelka, Robert Desrosiers.

I have no idea how I have got this far without naming the choreographers. An article in the *Toronto Star*, written by Paula Citron, began: "Betty and her boys will be in the spotlight next week." An accompanying picture shows me happily surrounded by "my boys"—David Allan, John Alleyne, James Kudelka, and Robert Desrosiers.

David Allan's ballet, *In Exultation*, was first on the program. Set to Handel's music, it was designed to show off the present generation. With thirteen dancers, ranging from Grade 9 (fourteen years) and up, it was led by Alexander Ritter.

This was followed by a piece by John Alleyne called *Blue-Eyed Trek*, a set of three *pas de deux* danced by Julia Vilen and Pierre Quinn, Jennifer Fournier and Rex Harrington, and Sally-Anne Hickin and Owen Montague, all of whom were graduates of the School who had become members of the National Ballet of Canada.

This reminds me of a joke that reveals a lot about the government's choice of ministers for particular portfolios. A certain provincial minister of culture said to me one day, "Betty, I know *pas de deux* means 'not for two' but when I see one it always seems to have two people dancing in it."

The third ballet, James Kudelka's *Signatures*, set to Beethoven's Fantasia in C, was an affectionate satire of the National Ballet's repertoire and the dancers who perform it. Kudelka explained to Paula Citron in an interview preceding the performance, "The audience will be able to recognize familiar dance imagery and snippets from the classics. . . . I'd like to give the new theatre some ghosts right from the start."

Of the final ballet Bill Littler, in his review of the first night, wrote:

> Nor did it come as a surprise to find the bizarre imagination of Robert Desrosiers exhibited in *First Year*, a panorama of the seasons with its visions of dancers in flippers and octopus tentacles, umbrellas and cat's heads snowed upon in an icicled cavern.
>
> All this from a ballet school? Yes, but a very special ballet school, referred to last night as "the house that Betty built" by Communications Minister Flora MacDonald.

Flora was a wonderful friend to the School. She had been with us on October 15, 1986, when I broke the ground for the theatre. It was a beautiful sunny day. She and the National Ballet School family shared a moment of closeness I will always treasure. She was also with us at the opening. I shall never forget her tribute to me that night: "She has given a lasting legacy to Canada. Would that the same thing could be said of all of us."

The School doesn't claim to create choreographers, but it does provide the environment—the fertile ground and nurturing that allow us to spot this rare talent and encourage it to grow.

That we succeeded in our efforts was confirmed by William Littler:

> Every last one of those choreographers and dancers was a present or past student of the National School and over the course of a single evening they presented just about the most eloquent demonstration imaginable of the School's impact on dance in this country.
>
> And those choreographers? Far from cut-outs from the same mould they presented themselves as dancemakers of singularly different taste and personality, united only in their desire to pay homage to their teacher, Betty Oliphant, and the school that trained them.

The successes of these four choreographers and other budding creative talents over the years proved important to me. For a long time, while I was a member of the Canada Council's Advisory Arts Panel, I was told by some of my fellow panellists that dancers could emerge from an institution such as ours but never a choreographer. I believe they thought that our strong emphasis on self-discipline and high standards would somehow destroy creativity. I remember these same people, usually young and artistically self-indulgent, telling me and W. O. Mitchell, a fellow panellist, that we couldn't understand their point of view because we were dinosaurs.

Exactly one decade before standing on that stage, knowing that my dream had become a reality, I had decided that a theatre was an essential part of a professional ballet school—although few have one.

In 1978 I was in Denmark at the request of Henning Kronstam, the new director of the Royal Danish Opera ballet company and school. He wanted me to advise him on ways to improve their training, which had been deteriorating over the previous ten years. The invitation was the result of my having undertaken a similar but more comprehensive task in 1967 for the Royal Swedish Opera ballet school when Erik Bruhn was artistic director.

On my return from Denmark, where I had had the time and distance to assess the strengths and weaknesses of our own organization, I wrote the following in my annual report to the board of directors:

> What are the strengths of the Danish School? They have a theatre. The children study and train in the Opera House. The walls of the interminable corridors are lined with posters and photographs that remind them of the great tradition that lies behind them. They are constantly on stage as part of the company, whose repertoire includes a number of works which have dancing roles for children, especially those of August Bournonville, the famous Danish choreographer. The students appear several times a week during a ten-month season. . . . Their mime, their make-up and their stage presence show clearly the value of this atmosphere for developing professional dancers.
>
> Let us contrast this with the opportunities given to our students to perform in public. If they are small enough for *Nutcracker* (God bless *Nutcracker*) they have two weeks of consistent stage appearances, rubbing shoulders with the people who have achieved the goal which they have set for themselves. . . . In addition to this, students of all ages get the opportunity to walk on as pages, citizens, attendants and spear-carriers during the seven weeks the National Ballet appears in Toronto and, occasionally, if somebody breaks a leg, they might be able to dance with the *corps de ballet*.

The visit to Denmark reinforced my desire to have a theatre and I was determined that we would.

This determination of mine was a cross which our board of directors bore bravely over the years. They visibly cringed as they estimated the cost of my request. I heard murmurs of "Betty has really gone too far this time," or "We will never be able to raise the money," or "We'll have to nip this in the bud." But, as always, when the chips were down, they rallied around.

Although the funding of the theatre was a protracted affair, Mary Anne Beamish, a freelance writer, described it briefly in *Dance in Canada* without any indication of the pain and suffering we went through for several years:

> The record of excellence and achievement of the National Ballet School in 29 years of existence cannot be contested. Founder Betty Oliphant's lauded artistic and pedagogical skills have produced a roster of outstanding graduates, now gracing many of the world's ballet stages. Less well known, however, is the political savvy and real estate acumen which have made her a property developer par excellence. The latest phase in the growth of the National Ballet School is an extraordinary 300-seat theatre or "stage training facility."

There is a little joke connected with this title. Because we did not have enough space to provide parking for a theatre, we had to convince the municipality that our building was for training purposes only. I was rapped over the knuckles by Bill Poole every time the word "theatre" passed my lips, but I hated the other description. It sounded so amateurish!

The article continues:

> The Ontario Government under William Davis was the first to pledge its support for one-third of the projected costs of building a stage training facility for the N.B.S. students and the Federal Government followed with a similar commitment. A Capital Campaign was launched to raise the remaining four million dollars from the private sector and the architectural firm of A.J. Diamond was engaged to design a full-sized stage with fly tower, a 300-seat auditorium with piano lift, a physiotherapy centre, a swimming pool, a whirlpool and ancillary facilities all within the confines of the house and its grounds.

This summary, although accurate, does not convey the time and effort we invested in the project. Our first attempt to find funding was deceptively easy, when on January 15, 1982, we received a grant from Reuben Baetz, then minister of culture and recreation for the Province of Ontario. It was September 3, 1985, before all the funding was in place. We spent the intervening time on an emotional roller-coaster, with our hopes being constantly raised and dashed. There were many dramatic moments but the two I remember best happened in the days leading up to our twenty-fifth anniversary gala performance, which, as I mentioned, took place at the O'Keefe Centre on November 21, 1984.

After receiving the initial provincial grant, we had been struggling for over two years to get a matching grant from the federal Liberal Party. You can imagine our horror when the Conservatives swept into power before we had achieved our goal. That was when our friends—including E. A. Goodman, the well-known lawyer; David Silcox, then assistant deputy minister, federal Department of Communications; and Bill Davis, retiring premier of Ontario—came to our aid.

With friends at the twenty-fifth anniversary post-performance reception. Vanessa Harwood, Erik Bruhn, me, Monique Michaud, and Celia Franca, November 1984.

Our aim was to finalize our plans before Premier Davis stepped down. Since the original commitment had been made by a minister of his government, we were afraid that a new premier might not be willing to honour it.

By this time we were a month away from the twenty-fifth anniversary performance, and rumours were flying that Marcel Masse, the new federal minister of communications, would be giving us good news at that time. There were several clues but no hard evidence that this was true. Two things happened that were significant. First, I had a phone call from one of Mr. Masse's aides, asking me if I would allow the minister to present me with a cheque on the stage at the performance. This should have calmed all my fears—except that the "feds" owed us a relatively small amount for a previous project, so I said, "It depends on the size of the cheque." The aide laughed uproariously and intimated that he thought I would be satisfied, but Bill Poole and I had gone through too much to believe that our troubles were over.

The second incident was encouraging, but it filled me with horror. I was invited to attend a dinner for Marcel Masse, hosted by Premier Davis at the Albany Club on October 20, the day before the performance. This was the day of our dress rehearsal. We had graduates from all over the world who would be performing pieces choreographed by their artistic directors, who had accompanied them. I wanted to decline the invitation, but knew I had to go.

Although agonizing over missing the rehearsal, I arrived for the dinner at 6:00 p.m. with my heart beating rapidly at the thought that maybe, just maybe, my hopes for a theatre were going to be realized. It became clear at dinner that this was true and that I would indeed be able to allow Mr. Masse on stage to present the cheque. At 8:00 p.m. Bill Davis said, "I think we should let Betty go; I know she is very anxious about her rehearsal." I could have hugged him, but instead thanked him profusely and dashed off, arriving at the O'Keefe Centre five minutes after the rehearsal had started.

In the thirty years I spent running the School, finances were always a terrible headache. Earlier capital projects, such as the expansion and the new residence, were no less painful and prolonged. Although smaller in scale, they still involved cutting through layers of bureaucratic red tape at all three levels of

252

government. Moreover, we constantly lived with the uncertainty of what the future would bring since our operating expenses were funded on a year-to-year basis.

It will be a relief to leave the issue of money and to move on to more pleasant subjects, but first I must say this. I spent over a decade with the Company, followed by my years at the School, trying to convince ministers, civil servants, board members, and members of the public that funding for the arts in our society is as vital as the funding of social programs.

I am deeply moved by the poverty and suffering in this country and feel that we are all responsible for trying to alleviate it. At the same time, I am appalled by the general lack of recognition of our need for spiritual sustenance—and I don't mean in the religious sense. In this society life seems empty to many of us, partly because of the emphasis on material things, but mainly because so little attention is paid to books, music, painting, dance, and drama.

From where I sit, it seems that people gifted in the arts are rarely given a chance to develop their potential. Their talent may lie dormant; their dreams may wither on the vine. They feel unfulfilled without knowing why. They have little or no exposure to the arts at home or in school, so it is hard for them to discover what they need.

Happily this is not the case at the School. But the constant fight for funds—along with the fact that grants to the artistic community are the first to be sacrificed in times of fiscal constraint—shows me that the encouragement of artistic talent has a low priority both within government circles and among the general public.

From the beginning Marian Horosko, associate editor of *Dance Magazine*, has been a great supporter of the School. When the Betty Oliphant Theatre was opened, her article in *Dance Magazine*, headed "Betty Builds Bigger," started with these words:

> Just when you think that the National Ballet School of Canada is perfect, Betty Oliphant, its founder, artistic director and ballet principal, adds something new to this remarkable school.
>
> Oliphant would be the first person to praise those who have contributed to the growth of the school, and those praised would be the first to tell you that it is Oliphant's extraordinary persuasive abilities that make her arguments

irresistible on the basis of logic, necessity, immediacy and artistic merit. That order of priorities is important, for while artistic standards are her first consideration, she has won the support of governments, private donors, and defiant boards with her direct yet affable approach, her clear and complete explanation of needs in her written reports, her stance on the timing of her requests, and she has then backed up all her proposals with proof of her past artistic achievements. What N.B.S. could give the rest of the dance world is a course by Oliphant in arts administration that would include educating boards in understanding dance, writing reports as if they were intimate letters to a privileged few, submitting a subject young or old to a direct gaze until a request is properly understood, and looking interested when someone is saying something absolutely asinine. Beneath all that administrative talent is a love of teaching that provides the energy, drive, and will to solve whatever stands in the way of providing what she knows is needed—without the interference of personal ambition. Perhaps luck and opportunity have played a heavy part in her success. But having a theatre named after her is a fitting tribute to the woman who brought dance to Canada and set a standard for all other dance schools to follow.

As a pioneer, and a successful one at that, I have had to put up with a lot of criticism and backbiting. I am able to cope with reading and hearing negative comments that come my way by acting on those that seem valid and dismissing those that, in my view, stem from jealousy or ignorance. Being human, however, I enjoy being appreciated, and the insight shown in this article gave me a terrific lift.

As the head of an institution, which is essentially a lonely job, I was deeply appreciative of the support I received from friends and colleagues on the opening night of the Betty Oliphant Theatre. Cards, letters, and telegrams poured in from all over the world, including the Soviet Union.

The week closed with a gala on Saturday, October 22. I was asked to give a press interview with Bill Littler at the time of the rehearsal of the finale. I was not concerned, as I knew the staff could cope with the rehearsal very well. In fact, this was a set-up to keep me away. Our intention was to have all the students on stage behind me and the performers. They would file in, starting with the youngest. This entailed organizing some hundred children, all dressed in the School uniform: a white blouse, a green blazer, and a pleated skirt in one of the old Irvine tartans.

That evening, at the end of all the curtain calls, I was left standing alone on stage. I seemed to be standing there forever. Luckily, I was welcomed with great enthusiasm, but I was waiting for the students to come out and was cursing the fact I had missed the rehearsal. Sensing that they had finally arrived, I turned to greet them. I was flabbergasted! There standing in a line were Karen Kain, Veronica Tennant, Rex Harrington, and all the other Company members who had taken part in the show. They were wearing their own or borrowed school uniforms. From stage left Jeremy Ransom strolled on, carrying a tatty bunch of flowers for me. He was doing all the things they knew I hated: smoking, chewing gum, and looking very untidy. I laughed so hard! I loved them all. I was especially moved by their gesture as I knew how

photo: Jeannette Edissi-Collins

Company members dressed as students at the official opening of my theatre, October 1988. Left to right, Kim Lightheart, David Meinke, Serge Lavoie, Veronica Tennant, Lorraine Blouin, Rex Harrington, Karen Kain, Cindy Macedo, Owen Montague, Clinton Luckett, Gizella Witkowsky, Sally-Anne Hickin.

tired they were. The week had been exceptionally hectic for them, since they had been rehearsing for their own season with the National Ballet of Canada as well as appearing with us.

I learned later that I had almost spoiled the joke. I had spilled something on my dress and, in the second intermission, went down to the wardrobe to get it fixed. Those who were not in the last ballet were putting on their uniforms and had to run and hide while the wardrobe staff kept me busy and hustled me off as quickly as possible.

This event resulted in a moving tribute from Veronica Tennant. After recalling our first meeting when she was ten, Veronica's tribute ended like this:

> . . . and much has happened since. On October 22, 1988, we seasoned performers shared the fabulous stage of the Betty Oliphant Theatre with the impressive present generation of N.B.S. students. All of us were proudly clad in the green uniforms of the National Ballet School. What fun we had planning this and what a wonderful surprise for Betty. And when our eyes met, that heart-filled second flashed with profound and stirring emotion.
>
> Thank you Miss O,
Veronica Tennant

At the opening of the theatre, I thought of the many challenges I had faced, and I remembered being told, when I arrived in Canada, that I wasn't needed.

In an article "An era ends at National Ballet School" (*Toronto Star*, October 14, 1988), William Littler commented on this hurtful remark:

> Whoever told her she wasn't needed knew little of the woman and less about her mission. The Betty Oliphant Theatre may be a monument of a kind, but the real monument is flesh, blood and ideals. May it endure, and may her example continue to inspire those who regard ballet as an art worthy of the best that is in us.

Appendix:
List of Awards & Honours

1967	Centennial Medal, Canada
1973	Officer of the Order of Canada
1978	Honorary Doctor of Law, Brock University
1978	Honorary Doctor of Law, Queen's University
1978	Molson Prize
1980	Honorary Doctor of Law, University of Toronto
1981	National Dance Award from the Canadian Dance Teachers Association
1982	Diplôme d'honneur, Canadian Conference of the Arts
1985	Companion of the Order of Canada
1985	Distinguished Educator of the Ontario Institute for Studies in Education
1990	Order of Napoleon by the Maison Courvoisier, France. One of the first two female recipients, and only the third Canadian.
1990	Toronto Arts Foundation Lifetime Achievement Award
1992	Paul Harris Fellow of the Rotary Foundation of Rotary International
1992	Commemorative Medal for the 125th anniversary of Canadian Confederation
1992	Honorary Doctorate of Letters, York University

Index

Photos are printed in bold. Titles of books, operas, magazines, films, and ballets are printed in italics.